Hannah, Anna, Michael & Mary:

*Mennonite, Hutterite and
Sons of Freedom Narratives*

Mary Eggermont-Molenaar

Memo Books

HANNAH, ANNA, MICHAEL & MARY:
MENNONITE, HUTTERITE AND
SONS OF FREEDOM NARRATIVES

© 2013 Mary Eggermont-Molenaar
All rights reserved.

Design & layout: Colin McDonald

No part of this book may be used or reproduced in any manner without written permission except in the case of brief quotations embodied in critical articles or reviews.

Eggermont-Molenaar, Mary, 1945-
Hannah, Anna, Michael & Mary: Mennonite, Hutterite and Sons of Freedom Narratives
ISBN 978-0-9812819-2-6

To:
My new friends in this brave new world

Also by Mary Eggermont-Molenaar

Montana 1911: A Professor and his Wife Among the Blackfeet.
University of Calgary Press, 2005 | University of Nebraska Press, 2005

Missionaries among Miners, Migrants and Blackfoot: The Van Tighem Brothers' Diaries, Alberta 1875-1917.
University of Calgary Press, 2007

Gustave Aimard: Feiten, Fictie, Frictie.
Special Snowflake, 2009

Index

List Of Illustrations 8
Preface 10
Acknowledgements 12

Introductory New Year's Letter 14

Chapter 1: Visit with Mike Chernenkoff 20

Chapter 2: Doukhobors 32
- Russian Orthodoxy one thousand years later 35
- Doukhobor Background 39
- Tolstoy, Klisty and Skoptsy 48
- Others on the Skoptsy 54
- Doukhobors to Canada 59
- Free Men, Sons of Freedom 66
- Eyewitnesses: John and his grandmother 71
- To and in British Columbia 78
- Sons (and daughters) of Freedom on CBC radio 96
- Mike's prison diary 101
- Apologies and movie men 109

Chapter 3: Hutterites 116
- A brief Hutterite history 127
- To South Russia 133
- To North America 135
- The Hutterian Brothers in the Military Prison on the Island of Alcatraz in the Bay of San Francisco by David Hofer (1917) 146
- Hutterites to and in Canada 152

Chapter 4: Mennonites   *162*
    Hannah   *165*
    To Poland and on to South Russia   *177*
    The 1874 wave: John's story   *181*
    The 1919 wave: Nestor Makhno   *184*
    The 1926 wave: from Canada to Paraguay   *187*
    The 1945 wave: Bartel moves from Germany to Canada   *188*
    The 1948 wave: from Germany via Paraguay to Canada   *190*

Chapter 5: Answers 1 and 2   *192*

Chapter 6: 2001 (South Russia) Ukraine Travelogue   *196*
    Trip to Ukraine   *209*

Conclusion: Answer 3   *248*

Bibliography   *252*

List Of Illustrations

Cover: Maarten Biesheuvel watching Mathilde

Signs upon entering Krestova   19

Perun statue   33

Mike at the premises of the former Tent Village   83

Non-Doukhobor school facing public highway   87

Former railway tracks in Slocan Valley   87

New Denver boarding school   97

Getting ready for a break: movie men, Mike, and Sam   111

Sam being interviewed   113

Hutterite cows   117

Hutterite visitor   119

At a colony   121

Childrens' dining room   123

At a Hutterite wedding   125

Device Menno Simons   *173*

Nestor Makhno   *185*

Light blue cathedral   *213*

Entrance harbour of Sebastopol   *217*

Interior of Tatar palace   *219*

Ruins of a Greek settlement   *223*

Children's' choir   *225*

Getting entrance?   *227*

Stalls at the school   *229*

School children   *233*

Grandfather's house   *235*

Outhouse at Deviadoso   *239*

Baba statue   *241*

Preface

After having immigrated to Canada in 1986, one of the first things my new friend Hannah cheerfully confided was: 'Mary, when you hear the word garden, you think of your backyard. I then think of the Garden of Eden.' Well yes, that word focuses my mind on the backyard and dependant of the context on mosquitoes, raspberries, grass and what have you.

'How so?' I asked her

In a nutshell it came down to the facts that Hannah's ancestors were chased out of 16th century Friesland, the area now known as the province of Friesland in the Netherlands. Her ancestors, over time known as Mennonites, had subsequently lived in Poland, that had become Germany and Russia that had become Ukraine. Hannah was born in Germany in February 1945, which became West Germany, and is now again Germany. From 1948 on she was raised in Paraguay, which is still Paraguay. Her mother and her six siblings had emigrated from there to Canada when she was eleven years old. All of this and more I guessed caused Hannah to think of a backyard as a Garden of Eden.

I just did not know what to make of this family history and also not of what follows. When Hannah saw my teaspoons in a little glass on the countertop in the kitchen, she said that her mother used to keep her teaspoons that same way. Once she offered me a slice of weird looking cheese. I declined, saying, 'What the farmer does not know, the farmer does not like (translation of a Dutch proverb).'

Hannah: 'My mother always used to say that.'

At a New Years Eve party Hannah brought cookies along. She proudly introduced them as New Year's cookies. I recognized them to be Dutch *oliebollen*, dough fried in oil, complete with icing sugar. Only, her *oliebollen* were smaller, golf ball size; Dutch ones boast tennis ball size.

What happened to *oliebollen*, they shrunk, the teaspoons, still gloriously on her mother's countertop, and the mindset of people whose ancestors have been on the move for over 400 years? It seemed that in her and in those of many others

I met in Canada neither the mental or spiritual make-up, nor little household customs, in many cases not even the language got lost through immigration. It seems that religion often serves as anchor for identity with the church as an ethnic or religious or national save-haven such as Polish or Chinese Catholic churches. Or combinations thereof.

Over the years I also met with numerous Hutterites, actually, my house became their camping ground, and a few Doukhobors - rather, members of the once radical and perhaps misguided division thereof, the Sons of Freedom. This book is a very personal narrative about my encounters with Mennonites, Hutterites and a few Sons of Freedom. It provides skimpy sketches of their ancestors' trials and tribulations that caused them to end up in South Russia, now Ukraine, and from there migrate to Canada. This book is also an attempt to answer questions that arose while familiarizing with my new 'Canadian' friends.

The final chapter is about the cruise through Ukraine Hannah and I made; a trip through Ukraine where the members of said three groups peacefully toiled in the 19th century and from where they left for Canada from 1874 on.

Acknowledgements

Thanks to the following people who told me their stories and made me understand where they are 'coming from.'

In British Columbia: Mike and Lara Chernenkoff, Sam and Rosemary Conkite, Nellie and family, and David L. Kirk from Victoria.

In Alberta and Manitoba: Anna[†] and Paul, Mathilde, Peter, Becky[†], Suzie, Esther, Clara, Mary, Andy, George, Theresa, David, Rachel, Martha, Miriam, Maria, Mary, John, George, David, Rosa, Mary, Joe, Cathy, Dave, Sam, Mary, Suzie, Kathy and Martin, all living at Hutterite colonies.
Also: Colin McDonald, Hannah and John Toews, Jos Eggermont, Harry van den Elzen, Anne-Marie Veress-Baez, Eleonore Aukes, and Hans Berkhout.

In Ontario: John Hewitt and Cornelius Jaenen.

In the Netherlands: Hans Visser (1936-2001), Dick de Boer, Henk Jan de Jonge and staff of the Municipal Archives of the city of Gorcum.

In Belgium: Paul Callens.

In the US: David A. Shank and William E. Farr.

In Austria: The staff of the Arnold Schönberg Center in Vienna.

Introductory
New Year's Letter

. . . so far about the family. Well, that will do, I would say. As for me, on a daily basis I take care of the dog and the the cat. Sometimes I translate drivers' licenses, diploma's, touristic guides, manuals and so on; on a regular basis I organize lecture tours throughout Canada for Dutch and Belgian authors and professors. And I write about Gustave Aimard (1818-1883), with Blackfoot about their matters or about my new Canadian friends, which is what I am doing right now.

This summer a travelling journalist dropped by. He phoned me in mid July, and said that he is always travelling and writing books about people in foreign countries. A while ago he was somewhere in Africa discussing his plans for a book about religiously oriented communities with a Dutch nurse. She suggested that he contact me.

I took the journalist, Boris, along to my Hutterite friends, Charley, Anna, and Mathilde. At their colony he expressed his wish to stay overnight. That was possible, but he was jokingly told that in that case he had to stay on for life. Friends in another colony who did not nurse such extended hospitality agreed to have him for one night. So he spent the night in a colony along the Milk River. Afterwards, he told me that he had had quite an experience: including been woken up by an enormous thunderstorm and terribly screeching shrieks. The next morning he had found out that a fox or a coyote had bitten out the throats of twelve geese in a meadow behind the house. Who would have liked to miss that!

As Boris also wanted to meet with Doukhobors, we got in touch with a Doukhobor couple retired in Calgary with the help of the curator of the museum in Arrowwood, a hamlet south of Sikskika Nation, 90 kilometres east of Calgary

This couple kindly suggested that we should attend the annual Doukhobor Sobranie in Grand Forks, British Columbia. On the 11th of August we left, not having any clue what a Sobranie was. Stupid, we just forgot to ask.

En route we first drove a few hours through a severe downpour. In Cowley, a Doukhobor hamlet west of Pincher Creek, Boris interviewed a Doukhobor couple whose name we got from the Calgary couple. They invited us to stay and have supper with them and their deceased daughter. Her large photograph stood on a chair at the table. Afterwards they prayed with us for the thunderstorm to stop. The prayer was heard, the skies cleared up, and we drove on.

After two days of driving, we arrived in Grand Forks where we booked two nights in a motel. That evening in a local pub I accidentally dropped my beer glass from the counter. It slid from the circular outer edge on an inner edge and went on: spinning, sliding, staggering, and then finally falling on the tiles right behind the barmaid. Startled she jumped up and shouted, 'And it is not even six o'clock!'

The performance of my unfortunate beer glass, shattering itself to pieces, brought about an immediate brotherhood with the local lumberjacks around the bar. From them we learned that evening a few things about the local Doukhobors, which form eighty percent of the local population.

'They call themselves pacifists, but as bosses they are very authoritarian,' the checkered jacks agreed among themselves. One offered to show us the stronghold of the Doukhobor extremists the next morning - the Sons of Freedom. We had to decline his offer, as we were planning to attend the Sobranie.

Upon arrival that next morning, John Verigin, the spiritual leader, stood talking with someone at the entrance of the meeting hall. We told him of the couple from Calgary who suggested that we should attend their annual Sobranie as a way to learn about the Doukhobors. Verigin nodded, but told us that we would have to introduce ourselves to the community and let us in.

A moment later we stood in a hallway of a kind of a rectangular community hall. Inside everything was painted white and there were no decorations, statues or icons. We looked around and started to bow, just as we saw other people doing before they entered the main hall. People seemed to wait until they were with a small group, and then before entering, they bowed to the people already seated. These would in turn rise, bow toward the newcomers, and only then the newly arrived proceeded into the meeting hall. Afterward we learned that this bowing is for God's spirit in the people, not so much for their physical presence.

The Doukhobors sat on long pews, men and women opposite each other. In the center was a table with bread, salt, and water - symbols of hospitality. At 10 a.m. the service started: choirs sung off and on - sometimes men, sometimes, women, sometimes youth. My impression was that any choir member could start a song and that the whole choir then joined in. The singing was alternated with family and community news from the floor. In the front row people once in a while engaged in an elaborate ritualized kissing. By noon a few girls about ten or twelve years old from Chernobyl introduced themselves and sang a few Russian songs. The Doukhobor community was caring for these girls, suffering from cancer; I guess that everyone felt a lump in their throat.

Boris and I had not thought to bring anything to eat so we gratefully accepted invitations to share lunches in the treed front yard. I spent time with a very nice family: a housewife, the husband employed in construction, and the children attending university in Vancouver. Boris ended up lunching with Eli Popoff, the Doukhobor historian, who later that evening would pay us a visit.

After lunch it was our turn to introduce ourselves to the community. Verigin Junior (Doukhobors have an inherited leadership) announced: 'And we have very special guests, a couple from Europe.' Boris rose from between the men on the benches across and loudly announced that 'we were not married.' Deadly silence among the two hundred worshippers! And we still had to come forward to the microphone. Boris talked about his books and about Africa where he had met a Dutch nurse who had given him my name. The community seemed to listen with pricked up ears, stiff spines, and square jaws.

Then it was my turn. What could I say? I told people that I was an immigrant from the Netherlands. With my accented

English, being an immigrant seemed to be my greatest commonality with this community: the men in farmers' shirts, the women in flowered skirts and blouses with beautiful white lacy headscarves. However, my revelation did nothing to lower the ears, relax the spines, or loosen the jaws.

'We are not married,' seemed to echo around, hitting the walls and bouncing back as 'They are not married.'

Pointing to Boris I said that I was only 'his driver.' I still saw straight faces and sensed stiff backs: 'and just in case you are interested, I have room fifteen and he occupies room eh ... eh . . .' 'Thirteen' went through my mind, but I did not say so, because while stammering, I realized that this was not true: While I was in room fifteen, he was not in room thirteen. I tried to visualize his door, zoom in and recall the right number to mind. There it was. It was number twelve. But by the time I remembered his room number I had already cut myself short, uttering lamely: 'His room is two doors from my door,' adding: 'at the Grand Victorian Motel.' Thunderous laughter.

The choir sang until 4.30 p.m., and was again alternated with more presentations and communications, most of it in Russian.

In the evening Eli Popoff, the historian, visited us at Boris' invitation. At our motel, under a roof of corrugated plastic, on a torn, plastic-upholstered couch, we listened for two hours to him expounding on Doukhobor history. As he was leaving, he invited us to follow him to Gilpin, a Sons of Freedom stronghold stuck between the railway tracks and the foot of a mountain. We accepted and drove behind him along very modest houses with quite neat little yards.

'At the other side of the mountain is America,' Popoff explained during a stop, 'not that the inhabitants care about that; they don't care about authorities.'

The next day we were invited to Krestova (also known as Novoe Poselka) - the other Sons of Freedom stronghold. From Nelson on we followed a Son of Freedom who guided us to a road that lead uphill from a river, forking into two branches. Entering was by permission only. Both roads were lined by houses built by the inhabitants themselves with, again, very well-kept yards. We arrived at the home of Mike Chernenkoff, a stocky, muscular man who made coffins for a living. After some chatting in his front yard, I asked if I could use his bathroom. He immediately invited us in, let me use the bathroom, and then he took a shower. Upon finishing, he walked from the bathroom through the living room in a housecoat and said something like: 'You see, I am fully dressed.' We took that for granted.

He then came back in a T-shirt and jeans. While he served us bread, cucumbers, cheese, homemade cherry jam and lemonade, he entertained us with stories about arson and nudity. He said that the police had handed out matches and told them that they would be sent back to Russia if they set fire to this or that building. And since that was exactly what the Sons of Freedom wanted, that is exactly what they did.

'But,' Mike said, 'Mother Russia did not want arsonists so we ended up in prison.' He had been in jail for eleven years.

I cannot say that I comprehended much of what he was saying, but we understood that arson had become more and more a means of protest for the Sons of Freedom, a fiery branch of Doukhobors I understood. That morning however, it had not yet become very clear to us against what, or where, his group had protested...

And so I went on in this New Years newsletter.

↑ Signs upon entering Krestova, photo Mary E.M.

Chapter 1: Visit with
Mike Chernenkoff

Although I did not mention it in the New Year's letter, some-thing happened during the lunch meeting with Mike Chernenkoff that, in hindsight, prompted me to start this book. Mike had asked us whether we were interested in his revision of the *Symposium Meetings* (1974-1982), a book of six hundred spiral-bound pages that Boris had bought from Eli Popoff the previous evening. It crossed my mind that someone who revises would also write.

'Revision? Do you write more often?' I asked Mike. He confirmed and showed us copies of his self-published monthly, *Istina (The Truth)*, in which everybody is invited to write. He gave me a few issues to take home. The articles are mainly in Russian, but as far as the English parts are concerned, the journal could as well have been named *Straight from the Hip* or *The Truth and Nothing but the Truth*. Editor Mike and his guest authors did not seem to shy away from penning down any thought whatsoever.

In one of the issues, I saw a few pages that apparently were copied from a book, in English, by a Dutch author who had spent his youth in Gorcum, the Netherlands. In it the author joyfully reflected on this hometown and his uncle Kees who had seen Tolstoy at the banks of the Seine. At the fireplace of Kees' father, the author's grandfather, in Gorcum, the author had met 'with Tolstoyan, conscription-fleeing Doukhobor pacifists.' One of the *Istina's* also featured pages and pages about Tolstoy's efforts to help the iconoclastic Doukhobors, or 'Spirit Wrestlers.

In order to find out more about the connection between Doukhobors, Tolstoy, and Gorkum I asked Mike about the author of these copied pages. Mike wrote back that the author was Pierre van Paassen and sent me a few more pages of Van Paassen's book, *Days of Our Years*.

In 1939 *Days of Our Years* was number one on the top-ten of non-fiction books. According to Payne Hacket, Hitler's *Mein Kampf* ranked number seven that year. In it Van Paassen tells that his uncle Kees had once given him a pile of books: Voltaire, Rousseau, Bayle, Proudhon, Lamennais, Saint-Simon, Goethe, and Tolstoy.

Reading more of Van Paassen books, it struck me that while he generously mentions names of family and villagers, he never names his oft-mentioned maternal grandfather who met with such a large variety of people: refugees from Persia, Tolstoyan pacifists, Salvation Army soldiers on their way to a leprosy colony in Java, Hernhutters *en route* to Canada, and even priests deserting the church of Rome. His grandfather had done so much and seemed such an interesting character, why was his name missing?

Hans Visser (1936-2001), biographer of the famous Dutch author Simon Vestdijk, helped me with this question. He investigated and had me know that the last name of Van Paassen's mother was Sizoo.

The exact connection between Mike the Coffin Maker, Van Paassen, and Tolstoy in the museum yard kept me busy. The Internet showed that a few people occupied themselves with Van Paassen's biography: a journalist in Jerusalem, and David Kirk, an emeritus professor of Sociology from Victoria.

I asked Kirk how the Van Paassen biography was coming along. On 27 January 1999 Kirk wrote that his wife Bev and he had been researching Van Paassen's life since 1989, but due to his wife's illness and death he hoped to have a truncated version ready by the end of that year. Kirk also communicated that Van Paassen did not immigrate to Canada with his parents when he was fourteen in 1914, but in 1911 at age sixteen with his younger brother. His parents had followed a few months later after the death of their youngest son.

But, the question why the name Sizoo was never mentioned by Van Paassen was not solved by this friendly note; the issue lingered on in my mind, and will only be solved by the end of this book.

Mike made coffins and Van Paassen's in-laws, as I found out through the city of Gorcum's archives, had been cheating on the coffin business. Further, both Mike and Van Paassen's in-laws had been in prison, Mike for nudity and his in-laws for cheating the coffin business. What kind of connection was that?

Next, according to a 1981 article by G.D. Homan, Van Paassen had been a staunch pacifist until 1917. Based on the following on lines from Van Paassen's *To number Our Days* and *Days of Our Years*, Homan writes about Van Paassen being requested to help raise funds for a British battleship, but the latter:

> asked to be relieved of his task. [Van Paassen] was a sincere Christian pacifist who believed that preaching the gospel of love and peace was incompatible with the raising of money for the purpose of constructing battleships.

Later I saw that Van Paassen had taken up active duty in the Canadian Armed Expeditionary Force as a translator.

According to Homan, Van Paassen had written, on the eve of World War II, that the real heroes of the Great War had been the conscientious objectors. But in 1941,

> while decrying war as a supreme evil and its existence as a betrayal of Christ, [Van Paassen] felt that the spiritual defence and progress of the world alone would not protect mankind from the onrushing forces which were intent on blotting out Christianity and democracy forever.

Millions of Van Paassen's books were sold and somehow the question of who he really was, has never been satisfactorily answered. Still he was known and people wrote about him, thought that he was a Jew.

For example in *The National Vanguard* of March 1984 under the title 'Journalist Not French:'

> In the letters section of the January issue, 'L. H.,' of Hazel Park, MI, quoted Pierre [Van Paassen], whom he calls a 'French Journalist,' tells of the massacre of German troops

in Syria during World War I. What was the real motive for telling this sordid little tale in his book Days of Our Years?[1]

Homan explains this so-called Jewish connection through Van Paassen's links with the Jewish congregation in his hometown, Gorcum, the Netherlands. He had been handing out copies of the paper *Pniël* to the local Jews because his mother believed that the Jews had to be converted to Calvinism.

As said, because of my growing interest in Van Paassen, Son of Freedom Mike and I kept corresponding. He once announced that he had to come to Calgary because his daughter Lara had to undergo eye surgery. In February 1999 I picked up Mike and his daughter at their hotel in Calgary. Lara was a cheerful young woman with Down's syndrome and very thick glasses. She greeted me in overwhelmingly friendly fashion while Mike muttered something about steel-wired dinosaurs along the road. Taking the hint, I drove them down Memorial Drive; a nice ride along the Bow River behind which the Calgary downtown skyline towered, sharply contrasting against a brisk blue sky. Next we passed the Calgary Zoo where giant steel-wired dinosaurs can be admired on an overpass.

---

1 *The National Vanguard* of March 1984 under the title 'Journalist Not French' continues:

> ...
> First one must look into his background. Study will reveal that this is not his real name. He is also not a Frenchman. Pierre [Van Paassen] is a pen name for Pinchas Paskowitz, a Dutch Jew of Lithuanian extraction. His 1940 book was a propaganda piece to aid Jewish interests by promoting anti-Arab feelings in this country, among other things.
> In the case of 'L. H.,' at least, it looks as though the Jew Paskowitz, alias, was successful in his attempt to stir up anti-Arab hate, thus promoting Jewish Middle East domination.
> W.R.S.
> Indianapolis, IN

This letter to the editor of *The National Vanguard* comes across as if W.R.S. from Indianapolis, had read the following sentences in Van Paassen *Days of Our Years* (1939):

> Dr. Josef Goebbels, who banned the newspapers for which I was writing, motivated his decision in the following notice, published in Die Angriff:
> 'The correspondent Pierre, a Dutch Jew of Lithuanian extraction, whose real name is Pinchas Paskowitz, is an ex-rabbi, who engaged in atrocity-mongering while on Reich territory.'

Lara then wondered whether Calgary had a space needle. Instead we went to the Calgary Tower which resembles more a darning needle. It does have an observation deck with splendid views and a revolving restaurant. As the revolving restaurant was too crowded, we went to the stationary restaurant at the top. There, a ceiling-mounted television featured a wrestling match of men in colourful silk costumes pounding each other. Swaying with raised fists, Lara cheered them on: 'Get him, get him!'

I gently poked in her side: 'Lara, you are here with your pacifist father.' Mike laughed good-naturedly, as he did when his daughter ordered a hamburger. Doukhobors are also vegetarians. The Sons of Freedom interpret the biblical prohibition to kill in the widest sense: 'One should not turn one's body into an animal graveyard.'

Upon arrival at my home, Lara insisted on watching a hockey match. While she was cheering the hockey players, I showed Mike some documents, among them a photocopy of a handwritten letter by Van Paassen that I had received from the Arnold Schönberg Center, Vienna, Austria.

'Mike, this is about your pacifist here!' From that letter it appeared that in 1942 Van Paassen was the national chairman of the Committee for a Jewish Army of Stateless and Palestinian Jews and that he had invited Schoenberg [Schönberg] to become a member:

> It gives me great pleasure to invite you, on behalf of my colleagues, distinguished figures of all walks of American life, to join the Committee for a Jewish Army, a non-sectarian and non-partisan body [...] our ultimate goal [...] a full-fledged Jewish Army of stateless and Palestinian Jews [...] We feel sure that you will agree with us that the Jews, who were the first victims of Hitler's aggression, must have a chance to strike back at the greatest enemy of their history.

Mike, reading this letter, asked what my plan was. So far I had been smitten with the Van Paassen story, but I felt that Mike was trying to bend my focus onto his curious past. I replied that:

I read about Pierre Van Paassen, a pacifist in your Russian journal, and wondered about the Christian pacifists he met at his grandfather's fireplace in Gorcum. Van Paassen also seems to have tried to establish a Jewish army. I saw Tolstoy's statue in the backyard of the Doukhobor museum in Castlegar and now I wonder about the connection with iconoclasm. Despite Doukhobors being against statues or icons, I knew that they had a big statue of Tolstoy in the backyard of their museum in Castlegar. It is made by Jurij Chernov (1935-) who based it on photographs of Tolstoy made by his wife Sofia. In 1987 the Russian government presented it to the Castlegar Doukhobor community.

You told me about having spent many years in prison for nudity and arson - but to me you look like a decent, well-dressed man.

I have been in colonies of Hutterites - how did they end up in Canada? A Mennonite friend told me stories about her pregnant mother who fled Russia with six siblings. She was born in Germany and raised in a dessert in Paraguay. What was that flight all about? How came she and her family ended up in Canada? I understand where the Indians come from (here!), and I can understand the talking about oil, gas, cows and grass.

I do not plan to write specifically about what the police did to you, or what you did to the police. I will just see what and who else crosses my path and only then I will write. I need some angle; I am trying to make sense of Canada as far as 'Canadians' cross my path.

We agreed that my plan was vague. After dinner I brought father and daughter back to their hotel. Mike invited me in. Moments later Lara was in her nightgown on her bed, watching and commenting on a program on President Clinton and Monica. She was all for the hearings to be OPEN; an adult women with an adult opinion, ventilating with a childlike enthusiasm.

'Open, open!' she encouraged the Washington senators.

Mike gave me a new pile of his papers, among which was a neatly typed light-blue diary in Russian from the time of his incarceration somewhere in British Columbia: 'I wrote it originally on the back of stickers and toilet paper. It was unused.'

'For the time being it will go on my pile of papers,' I replied. However, I read some of Mike's papers before adding them to the pile. So, when I picked up Mike and Lara the following morning for sightseeing downtown, I asked him about one of the people mentioned, Lebedoff. By then it can be said that my mind was successfully turned to Mike's affairs.

Mike: 'We were stupid. Lebedoff first said that he worked for Verigin, and later for Sorokin. But the latter was not true. Sorokin warned us about Lebedoff, but we would not listen. Just like us, Lebedoff was incarcerated, but that was only to fool us. Later Lebedoff picked up his own work, and kept saying that he worked for the leaders. Many dropped him. Lebedoff only had a small group of followers. He is dead now.'

I felt stupid as well: I did not understand a word of what he was trying to tell me and asked again about the light-blue book he had given me. Thinking about it caused Mike to be overcome by an avalanche of memories about being force-fed: 'I saw there [in a hospital] that they tried to push a tube through someone's throat. First they put the tube in cold water, so it is no longer flexible. Then they sharpen the tip, so it causes as much pain as possible when they insert it. [With] it they drilled holes in the stomach walls of the prisoners.'

In that way we chatted on for one more hour and then watched the rest of the Clinton affair with Lara. The following morning it turned out that Lara's eyes would not benefit from laser treatment, so father and daughters (there was another daughter, but she was all the time elsewhere) drove back to their mountain slope.

By the end of February 2000, I got more mail from Kirk. 'It is not simple to write Van Paassen's biography,' he informed me. 'Van Paassen had a wonderful imagination. That is fine when you are a writer, but what is fact and what is fiction? For example, in 1936 he was dismissed by *The Star* because he had sent his articles from France and not from Spain as he should.'

Kirk and his late spouse Bev had found out that the accusations of the editor of *The Catholic Register* never had been proven and that this journal wanted Van Paassen out of the way because of his anti-Franco and pro-republican articles.

Kirk cheerfully added that Van Paassen never would have written *Days of Our Years* if he had not been dismissed.

It is true that Van Paassen's imagination was wonderful as far as his origin is concerned. I knew, for example, from several sources, the archives of the city of Gorcum among them, that his uncle Kees had been an imaginary uncle. Still, it was to be regretted that Van Paassen mixed his historical accounts, such as the one in the 1943 *The Forgotten Alley* with imagination as he wrote the following:

> **Yet, what are the facts? Thousands of the humblest and poorest Jews, inoffensive and innocent men, women, and children, are being murdered each day, smothered to death by poison gas, electrocuted in abattoirs, buried alive, mowed down by machine-gun fire.**

Did his audience know about his 'wonderful imagination,' and did that contribute to the fact that not much heed was paid to his gruesome enumeration and his statement that 'now' already three million Jews have been killed?' As Kirk was busy with a biography of Van Paassen, I decided to leave the Gorcum author alone, while Mike did not leave me alone.

Earlier on, in March 1999, Mike had sent me his article about a 1953 affair. Then the British Columbia government had allegedly kidnapped Doukhobor children. He also enclosed a letter from a Doukhobor to a former leader, Peter Petrovitch Verigin. One week later Mike sent me an *Open Letter of the Doukhobors* to their fellow countrymen the Quakers, containing a complaint concerning a Quaker in the service of the British Columbia government.

I now wondered what Quakers had to do with Doukhobors. In hindsight my life back in the Netherlands started to look more and more neatly arranged. Also, much of what crossed my path in Canada seemed linked with Tolstoy; it was time to take this Russian count from the bookshelves. And that was not easy. The University of Calgary Library had shelf after shelf of books on, and by, Tolstoy. After some hesitation I took home the oldest-looking, thickest, two-volume 1908 and

1910 Tolstoy biography by Aylmer Maude.[2] Leafing through it, it became clear to me that Tolstoy's home life had been hell. Who created that hell? In *My Life* Sofia Tolstoy repeatedly blames her husband's shift from being a fiction to a religious writer. Because of it her 'life and happiness' had clouded over and her life had been better without this 'Christianity.' Somehow the image of Tolstoy's hell reminded me of Van Paassen, who had been creating an army and in one of his books describes war as hell.

Pacifism, hell, army, incarcerated Doukhobors, and Quakers and there was something else. Between the 1780's and 1870's, the ancestors of the people I had met so far in Canada, Mennonites, Hutterites, and Doukhobors, all had lived in South Russia, which is Ukraine since 1991. They had been toiling peacefully there for nearly a century but had then moved to Canada.

In July 1999, I had to put Maude's Tolstoy biography back on the library shelf as the summer had arrived and brought along a few friends from the Netherlands. As soon as Frans and Mieke had overcome their jet lag, we took off and went from Calgary along the southern route to British Columbia. Our first stop was Kimberly, a German kitsch-town where the food is unexpectedly fantastic. We then made our way to Nelson to visit Mike and Lara.

Mike had written that he had suffered a stroke but insisted that we visit him nevertheless. I had replied that we would certainly do so, but after that had not heard from him since. As Mike had no telephone, we had not been able to announce the time of our visit, or ask how to get there. After some driving back and forth on a blazingly hot mountain slope, I recognized the same road sign from the last year and then Mike's house, a grandchildren's swing in the front yard.

---

2   Aylmer Maude (1858-1838) and his wife Louise (1855-1939) were part of a thriving group of English in Moscow and Tolstoy's main translators during his lifetime. They also assisted with the 1899 Doukhobor emigration to Canada. In *My Life*, Sofia Tolstoy describes Maude and Chertkov as vultures, both eager to claim 'the monetary advantage from translating Resurrection, the profits whereof Tolstoy had destined for the immigration of the Doukhobors. Sofia T. found Maude a 'more decent and less money-grubbing person than Chertkov,' who had 'withdrawn his bid and yielded to Chertkov.'

We knocked on the front door. Nothing happened. Another knock. Sounds of rummaging. With some effort I pushed the door open, thus shoving the two dining room chairs standing behind it back into the living room. Dressed in a bathing suit Lara was mopping the floor.

'Dad!' she said, turning her head back enthusiastically when she saw me, 'your girlfriend from Calgary is here!'

Mike stepped out of his office where he had a generator-powered computer. Meanwhile Lara had disappeared to return moments later, neatly dressed, and continued her mopping.

'I was just writing a letter to you. You were supposed to come down in July.' 'It is the 28th of July and here I am with my husband and our friends from the Netherlands.'

We sat down at the table. Mike's health had visibly deteriorated. He seemed a bit sullen, but also aware of it. He said he was glad for our visit and that he could no longer find words easily. Lara mopped on. When she arrived at the dining room table, we had to continue the conversation with pulled up knees, so she could continue underneath. Mike mumbled that she maybe should finish it later. Lara reacted cheerfully that 'she was mopping. You told me to do that, didn't you?' and wanted to finish her job. Mike acknowledged that her reasoning was irrefutable and with some effort he too pulled up his knees. Mopping along Lara suggested:

'Dad, why don't you ask Mary to marry you?'

Husband and friends nearly swallowed their tongues. Mike looked a bit taken aback at his daughter. Lara explained her father that he needed a wife and she a mother, and that her new mother should mop the floor. We laughed our heads off. It was still very hot and dry and for quite a while my tongue had been glued to my palate. I proposed to have a drink at *Nellie's Kitchen*.

'Do you know her?' asked Mike.

I said yes, meaning that I had heard of her existence. Near his house I had seen a trailer with a sign *Nellie's Kitchen* and Mike had told me that he sometimes had dinner at her place. Lara resolutely put her worn-out mop in a corner and we all strolled to the trailer. Mike entered *Nellie's Kitchen* first to return outside a moment later with a big, warm-hearted woman, who invited us into her living room. There we met her daughter, her granddaughter, and a quiet old woman whom Nellie introduced as her *Zwägerin* (sister-in-law).

It dawned on me: this was not a trailer-pub, but a private household. I apologized for my proposal to get a drink at her place. Nellie laughed and said that yes, long ago she had served a few drinks for payment. A joker had then nailed the sign to her trailer, 'that's how come.' Fortunately, she still asked us if we wanted a drink. Yes, I could not think of anything else by now. We were served lukewarm Cokes as then, people on that mountain slope did not have electricity, fridges, or phones. Later on that would change. While Nelly poured Cokes, Lara reiterated her suggestion that her father should propose to me.

Nelly replied: 'She already belongs to someone,' pointing to my husband. Lara's brows furrowed but quickly came up with a solution; Jos could marry our friend Mieke, but then her spouse Frans would pose a problem. Lara pondered on. A bit later, while munching raspberries in Mike's backyard, she had her eureka moment. As soon as Jos and Mieke were married, Lara thought, Frans just should figure out by himself how to get his floors mopped: he seemed to her to be an able-bodied man.

As we were leaving a young man walked up the pathway. He also had Down's syndrome as well and a powerful handshake. We heard he was Lara's friend and lived at the end of the road. After a brief chat he wished us a joyful journey

Back home a few weeks later, we received a letter from Mike with an apology for the behaviour of his daughter Lara and the news that her friend had died and that she wanted to attend the funeral. Actually we had enjoyed Lara's behaviour: say what you think, think creatively and come up with solutions.

'Which friend?' I asked Mike. 'The friend you met,' Mike wrote back. 'People with Down's syndrome do not become old. Suddenly it all ends.'

Everything ends and how will a young Down's syndrome woman on a mountain slope without electricity find a new friend? How and why had her people ended up on this mountain slope? Why were they rounded up in the Moscow area and later exiled to south of Kiev? How and why had the two other groups, Hutterites and Mennonites, also ended up in South Russia around the turn of the eighteenth century? Why did most of them leave for America and Canada at the same time - around the 1870's? Answering these questions and exploring where these groups came from in the literal sense of the word became my plan.

Chapter 2
Doukhobors

Many Hutterites and Mennonites left South Russia around the 1870's. The Doukhobors only left in 1899. But, before we get there, first a closer look into Doukhoborism: which turned out not to be an easy task.

Their ancestors lived in Russia and converted to the Christian faith around the year 1000.* From the seventeenth century on splits occurred. Around 1805 they were expelled to the south, and from then on further south, until they left in 1899.

Reid writes in *Borderland* that in 980 Volodymyr (c. 958-1015) became Grand Prince in Kiev at a time that Christianity already had made itself felt in Russia: indeed, Volodymyr's grandmother Olha had privately taken baptism some years earlier. Originally Volodymyr had been an enthusiastic pagan 'who had set up idols on the hills outside the .... castle:† Perun, made of wood with a head of silver and a moustache of gold, Khors, Dahzbog, Stribog, Simargl, and Mokosh. The people called them gods and sacrificed their sons and daughters to them.'

But Volodymyr felt that his country needed a more advanced religion, and consulted with the Muslim Bulgarians. He listened to them, 'for he was fond of women and indulgence, [...] but circumcision and abstinence from pork and wine were disagreeable to him.' Volodymyr then investigated the Jews and the Catholic Germans, but saw no glory in the ceremonies in their temples. However,

The Hagia Sofia bowled the Kievans over: 'the Greeks led us to the edifices where they worship their god, and we knew not whether we were in heaven or on earth. For on

---

* When the Eastern Church separated from the Western in 1054, the Russian Church took sides with Eastern Orthodoxy and became the Russian Orthodox Church.

† [ellipsis from the original]

↑ Perun statue, photo Mary E.M.

earth there is no such splendour or beauty, and we are at a loss how to describe it. We only know that God dwells there among men, and their service is fairer than the ceremonies of other nations (Reid in *Borderland*).

In 988 Volodymyr subsequently ordered the Perun statues to be thrown into the Dnieper and had the Kievans herded into a tributary of the Dnieper for baptism: 'some stood up to their necks, others to their breasts, [...] there was joy in heaven and upon earth to behold so many souls saved.'

Whether it went like that, that Volodymyr had been shopping around for a religion that fitted him I don't know. Anyway, he had introduced a religion based on Greek Orthodoxy, which started to show some splits 600 years later when its rites were changed by patriarch Nikon (1605-1681). More about patriarch Nikon and his changes hereunder, first a very brief investigation into Orthodoxy.

Russian Orthodoxy one thousand years later

In order to see what an Orthodox service is like, I got myself invited to a service in Calgary. As I couldn't find the church, I entered a bit late, but only very shortly after the service had begun. At the entrance hall was a booth where candles were being sold. Inside, the parishioners attended the service standing on their own two legs. At the far side of the nave was an altar with a wooden screen wherein two carved doors between the icon of the Mother of God, on the one side (left), and the icon of Christ, on the other. Through the latticework of the doors one could see a priest, his head covered with a stiff, stand-up bonnet, rummaging around. During the two-hour service this priest often went to and fro through these doors, but never without first having kissed them.

In a corner, behind an enormously large sculpted Jesus, stood a young priest monotonously reading, for me, incomprehensible texts. Occasionally a parishioner started to sing, to be followed by the congregation. It reminded me of the way Grand Forks Doukhobors had sung; someone just started and the community joined in. Here in Calgary, during the singing the priest stepped down from the altar and walked along the walls of the church swinging an incense burner; the congregation turning as he approached, bowing for him.

Back again behind the doors the priest occupied himself with incense and candles, while a bible, later on I heard it was a Gospel book, on a stand was quickly set up. The priest then walked up to this enormous, red velvet, copper-locked book at the altar and read from it. The priest subsequently walked about in front of the altar with another book, disappeared, and reappeared with a chalice of wine. From this a number of people, children included, got a spoonful: the two altar boys keeping napkins under the believers' chins.

A warden walked up and down with a bowl of wafers. After distributing them, he kissed the latticed door before going through it, to appear immediately again, with even more wafers. Later I learned that these wafers were flatbread baked by the priest himself: apart from him no one had touched them with his or her hands.

During the two hours service everyone stood: there were no pews, just a few simple chairs lining one wall. Very few people sat on them. Fifteen minutes later, seeing that most of these chairs remained empty, I joined the few. After a while the warden saw me sitting, approached me, and asked with a loud voice whether I was 'A WOMAN?'

'Yes sir.'

'AND YOU WEAR PANTS IN THE HOUSE OF GOD?'

It was true: I, a woman, was wearing pants in the house of God. My best pants, bought all the way in Voorschoten back in the Netherlands, and kept for special occasions. The woman on the chair beside me rolled her eyes in solidarity (with me). The parishioner that had invited me to this service later apologized for the warden's behaviour, saying that she should have told me what to wear:

We are Orthodox, and *they* want to keep everything the old way. When I was eight months pregnant and did not feel very well, I sat down after one hour. The warden approached me and said that during the service I had to stand up. I complained and the priest said that during my pregnancy I was allowed to sit down.

The 'we' and 'they' in one sentence struck me. I was not pregnant, felt very well having been through my last pregnancy thirty years ago and thought it a shame to have these chairs around unused. Does this church have stocks in varicose vein stockings?

Not long after, during the same service, the warden approached me again. This time he shouted that I sat with my 'LEGS CROSSED,' which was not allowed either. The woman next to me rolled her eyes in even wider circles.

After the service wine, beer, coffee, cookies, soup, candies, sandwiches, tea and pies were served in the church's basement. My Orthodox friend told me that she was from Azerbaijan and had Russian, Ukrainian, Cossack, Gipsy and Syrian blood in her veins and:

before Azerbaijan split from Russia, I was just a Russian. Azerbaijan is now nationalistic; now it is important what kind of nationality one has. I was Moslem, just as my

father, but decided, just as my sister did, to become a Christian too. My brother still is a Moslem. My father had no problems with it.

She went on about her aunt, a Molokan, and repeated how, before the split from Russia, everyone just could be 'whoever they were.'

'Molokans are milk drinkers, aren't they,' I asked her. 'What is so special about Molokans? Tolstoy writes somewhere in *The Cossacks* that Molokans speak pure Russian, are Christians, have mixed with aboriginal groups and took their habits, liked freedom, idleness, hunting, and warfare. To be drunk is a ritual for these people: to be not drunk would be seen as heresy among them.' Much later I read in Sofia Tolstoys' *My Life* that the Cossack Old Believers live spaciously and cleanly, are well-fed, that the women do not work in the fields, but only at home. Sofia Tolstoy lists what these people eat, melon and cream from boiled milk and so on, noting that she did not get anything because they did not share their eating utensils.

Out of breath, I took a big sip of wine. My hostess said that this description did not remind her of her aunt: 'Molokans drink milk during their service, not wine like we do, because that symbolizes the blood of Christ. They are vegetarians.'*

I asked her why the people in the service I had just attended, cross themselves, touch the floor, and kiss the icons - sometimes seven times in a row.

'We bow as deep as possible for Christ. One touches the floor in order not to lose equilibrium.'

'It must be good exercise,' I observed.

'Yes,' she said, 'the Moslems have exercise anchored in their rituals. Mohammed thought that people were too fat and too lazy and that is why he ordered them to be on their knees five times per day and touch the floor with their head. And they are circumcised. Their penis rubs in their underwear the whole day; that causes it to be insensitive and that is why they can keep up their erections a long time. Women like that.'

I silently wondered why she had become a Christian. By the time we left, she introduced me to the priest who had led the service. There was no way around it, he stood right in front of the exit.

* Sonja Tolstory writes in *My Life* about the Molokans: 'A religious group similar in beliefs to the Doukhobors, but who accepted literacy and the reading of the Bible (307).' 'At that time Lev Nikolaevich had a visit from some Molokans whose children had been taken away so that they would be raised in Orthodoxy and not by their parents in sectarianism. As I recall, they put up the children in a nunnery (931).' Sonja T. goes on to tell how her daughter Tat'jana pleaded with Orthodox clergy to let the children return to their parents.

'Welcome,' he said affably, at the same time gesturing at my best pants and hissing in my friend's ear 'What is that!?'

We both apologized for my attire. I said that I was not familiar with their dress code and she said that she should have told me. In the short chat that followed I told the priest that I had come to see the church from which the Doukhobors had split.

The priest answered: 'Jesus said to Peter, I will build my church on this rock. He did not say, "I will build my church on these rocks." The Roman Catholic Church has lapsed. We are the only true church.'

In between his farewells to other parishioners I had a chance to ask him about the angled crossbar under Jesus' feet in his church.

'That is a footrest, pointing at the right to heaven, because the robber at His right hand was a good robber. He believed in Christ. The left side points downwards to the robber at the left ...'

But then more people, leaving the basement, cut him short. As they passed the priest they put their hands in a bowl shape, which the priest took and kissed. So while I sadly missed the end of the robber story, I left the loud-mouthed warden and the hissing priest and felt an urge to split, dance and jump.

Doukhobor Background

The history of the Doukhobors is for a great deal recorded in a thick book titled *Symposium Meetings 1974-1982*, with the lengthy subtitle *Report of the United Doukhobor Research Committee in the matter of Clarification of the Motivating Life-Concepts and the History of the Doukhobors in Canada. A compilation of officially recorded oral presentations and written submissions*. I have never seen a more democratically composed history book.

In it, Popoff (*S.M.*, 46) writes that the Doukhobors' spiritual forebears are considered to be like the Jewish youths, Shadrach, Meshach and Abednego, who in the *Book of Daniel* were thrown into a fiery furnace. Popoff mentions a number of non-conformists 'whose beliefs continued the patterns set by the medieval Christians such as the Paulicians, Albigenses, Waldenses and Bogomils, who were all harshly persecuted.' Among them, he argues the Bogomils 'remained strongest in Bulgaria, from where they spread into Russia.'

Popoff goes on the say that early Doukhobor leaders such as Kolesnikov and Kapustin, 'concept of the Spirit of God being manifest in man', supposedly composed or edited Doukhobor psalms. He concludes that Doukhoborism was imported by Bulgarian Bogomils, but that their psalms were native.

According to Legebokoff (*S.M.*, 27-8), Doukhobor history is to be found in the *Psalms of Life*, in a document written in 1791 and Novitskiy's 1832 book, *The Doukhobors: Their History and Beliefs*. Legebokoff but warns that:

> It must be noted that Orest Novitskiy was of the Greek Orthodox faith. He had never visited the Doukhobor colonies and he did not have a single interview with any Doukhobors. His book was based on government edicts, church records and statements on Doukhobors made by historians and so on. We can assume that Novitskiy himself did not think up the false statements, but that the sources he got the material from already had things falsely recorded.

Novitskiy subscribes to the theory that one of the first individuals, mentioned as an originator of Doukhobor thought, was an unnamed [Quaker] 'Retired Junior Officer' who lived in the Hunter's Village, in the Province of Kharkov.

Legebokoff (S.M., 28) continues with the theories of another historian, Fyodor V. Livanow (1869), who contends, that the Doukhobor tenets or articles of belief originated with the Bogomils and that all the ideas in circulation came to a head when [Russian] Archbishop Nikon introduced a number of reforms in the seventeenth century.[3]

So, while people were Russian Orthodox, other ideas circulated and these came to a head when archbishop Nikon wanted to change some rites. About half of the Russian population was in one way or another against these reforms and became known as the Raskol'niki (Dissenters) and Starovertsi (Old Believers). The newly contrary tenets were prominent in the provinces of Kharkov, Ekateroslav and Tambov and, as said, had similarities with those of the Bogomils, Paulicians and the Quakers. We have to go back in time.

Keck (1998) writes that the Bogomils derived their name from the priest Theophilus Bogomil from Trace and Philippi. In the 11th century Bogomilism spread from the Balkan to Asia Minor and Constantinople; in the 12th century it influenced the Kathar doctrines in the west and by the 13th century it had spread from the Black Sea to the Atlantic Ocean. As already in 1180 St. Symeon of Servia started to suppress the movement, the Serbians and Bulgarians started to settle in Russia.

This may also explain why their ideas, later known as Doukhobor ideas, emerged at so many places at the same time.

Anyway, when the Patriarch Nikon introduced a number of changes in the liturgy, the time was ripe for revolt. According to Von Haxthausen in *The Russian Empire I*:

> Bogomils are said to have descended from the Paulicians, a historical sect dating back to the seventh century of Christianity. The Paulicians (and others like them), formally opposed institutionalized worship, hierarchal structure, elaborate rituals, and sacraments, they emerged as soon

---

[3] In 1656 he also founded the New Jerusalem Monastery, 55 km NW of Moscow.

as Christianity was legalized by the first Christian Emperor Constantine (306-337).

The Patriarch Nikon [...] sent learned monks to Mount Athos, to consult the most ancient manuscripts, [... and] produced [...] the restored texts and the amended liturgical books, which in 1659 he ordered to be generally introduced, annulling those previously in use. Others alleged that Luther had in like manner declared that he merely restored primitive Christianity, whilst overthrowing everything, and abolishing the Mass, five Sacraments, etc.

Archbishop Nikon also prescribed that believers had to make the sign of the cross with two instead of three fingers. But, there was an Archpriest Avvakum and many others, who did not agree with Nikon's innovations. According to Von Haxthausen, the new, printed liturgy was condemned by those who hitherto only had had hand-written copies as transcribed in their nunneries. A large number of believers warily wondered about these innovations. Thinking them to be devilish seduction, they kept to the old rites. That is how they became known as the Old Believers or Starovertsi. Sometimes, as said above, they are also referred to as Raskol'niki, which means 'heretics or dissenters.'

Von Haxthausen writes that it was not only the reforms of archbishop Nikon that brought about the schism in the church. One Raskol'nik confided to him about the 'beard issue':

> It was not Nikon who separated us so completely from other Russian brethren, but Tsar Peter I [1672-1725 - Tsar from 1682 to 1696] effected this through the introduction of Western ideas: the order to cut off the beard was only an outward sign. Earlier, Tsarina Sofia [regent from 1682 till 1689] ordered the rebellious Archpriest Avvakum and his followers to be tortured.

According to Peacock in *Songs of the Doukhobors*, at that time there were already hundreds of thousands of sectarians. Some of them preferred to commit mass suicide, locked themselves up in prayer homes and set them afire. Avvakum was chained, imprisoned, beaten up, spit on, and then banned to Siberia. Sometimes Avvakum wondered whether all of his sacrifices were worth it, as changes in the liturgy were mostly accepted. However, his spouse urged him to keep faith, because 'Christ will not leave us.' Avvakum kept writing which caused him more trouble. On 14 April 1682 he was locked up in a wooden shed and burned alive.

Nikon's reforms led to a manifold schism in the Russian Orthodox Church; some of these sects, such as Skoptsy and Khlysty, led to Doukhoborism. One Doukhobor psalm indicates their communal origin from the early jumping and dancing sects: 'From jumping, dancing and other evil-inspired erratica ('pakklikooshki') we have disassociated ourselves.'

Chernoff (*S.M.*, 182) citing from the Russian *Bolshaya Rooskaya Encyclopedia* (1903), adds another common feature (besides jumping and dancing):

> From the Khlisti, Poborokhin (the then leader of the Molokans) took the concept that this 'Christ-Wisdom' continues to be reincarnated in God's chosen prophets. He considered it to have been reincarnated in himself. From among his faithful he chose 12 archangels and 12 angels of death.

Soukoreff (*S.M.*, 38) about the Khlysti connection to the Doukhobors:

> There still exist factual reports that give witness to the claims that the Doukhobors essentially evolved out of a group referred to as 'Worshippers of Christ-Incarnate.' Their largest numbers were within a sectarian movement called 'Khlisti,' or literally 'Self-Lashers,' because of one of their ceremonies wherein they lashed themselves with small whips in order to subdue or drive the devil-part out of themselves. A part of this movement also had a ceremony called '*Radeniye*,' which probably can be explained as a ceremony for a 'joyful quickening' of the spirits [. . .] Historians confirm that the Doukhobor movement took on more rational concepts in their interpretation of the proper manifestation of Christian beliefs, and they disassociated themselves from the mystical and fanatical elements of this broader dissident movement.'

Inikova writes in *The Doukhobor Centenary in Canada* that the name Doukhobors appeared for the first time in a report 'by the Slovenian Archbishop Nikifor to the Synod of March of 1786.' According to Lebedoff (*S.M.*, 16-17), it was Archbishop Ambrosius of the Province of Ekaternoslav who in 1785 referred to the forefathers of his group as the Doukhobortsi or Spirit-Wrestlers. This name was accepted by the group, then known as Old Believers: 'Yes, we are Spiritual Wrestlers because we are wrestling against all the evils inherent in the world.'

Peacock writes in his introduction to *Songs of the Doukhobors* that the People of God, their earlier name; 1) believed that God existed in man as a spirit; 2) that to kill a man was to kill God; 3) that the spirit did not exist in things like icons; 4) that Christ was naturally born, 5) and that after the crucifixion his spirit arose, not his body.

As splits from religions often splinter, in this case a group, the Molokans (Milkdrinkers) split off from the Spirit-Wrestlers as they held on to the Bible. Poborokhin, their leader was later arrested and his son-in-law became leader. From the 1880's on this group left for California and can still be found there.

The remaining group, the Doukhobors did not adhere to the Bible because one of their leaders, Daniel Filopovitch thought it to be a Maker of Controversy and threw the Bible into the Volga. All in all the splits from Greek Orthodoxy kept causing uproars and uproars have to be contained.

In 1801 Russian Senator Ivan Vladimirovich Lopukhin made an inspection tour in the Province of Sloboda-Ukraine. After having met there with the Doukhobors, he petitioned Tsar Alexander I (1777-1825, Tsar from 1801 on) to 'allow their relocation to the Tauride Province.'

Under the leadership of Saveliy Kapustin, the migration started immediately. Kapustin was born in 1743, had married into the Kalmakov family, had taken their name and in 1792 his son Vasiliy was born.

When Tsar Alexander I (1777-1825) visited them in the Crimea, he was impressed by their simple, communal lifestyle. Following a Doukhobor petition to free exiled Doukhobors in Siberia, he decreed on 23 May 1818 that all Doukhobors exiled for their beliefs should be freed immediately.

Around 1833 about 4000 Doukhobors lived in the villages: five along the upper reaches of the Milky river - Bogdanovka, Spassovka, Troitskoye, Terpeniye - and four near the lake formed by the Milky River before entering the sea of Azov - Rodionovka, Efremovka, Goreloy and Kirilowka.

In *A Mennonite in Russia* Epp (1991) writes that Alexander I's impression was not shared by Cornies, the local Mennonite leader. Epp contends that in 1816 rumours arose about Doukhobors harbouring deserters and outlaws and committing serious crimes, including murder and burying elderly people alive. The rumours also said that Kapustin/Kalmakov's son, Vasiliy Kalmakov, was a dull-witted, self-indulgent drunkard and that the latter's son, Ilarion Kalmakov, was also a confused and impotent alcoholic. Lastly, it was put about that during Ilarion's reign a mass grave of Doukhobors who had rebelled against the communities' policies was found. These stories are also in Peacock's introduction to his *Songs of the Doukhobors*.

Because of all these rumors Emperor Nikolai I (1796-1855, Tsar from 1825 on), successor of his brother Tsar Alexander I, issued another edict in 1839. This one exiled all the Doukhobors from the Milky Waters to the southern borderlands beyond the Caucasian Mountains, where they were to be kept under strict military guard. This migration started in 1841 and ended in 1845. Shortly before they had to leave, Von Haxthausen visited them and noted that they took the news of being exiled again quite calmly. The Doukhobors' new settlements were within Georgian-Emerit, in the Akhalsisk district, near the Turkish border.

After this forced migration, the Doukhobor lifestyle no longer gave cause for concern. Epp (1991) cites from a report that from then on they led exemplary lives and were strongly opposed to drunkenness and debauchery. The report states that Doukhobors had no churches, sung congregationally at gatherings, recognized Christ only as a priest and teacher, had communal ownership, were kind even to animals, had no formal weddings, and that baptism and holy communion were not practiced.

Just to check these facts, I called on Mike in December, who since his stroke had a telephone - his children had insisted on it:

'Baptism? Well no, we don't do that.'
'Holy Communion?'
'Hehh?
'Marriage?'
'Well, for instance when we have a couple that wants to be married. We bless them and that's it.'
'Where do you bless them?'
'We bless them in someone's home. Some who leave the Doukhobors might marry in a church. But that does not happen often'
'What about Christmas?'
'Christmas has nothing to do with Christ. That is just an excuse to get drunk.'
'New Year?'
'At 11:00 a.m. we have a prayer meeting and in the evening we come together at 10 and wait for the New Year. At 12 we sing some more and then disperse.
'How many were there?'
'We were with 150 [Sons of Freedom].'

On with the Doukhobor history. In 1864, when leader Peter Kalmakov, Ilarion's son, died at the age of twenty-eight, his wife Lukeria Hubanova, succeeded. Lukeria had chosen to be succeeded by Peter Vasiliy Verigin after her death (in 1886), a young man related to the Kalmakov family. He was married, and had two children, but the girl died young.

Lukeria's choice of Peter for her successor caused a split: 700 families consented to the decision and were known as the Large Party, later known to as the *postniki* or *fasters*. About 200 families known as the Small Party, later known as the *mjasniki* or *meat-eaters* (and the Doukhobor administrative unit) did not agree, and instead opted for Lukeria's brother, Michael, denouncing Peter as someone who would incite religious insurrection. The ensuing upheaval was so big that the Russian government, interested in keeping up the status quo - Michael had been running the administrative centre - sent a Cossack army down and exiled Peter Vasiliy Verigin to Shenkursk, Siberia. That was in 1887. In 1902 he would be freed and let go to Canada.

As from 1883 on, Doukhobor youth were conscripted by the Russian army Peter V. Verigin sent directives from Shenkursk that the youth should not serve in the army. The directives only reached the Doukhobors between 1893 and 1895, which says something about the Russian postal services at the time. So, from 1896 on, young Doukhobors were sentenced to penal battalions in Siberia. 'The first party to reach the City of Yakutsk, in Siberia, arrived there on September 26, 1897,' (Soukeroff, *S.M.*, 42).

At the same time, on 29 July 1895 Doukhobors in Tiflis, Elisabetpol and Kars gathered around outdoor fires, prayed, sang hymns, and burned their guns. In Spasskoe the Doukhobors gathered fifteen wagon loads of firewood, gallons and gallons of kerosene, and all their weapons together and set them ablaze at midnight. The enormous jet of fire that lit up the sky and the sound of weapons exploding throughout the night roused neighbouring Georgians and Armenians, and by dawn the police had come (Sanborn in *The Doukhobor Centenary*). Sergej Tolstoy adds the following story to the turmoil. In *A Journey to Canada* he writes that the police in the Tiflis Province knew about the burning of arms, but not in the Elizavetpol' en Kars Oblast. And, that the meat-eaters had alleged that the fasters were going to attack them. These allegations were not checked, Cossacks were sent to the Akhalkalak district with their whips and later rampaged the village. The Tiflis Doukhobors were then exiled to Georgia, where they had neither land or employment. The Elizavetpol and the Kars Doukbobors could stay in their homes, but under strict police surveillance.

Over the next year 350 Doukhobors died of disease and hunger. The Doukhobors had found the martyrdom that Verigin had encouraged them to seek (writes Sanborn).

It was at this time, 1895 (Sep. 10), that Tolstoy, in reply to Birjukovs work about the plight of the Christians in Russia and Chertkiv's appeal Help, started to write articles about the Doukhobor plight in *The Times* in London. And so comes that

Tolstoy and, as we will see, also his son Sergej step into this story about the Doukhobor's.[4]

---

4   Sergej Tolstoy (1863-1947) studied at the Department of Natural Sciences in Moscow and music. He married Marija Rachinskaja (1865-1900) in 1895, and Countess Marija Zubova (1868-1939) in 1906.

Tolstoy, Klisty and Skoptsy

As said, at the start of my investigation the name of the Russian count Nikolaevitch Tolstoy kept popping up in Canadian Doukhobor circles as well as in the writings of the Dutch-American author Pierre van Paassen. According to Inikova in *The Doukhobor Centenary*, the followers of Tolstoy believed that the Doukhobor teachings were 'virtually identical' with those of their mentor Tolstoy, but, also that: 'the Tolstoyan dream of building the Kingdom of Truth on earth cost the Doukhobors dearly.' Next question, where did Tolstoy come from?

Maude (1908), discussing Leo Tolstoy's possible ancestry writes:

> In the annals of the Russian nobility it is recorded that a man named Idris came from Germany in the year 1353 with two sons and 3000 followers, and settling at Tchernígoff in Little Russia was received with favor by the reigning Grand Duke, who granted him much land.

Perhaps it was in his genes; Tolstoy's earliest known ancestor also had attracted followers. Maude does not reveal what kind of followers this Idris had nor why he left Germany but continues about Idris' great-grandson Andrew, who migrated to Moscow. There he was 'well received by the reigning Grand Duke Vasíly, who conferred upon him the name Tolstóy.' According to some other accounts writes Maude, the original German name of the family was Dick, of which Tolstoy (meaning: thick) is a translation.

This account is in an odd way confirmed by Pierre van Paassen *In That Day Alone* when he refers to a certain Willem Bos, a Gorkum bookshop owner. Van Paassen wrote that Bos had told him once that the Tolstoy family originally hailed from the Netherlands - a theory that has found some support in more recent years.

Peter Tolstoy, Maude goes on, served the Russian government around 1645, visited the Netherlands and France in the company of Tsar Peter I and also managed to lure Alexis, the run-away son of Tsar Peter I, back to Russia. Later on Alexis was executed in a secret trial in which Peter Tolstoy participated. As his help in this matter was greatly appreciated, it earned him large estates and a promotion to the headship of the Secret Chancellery. Catharine the Great made Peter Tolstoy a count on the occasion of her coronation, which title was transferred in 1770 to grandson Elias, Leo Tolstoy's grandfather.

Leo Tolstoy was born in 1828. He was one and a half years old when his mother died and nine at the untimely death of his father. Tolstoy's oldest sister, married to the Count of Osten-Saksen, became his and his younger siblings,' guardian. Maude focuses on numerous happenings in Tolstoy's childhood, some of which might have shaped Tolstoy's pacifist mindset. For example, Tolstoy's oldest brother, Nicolas, lasting influence. Nicolas invented games such as the Ant-Brother game:

> It was he who, when I was five and my brothers, Dimitry six and Sergéy seven, announced to us that he possessed a secret by means of which, when disclosed, all men would become happy, there would be no more disease, no trouble, none would be angry with anybody, all would love one another and all would become 'Ant-Brothers.' We even organized a game of Ant-Brothers, which consisted in sitting under chairs, sheltering ourselves with boxes, screening ourselves with handkerchiefs, and cuddling against one another while thus crouching in the dark.

Nicolas' conditions to become a member of the Brotherhood were:

> to stand in a corner and do not think of a white bear, walk without wavering along a crack between the boards of the floor, and for a whole year not to see a bear, alive or dead or cooked [. . .] Nikólenko, as I now conjecture, had probably read or heard of the Freemasons - of their aspirations toward the happiness of mankind, and of the mysterious initiatory rites on entering their order; he had probably also heard about the Moravian brothers.

Maude's editor explains in a footnote that 'ant' in the Russian language is a *mouravéy*. So Russian children, such as Tolstoy and his siblings, did not play 'Indian,' they played 'Moravian Brother.'[5]

Cuddled under a chair covered with boxes, Tolstoy became acquainted with the faith and fate of people with schismatic beliefs. According to Maude (1908) Tolstoy was baptized into the Orthodox church. But in *Confessions* Tolstoy admitted that from the time that he began reading philosophy, he no longer attended church services, and like Rousseau and Voltaire, amused himself with ridiculing religion. He did believe something though, but could not explain what exactly. He tried to better himself and drew up his own rules. Studying at the university was not much to his taste - in 1844 he accomplished one year of Eastern Languages, failed in German, and then switched to Law School. But, after two more years he stopped his law studies, having seen more of student life than of Law School.

The 1849 Hungarian revolution caused Tolstoy to become a member of the Horse Guards. He registered as a *Junker*, what meant that he had to live with military officers in order to become one himself.

---

5 Moravian Brothers, also known as Hernhutters, are members of a church, founded in 1457 by followers of Joannes Hus, a catholic priest and professor at the University of Prague. Hus argued that the gospel should be available in the vernacular, that everyone should be able to have communion by bread and wine and he was against a number of practices of the Catholic Church. Hus and his followers ended up on pyres. However, by the end of the fifteenth century the ashes seemed to have fallen on fertile soil.

Then, in 1517 on the night of the 31st of October, the day before All Saints Day, Luther nailed his ninety-five theses on a church door in Wittenberg. The next day an influx of pilgrims was expected. Luther objected to the crazed practices of the Catholic Church, such as selling indulgences, worshipping relics (many of these relics are now known to have been pig bones). Of course the church leaders did not like his criticism; periods of persecutions followed and much later the Thirty Year's War of Religion (1618-1648) broke out.

At the Treaty of Westphalia, 1648, it was decided that in the future everyone had to have the religion of the leader of his country. This decision caused the Moravian Brothers to flee, under the guidance of Bishop John Amos Comenius, to Poland. Others acted as if they were Catholics and still others used subterfuge.

At the start of 1700 a number of Moravian Brothers found a home at the Count Nicholas Ludwig Von Zinzendorf estates. There they founded the village of Hernhut and drew up their constitution, *The Lord's Watch,* which is still in power today.

In this *Junker* period Tolstoy played cards, managed a post office, enjoyed many women while paying for the fruits of his intimate relationships. When not travelling, he resided in the Cossack village of Starogládovksk, which he describes in *The Cossacks*. Among the Cossacks he found members of the Old Believers' sect who had fled the persecutions of the Tsars and had settled among the Muslim Tchitchénians, somewhere near the Térek River.[6] Tolstoy enjoyed talking with their leader, Aglaya. Tolstoy though was exposed to more than the Moravians or Old Believers.

Alexandra Tolstoya (1884-1979), Tolstoy's youngest surviving child, mentions in *The Tragedy of Tolstoy* several sectarian visitors that visited her father: 'Last year one of the Skoptsy, Andrei Yekovlevich Grigorieve, came along.' About Andrei, she notes, that his family came from Prilepsy, a town in Mtensk and that his father was good at drinking and swearing. But then, one day he bought some timber from a certain Semen Tomofeyevich Rastorguyev, a Khlisty. Khlisties did not drink wine, thought that people had 'to be born again,' and that Orthodox people were alcoholic as well as oppressed people. Andrei's father became a Khlisty himself.

Andrei, then fourteen years old, also wanted to become a Khlysty, but had to marry first. He did so and became a member of the sect on the condition that he would live with his wife as if she were his sister. While living with his 'sister,' the world started to look like a sad place to Andrei: so he left the Khlysty and became a Skoptsy. At this point in his story Tolstoy asked Andrei, 'Was it then when they did it to you?'

Andrei replied 'that had not been the case: they were cowards and it was only the bold ones who did so.' Andrei

---

6 In *The Cossacks* it is said the Old Believers are Christians and Dissenters. According to Seaton (1985, 56, 107, 124) the Cossacks originally had primitive and superstitious beliefs, while among each other they were honest and deemed cheating and cowardice as the greatest vices. [One wonders how much more primitive a belief can be!] After the persecutions of 1667 many Raskol'niki found refuge among the Cossacks and others went to the Terek area, "Old Believers that openly professed their faith were always numerous among the Cossacks." The Grebénsky Cossacks Tolstoy met with, originated from or had taken over the Molokan religion. Apart from basing their beliefs on the bible and rejecting priesthood, dogma's, rites, sacraments and icons, they drank milk.

had it done in the province of Ufa. Andrei went on to tell that his first brother had died, that the other brother had to enter military service, and that he was put in prison because he was a Skoptsy. He was put in irons, had half of his skull shaven, and people had been throwing mud at him because he had castrated himself. In the end he was sent into exile for thirty-six years. Tolstoy then had asked whether he had any regrets, but no, Andrei did not because otherwise he would have lived a life of weakness:

> My nephew is weak; he drinks, and swears with many kinds of words. He even beat me [...]. He hit me once, and I went off my feet; he hit me again, I went farther off; and when he hit me for the third time, I fell off the house steps. He beat me - and from that very time he softened! I thanked him for beating me, and after that he began to understand much that was good. I would have been glad if he had beaten me earlier.[7]

Andrei, when asked whether he now had a household of his own, had answered that he did not.

Andrei's story is quite vague, but one thing stands out; mud was thrown at him because he had castrated himself to be taken in by the Skoptsy.

---

[7] In *That Day Alone,* Van Paassen writes about another visit to Willem Bos' bookshop in Gorcum. Uncle Kees had told there about a farmer who was always beaten by his master and who in the end was embraced by this master and begged for forgiveness. 'Upon hearing the end of the peasant's story, Uncle Kees said, that Tolstoy got up in great emotion and walked around the room a few times and then burst into tears, but they were not tears of sorrow. They were tears of gladness.' *That Day Alone* was published in 1942. In *The Tragedy of Tolstoy,* published in 1933, 'Tolstoy was laughing from joy' at the end of Andrei's story. Could it be that Van Paassen had read Tolstoy's daughter's book?

Others on the Skoptsy

Goldberg dedicates a few pages in *The Sacred Fire* to the Skoptsy, who called themselves White Pigeons, 'that is, the pure.' According to the Skoptsy the Bible is a falsification; their scripture is the *Book of the Dove* that was already around at the time of Tsar Peter I (1672-1725), whom they called their Christ. Sexual union is the original sin, committed by Adam and Eve; Jesus Christ was sent on earth to mutilate himself, but failed to do so and was succeeded by 'an even greater son of God;' Szelivanow, the founder of their sect. Szelivanow stressed passages such as, 'If thy hand or thy foot offends thee, cut them off and cast them from thee . . .'

Other biblical quotes favoured by the Skoptsy were 'blessed are the barren wombs' and 'there will be some eunuchs, which were made eunuchs of men.' (Which is strange, as Skoptsy simultaneously think the Bible a falsification.)

However, the Skoptsy sect increased because everyone who brought in twelve converts was 'given the distinction of Apostle-ship.' Some people had to mutilate themselves; others were forcibly mutilated. If, because of an unsuccessful procedure, all desire was not completely lost, one spoke of the Lesser Seal or *Malay Pechat*. In the case of all desire being lost (because all the genitals were completely removed), one spoke of the Greater Seal or *Belaya Pechat*.

Goldberg writes about the congregation's wild orgies, called *The Ship*. He witnessed one such 'service,' and gives the text of one of their songs which starts with these lines:

> Hold fast, you men of the ship,
> Do not let the ship perish in the storm
> The Holy Spirit is with us . . .

. . . which continues with lines of the same tendency. Goldberg continues that the men started to sing, the women took over and that the congregation then:

> . . . fell into a dance [. . .] wild leaping and whirling [. . .] general kissing. In their worship, they chose a maiden, a *Bogoroditsa*, a 'mother of god,' who was expected to give birth to the new Christ [...]. She was then undressed and immersed in a tub of warm water [. . .] while the old

women amputated her left breast. The bleeding virgin was then placed upon an altar, and an almost inhuman orgy followed. The amputated breast was hacked into tiny pieces and grabbed by the worshippers to be eaten while still warm [...]. Before the close of the year, she would report at the meeting-place with her child [...]. On the eight day of the child's life, his left side was lanced by a finely pointed spear, and the warm blood that flowed from the wound in the infant body was drunk in the communion service. The body itself was dried and pounded into a powder. Out of this powder cakes of bread were prepared, to be offered the worshippers on the first day of the Easter season.[8]

Von Haxthausen writes in *The Russian Empire* that a large portion of the jewelers and goldsmiths in St. Petersburg, Moscow, Riga, and Odessa belonged to the Skoptsy. In Orel entire village communes were found, albeit on first sight only their 'normal' households are to be seen. The Skoptsy children that were nevertheless born, sprung from young lads and men in the neighbourhood.

In a footnote Von Haxthausen adds what his secretary learned about the Skoptsy and Khlysty: which is the same story as that related by Goldberg. Also, according to the secretary, at the age of nineteen or twenty these women looked as if they were fifty or sixty years old.[9]

Goldberg and Von Haxthausen were not the only ones fretting about the Skoptsy. Wilson states in *Rasputin and the Romanovs* that the Skoptsy women were only superficially mutilated, so they still could work as prostitutes to fill the

---

[8] Comment of Cornelius Jaenen, who was so friendly to proofread part of the text of this book, 'this sounds like 2nd century anti-Christian propaganda!'

[9] In this regard, Van Paassen *Earth could be Fair* comes to mind when he cites his imaginary uncle Kees who said that the Russians are the most unpredictable people on earth, because:

They take the Gospel seriously. Why? They take the Gospel seriously. Who was it that said that about the Russians being the only people who have preserved the true likeness of Christ in their bosom and whose destiny it is therefore, some day, when the peoples of the West have lost the road, to direct them into new paths of salvation? Who was it, again? Oh, yes, of course. I have it: one of those Dukhobors who stayed at grandfather's house when he passed through Holland on his way to America. Piotr Verigin was his name.

Skoptsy treasury box. Wilson mentions a few Skoptsy, such as Count Elanski and the head butler of Tzar Alexander I. Supposedly, Count Elanski proposed to convert all members of the Russian government, to free them of worldly emotions, and was subsequently banned.

In order to have a closer look at Andrei's first calling, being one of the Khlysty sect, I came across a book written by Maria Rasputin, daughter of the infamous Rasputin. Rasputin and Barham write in *Rasputin, the Man behind the Myth* that Danilo Filipov founded the Khlysty sect and his followers were fasting, self-flagellating fanatics. Readev, Filipov's successor, having said that the Holy Spirit himself had given him his inspiration, had established a harem of thirteen women with whom he satisfied himself *en masse*. Maria Rasputin's father, Grischa Rasputin, once had been going door to door to ask for food. He had come across a couple with an ailing daughter, who was somehow cured in his presence. He was then led by her mother to the *vozhd*, a Khlysty priest, who told him that the human body is a temple of God, that certain followers of Krishna meditate in the act of copulating, and that the *agape*, or 'love feast,' of the early Christians was banned by the Council of Carthage, in AD 397. Therefore, their [Khlysty] concept was not a new one.

Grischa Rasputin was subsequently invited to a service, where worshipping started with a prayer of the *vohzd*, followed by an admonition to love each other, a frenzied dance, and a woman breaking from the rows embracing the *vozhd*. Rasputin underwent a similar treatment and had to perform double, no even triple duty, with the women who had been forced to wait for their turn with him. Just as Rasputin was beginning to feel that he had no more 'to give,' the *vozhd*, who had donned his robe, spoke from his position in the centre of the room: 'Ye children of God, the ceremony is ended. Go in peace.'

The next morning the husband of his hostess went to the fields to work and when Rasputin, upon leaving, wanted to thank the wife:

He found her standing politely, though rigidly, to receive his thanks. His impression was that if he had approached

her with some sign of wanting to renew their lovemaking, she would have been as offended as any honest housewife at such temerity.

Maria Rasputin describes another more Khlysty ceremony in which her father had participated:

> All the participants were unclad from the start and the prettiest of the women was chosen to serve as the altar itself, not to mention the chalice. The sacramental wine was poured into her navel, from which the priest drank; he recited the Lord's Prayer in reverse, and began performing acts of perversion with his female 'altar' before Grisha's horrified eyes [. . .] and he found himself engaging in the general debauchery despite his initial revulsion.

The next morning he left with 'an entirely changed outlook on life, and his communion with God renewed in all its former plenitude.'

Also according to outsiders, Wilson for example, Rasputin was and remained a Khlisty all his life. Liepman states in *Rasputin and the Fall of Imperial Russia* that Khlisty means 'Man of God' and that Rasputin learned the rituals in the Verkoutry convent where Orthodox heretics were incarcerated with Khlisty. Liepman's description of such ceremony very much matches Maria Rasputin's description.

In *The Reign of Rasputin: an Empire's Collapse*, Rodzianko writes that the President of the Duma, the Russian Parliament, who would have liked to get rid of Rasputin, had written:

> I had in my possession scores of letters from mothers whose daughters had been seduced by Rasputin. I had also in my possession photographs of a 'Khlysty Ship.' In the centre sat Rasputin, surrounded by about a hundred of his followers, all of them young men and women.

This writing did not help the Duma President to get rid of Rasputin, as the latter was able to stop the bleedings of the Tsar's son.

As Alexandra Tolstoy noted in her chapter *Visitors*, many people came to her father's home to talk with him: 'Old pilgrim women in bast shoes and with knapsacks [. . .] peasants from near and far villages, the half-wit Parasha [...] the crazy peasant covered with rags and lice.'

Listening to the peasants' stories will have familiarized Tolstoy with a number of 'Old Believers' tenets - the gist of which may have helped to shape his own doctrines. As said, according to Inikova in *The Doukhobor Centenary*, the followers of Tolstoy believed that the Doukhobor teachings were 'virtually identical' with those of their mentor Tolstoy. Taken into account who visited Tolstoy and enjoyed his full attention, that is perhaps not surprising.

As also said, upon learning of their plight, Tolstoy, aided by his friends Birjukov (1860-1931), Chertkov (1854-1936) and Tregubov (1858-1931), started to publish about them. Subsequently these three were quickly exiled from Russia.* Tolstoy, according to Sanborn in *The Doukhobor Centenary*, was left unmolested due to his tremendous prestige at home and abroad.

Punitive action against the Doukhobors on behalf of the government did not work and discharging them from army service was rejected 'for fear that others would follow their lead.' Having them leave Russia seemed to be an easier option. Sanborn assumes that the government was relieved when the Doukhobors requested permission to leave Russia.

* His, and Birjukov's and Chertkov's, signatures on a public appeal in aid of the Doukhobor emigration brought Birjukoc exile to Kurland (now Estonia). Later he worked with Chertkov in England.

Doukhobors to Canada

The Doukhobors petitioned Tsarina Maria Fedorovna (1847-1928) for emigration and got her blessing. They then consulted Tolstoy, who in turn consulted their exiled leader, Peter Verigin. Both were against the emigration. Tolstoy sensed though that the people dearly wanted to leave, and he consulted his friends Chertkoff, Hilcoff and a few English Quakers. The Quakers suggested the group move to Cyprus, which was not so far and was English territory. This happened in August 1898, but of the 1126 people that went, about sixty died because of the climate. As agriculture in Cyprus proved too troublesome, the Quakers took it upon themselves to help the Doukhobors relocate.*

People as Kropotkin (1842-1921), Peter and Arthur St. John, a Quaker from Toronto, then suggested the Canadian prairies as a suitable place (Mealing in *To America with the Doukhobors*).† The Canadian government reacted positively to the idea, according to Sergej Tolsoy, because the requests first came from England. Anyway, on February 24 a memo was received from the Tiflis governor's office, conveying that (in full in Sergej T.'s *A Journey to Canada*):

> The Doukhobor fasters may go abroad under the following conditions: a valid passport, one has to pay their own travel costs and sign a guarantee that they will never come again within the borders of the Empire. Adding: 'on the understanding the penalty for violation of this last point will be exile to remote regions.'

Tolstoy wrote the novel *Resurrection*, profits of which he destined for Doukhobor immigration and also informed Queen Victoria of the Canadian plan.[10] Tolstoy asked his friend Leopold Sulerzhitsky (1872-1916) to organize and

* In *My Life* Sofia T. relates a visit from a Nicolas Russell, born Nikolaj Konstantinovich Sudzilovskij (1850-1930). "Everything he said about the locale," writes Sofia T. was very tempting, but it was too late, "since it had all been arranged by that time for the Doukhobors to go to Canada."

† Sergej T. writes that Kropotkins first discussed this plan with University of Toronto professor James Mavor and then suggested the plan with the Quakers and with Russians in England.

---

10 In the Netherlands Felix Ortt, a Dutch 'Christian Anarchist,' wrote in Dutch a brochure, *Christelijk Anarchisme,* in which he explains the Doukhobor tenets. The profits of this brochure went to the emigration costs of the Doukhobors. Ortt (1898, III) finishes his plea for help for the 'Duchoboren' noting that 'Wladimir Tsjertkoff, (Gable house farm, Sandon, Chelmsfort, Essex), who is banned from Russia because he publicly took the Doukhobors' side, collects gifts for them and that the Editors of "*Vrede (Peace)*", Leidsche Vaart 234, Haarlem, do so too.'

accompany the first boatload of people, and stay with them until they were settled satisfactorily. According to Mealing, Sulerhitsky had been a man 'without a clear role in life.' A footnote in Sofia T's *My Life* mentions that he was a theatre director. Anyway, upon Tolstoy's request he not only functioned as 'a kind of on-the-spot Tolstoy, but also as business agent, pastor, interpreter, trouble-shooter, nurse, teacher, and finally chronicler.'

For some reason Mealing does not mention that Sulerzhitzy was not alone in being charged with aiding and accompanying Doukhobors at the time of their immigration to Canada. In November he and Sergej Tolstoy left Yasnaja Polyana, the Tolstoy estate, traveled one and a half-day by train and then rode a few more days along the Georgian Military Road to Tiflis. Sergej T's *A Journey to Canada* gives a host of details with regard to rounding up the exiled Doukhobors, housing and feeding them until the ship, the Lake Huron was ready to leave. On December 10 Sergej wired to Chertkov in England: 'The Huron has sailed with about 2,020 souls.' On the 11th of December he wrote in his diary, 'Batoum feels empty after the Huyron's departure.'

Sulerhitsky's diary of the Doukhobor-migration was published under the title *To Canada with the Doukhobors*. He started his travel diary with:

> I shall not speak here of the events of 1894, when some of the Doukhobors (about 4,300 persons) were taken from their homes in Kars Province (Wet Mountain Area) and settled (exiled) in the Georgian villages of Tiflis Province. Nor is this the place to tell about the conditions they faced in the burning hot, fever-infested valleys of Tiflis Province.

Sulerzhitzky goes on describing the preparations for the leap over the ocean to Canada; how the people travelled to Batum at the Black Sea, how they kept themselves alive in a big, damp hall and how, on a certain day, a young man, whose wife was about to give birth, shyly approached him. Sulerhitzky was amazed that this story was brought with so much bashfulness. But then it appeared that three years earlier the group had decided to abstain from sex, so no babies would be born prior to emigrating. A corner was secluded, the child was born, and none of the fellow migrants volunteered any comment.

As there was not much money for the journey, Sulerzhitzky had rented a boat under the condition that he would be allowed to build 2140 sleeping cots in it. He had also made it known that the Doukhobors did not need any staff to serve them. Train tickets to Batum cost 2000 rubles; food for the journey from Batum to Canada 1000 rubles; the rent of the ship 56,000 rubles; the train in Canada 20,000 rubles: totalling 80,200 rubles. At that time a ruble was worth $0.50 CDN.

While the people waited in the hall, the ship was outfitted: sleeping cots were built and bedding, pots, and pans were brought aboard. As soon as the boarding process started it became clear to the organizers that the Doukhobors were not a homogeneous group.

Upon being asked what berth they were supposed to have, some said, 'We are from Orlovka and our elders said that once aboard, we had to keep left - but at that side the people of Tombovka and Efremova are already seated - what a disaster.' In turn, the Tombovkas said that the Orlovkas had to go to the second level. Anyway, it was generally agreed that the Resantsev family had to stay behind as one of them had scarlet fever.

Nevertheless, on 10 December 1898, propellers touched the black waters, the Doukhobors sang a psalm and then 'the ship [moved] ahead at full speed. The singing stopped. The petrified crowd, faces wet with tears, silent, holding their breath, looked at the mist-covered, mountainous shore. In the stillness a woman could be heard crying somewhere by the mast.'

Sulerzhitsky also mentions the little boy who died during the trip of leukemia and had a burial at sea; the misery when it became very hot, and a violent storm hit and lasted for days at a stretch. Finally, on 12 January 1899, the ship entered the Halifax harbour for quarantine inspection, and then went on to St. John.

Sulerzhitsky sketches the do-gooding ladies of St. John, who offered candies to the immigrant children - a gesture not much appreciated by the Doukhobor mothers. The welcoming crowd was a bit taken aback by the way Doukhobor greeted each other, bowing to each other in order to greet the Christ in each one. After a long train ride and a stop in Winnipeg, the immigrants arrived at the spot that the Quakers had sought out for them.

Son of Freedom Mike wrote the following about his parents' settlement in Canada in a letter to me in 1999:

> My family came with first Doukhobors from Georgia from a settlement called Bohdanovka, at the time of the persecution and Tolstoy's help. My dad was 11 years old when he came to Canada, mother was younger by 3 years. The first settlement was in the North West Territories, before they were named Saskatchewan and Manitoba. Then they lived in Pelly, Sask., and Arron, Manitoba, for a few years until the government robbed them of the land and the settlements. Then they moved to B.C. for a few years, then moved back to Sask. for some arrangement the government made with the Aboriginals. I was born here adjacent to the Indian reserve in 1924. We got along very well with the Indians and went to their picnics and rain dances. Here we lived until we had over 9 boys of this settlement arrested and sentenced to 9 months for refusing military service, which involved my brother also. Then as soon as the boys did their time the families left for B.C. in 1940.

Hawkes writes in *The Story of Saskatchewan and its People*, about a 'returning officer in the Territorial election' in a district that extended to the Swan River, who met with Doukhobors, 'who were looking for running water, wood and good soil.' They 'were not particular where it was as they intended to live within themselves.' After suitable locations far from railways and projected railways were found and the Doukhobors had settled, Hawkes notes:

> Their houses and buildings were well built of logs and clay, a fact that is partly accounted for by many of the Doukhobors being skilled mechanics. The houses in the villages were in double rows with stables, etc., behind, and wide streets between the rows. The buildings were whitewashed, and there were net fences; trees were planted in front of the houses [...] the villages ware connected with

good roads, many miles in length; and the Doukhobors were the first to have telephones between the villages [...] built, owned and operated by themselves. Their system of government consisted in electing three councillors in each village who were invested with supreme control. They could marry and even divorce couples, who were found incompatible.

From the start of Doukhobor settlement in 1899, journals and weeklies featured articles praising the 'Doukhobors' prominent but fine features from which one could read that they lead virtuous lives' (Jaenen in *The Doukhobor Centenary*). Journals and weeklies raved about the fact that the Doukhobors could have gone to France but had chosen British' liberty instead; that they were clean and religious; that one could count on them, and that people who depicted them as fanatics were not themselves civilized.

However, clergy started to have their doubts about the Doukhobors' intentions. A report, in French, from the archdiocese of Saint-Boniface (1902, 21) reads:

> The Doukhobors occupy a privileged situation in our social state. This eccentric tribe that seems to have fallen off another planet, with cult nor code except for the most refined egoism, without a doctrine other than vague echo's of Tolstoy's daydreams is refractive to our laws and even to the superior sentiment of the integrity of its adopted fatherland. They do not have schools, they object to subject to laws concerning marriages, births and death.

Comments from the Protestant side, by a Presbyterian minister, were that the Doukhobors should be put through the 'great Anglo-Saxon mill and be ground up; in the grinding they lose their foreign prejudices and characteristics' (Jaenen).

Hawkes noted that even early on also problems with the government were brewing: the Doukhobors caused great trouble for the 1901 census. They also resisted the registration of births, marriages, and deaths: saying that God knew all these things and it was nobody else's business. Then Doukhobor elders got word from the government that they had to keep to the laws of the land and had to have themselves individually registered.

Doukhobor spiritual leader, Peter Verigin, released in 1902 from exile in Siberia, urged everyone to just do that: to register. He was of the opinion that his people could as well live communally on registered land and that it could take thousands of years before mankind would acknowledge that fences and borders make no sense. Two thousand of his followers registered. So, everyone between eighteen and sixty years, that had registered, could purchase a lot of 160 acres at a cost of $10. However, they had three years to improve this land and pledge an oath of allegiance to the king.*

* By 1906 Saskatchewan had a flourishing Doukhobor community.

Meanwhile, in 1905, the Russian Tsarina gave birth to her son, Alexis. On this occasion several exiled groups were given amnesty. Peter V. Verigin sent Ivan Evseyevitch Konkin to Yakutz in Siberia to notify the exiled Doukhobors of the happy news (Popoff in *S.M.*, 148). However, before going to Yakutz, Konkin first went to see friends in England, and then went to France and by the time he arrived in Yakutz the exiled Doukhobors had already heard the good news and had already traveled to Irkutz. When Konkin caught up to them, they were camping under dire circumstances. Still he told the exiled Doukhobors that Verigin urged this group not to come to Canada too hastily. He advised them to request the Russian Governor-General that they could remain, settle along the Amur and start a self-contained community because there were problems with swearing to the Canadian Oath of Allegiance.

After everything they had been through, the Yakutz Doukhobors did not think that swearing an oath would cause them a problem; they promptly migrated to Canada in 1906. This caused 'a problematic relationship with Verigin and also some coolness with the rest of the Doukhobor community' (Popoff in *S.M.*, 149).

In the eyes of the ex-Siberian newcomers the lifestyle of the Canadian Doukhobors was wasteful. This group still resides in Saskatchewan; they, and those that took the oath of allegiance, refused to have their lives ruled by Verigin and are now known as the Independent Doukhobors.

Free Men, Sons of Freedom

Peacock's third group that started to harbour problems were those that did not enjoy the community's prosperity and some grumbled about Peter Verigin's material well being.

Already in 1902 the Free Men, later called the Sons of Freedom, did not heed Verigin's call to register and started a trek led by Vanya Podmoryov, an elder who had been a close friend of Peter Verigin. During the discussion about registering for free land, the idea had come up to that they should free cattle and horses because animal husbandry was a form of slavery and that they should go on a pilgrimage. Asked by Verigin's younger brother about the reasons for this trek, Podmoryov had said that it was meant to free their leader Peter Verigin from Siberia. As noted above, the Russian government indeed freed Verigin in September 1902.

Laktin (*S.M.*, 115) adds that Podmoryov had visited Verigin in Siberia, who had told him that the Doukhobors would move overseas and that they would witness 'a turbulent stream' and 'should jump into it.' According to Laktin, Podmoryov had not been the instigator of this trek; he had just recognized the several thousand trekkers as the 'turbulent stream' he had to jump into. During the trek he insisted that 'the Doukhobors were performing' a task they were destined to do. Whether the trek was a fulfilling prophecy or not, it helped to free Peter V. Verigin.

Fulfilling a prophecy

Popoff (*S.M.*, 292) provides the most traditional Doukhobor justification for nudity, fulfilling a prophecy. The former female leader Lukeriya Kalmakova, who died in 1886, 'had ordered two of her women servants, who served at her 'Sirotskoy' residence, the administrative centre, to undress and appear naked in front of a mass meeting of the Congregation.' Elders had insisted, according to Mr. Popoff, that this really happened:

> When the two naked women appeared before the Congregation, Lukeriya Kalmakova purportedly had stated: 'the time will soon come when you, brothers and sisters, will migrate across the ocean, and in your life there,

there will appear among you a group that will be referred to as 'The Naked Ones.'

Popoff also notes that:

from this prophecy fanatically inclined people have time and again repeated as one of their reasons for nude parades: 'The reverend Doukhobor leader Lukeriya Kalmakova had prophesied that this nudity among the Doukhobors would appear, and so we are merely fulfilling this prophecy.'

Unfortunately, according to Popoff, no attention was paid to Kalmakova's concluding words:

May God give the insight to people to refrain from joining this group of naked ones because if these people do not come to their proper senses, they will end up in very lamentable circumstances. They may become like our homeless, lowest caste gypsies, the roving kind who have no stable abode.

Fulfilling a prophecy and vulnerability

A recollection by Kootnekoff (*S.M.*, 113) illustrates that disrobing was not meant to facilitate the lives of bandits and also not mainly inspired by the urge to have a prophecy fulfilled. According to Kootnekoff, Vanya Podmoryov, who had been a close friend of Peter V. Verigin, had told him that a number of elders felt the need to show that their ideals and principles were higher to them than material belongings.

Vasily Petrovitch Podmoryov (*S.M.*, 122), grandnephew of Vanya Podmoryov, narrates how in the end the marchers disrobed - the weather had turned ugly, the trek led nowhere, and the police were watching. 'Vanya Podmoryov came up with the suggestion: 'We have proven that worldly possessions were of no importance to us when we stated on our trek, now we have to give our remaining clothes on our backs to the authorities.' Marching up to the police, he began taking off his clothes.'

Others followed him and in the end people were herded into a train with six empty boxcars. When Verigin heard of it, he bowed to Podmoryov, thanked him for listening to his inner voice and fulfilling God's will. Verigin also thanked the people that had stayed at home, for looking after the possessions of the Doukhobor trekkers.

Novokshonoff (*S.M.*, 106-110) is asked about the reason nudity started among the Sons of Freedom. When he himself had posed the same question to the Sons, the answer had been that they 'had been trying to return the paradise that was lost by Adam and Eve. Adam and Eve, they had said, stayed naked and were not conscious of any shame till the time they ate of the forbidden fruit. After that, they became conscious of shame and paradise was lost to them.'

The Sons' spokesman had also explained that: 'nakedness was our greatest safeguard. If a bandit meets a clothed person, his first command is 'Hands Up!' This is because he fears that a clothed person may have weapons hidden in his clothes [. . .] If a bandit accosts a totally naked person, there is no reason for the order 'Hands Up', nor is there any necessity for a search, as all is in the open.'

The Sons of Freedom, or *Svobodniki* (freedom seekers) started to plough their land with wooden shovels in 1903. They did not wear leather shoes, and avoided the use of metals in order not to bereave Mother Earth of her minerals. Further, while they did not want to be slaves themselves, they also did not want to be slave drivers - they let their cattle loose.

They did well: according to Novokshonoff (*S.M.*, 111), Peter V. Verigin, by now called Peter- or Verigin-Lordly, while doing his rounds through the Canadian villages, complemented the members of the *Troozhdeniye* colony in Saskatchewan. He said: 'A truly remarkable crop of grain, provided of daily sustenance, and it appears it is now time to put the heads down.' For most Doukhobors his comment referred to the fact that it was time to cut the grain.

But the Sons of Freedom arrived at a different interpretation of his words. 'Either they felt people were overly worshipping a material manifestation . . . .. As a result they gathered together at night and destroyed part of the harvest.'

When Verigin-Lordly heard of it, he must have said something like 'Yes, you have to watch out for these Sons of Freedom. They may even come out with their red-rooster tactics' (Novokshonoff in *S.M.*, 111). Next sheaves of grain and equipment were burned. As a congregation of the villagers of Troozhdeniye found it not their business to punish them, the arsonists were reported to the police. Two men were arrested and sentenced. Stories about their treatment while incarcerated contributed to further martyrdom and more protests, nude demonstrating, and arson.[11]

Meanwhile Verigin-Lordly lived a different life, one not so much with his head down! Hawkes about him in *The Story of Saskatchewan*:

> **He lived in great state near [the town of] Verigin. He had a fine large house, with all modern conveniences including a Turkish bath. He generally drove about with his secretary and three or four handmaidens in a swell democrat with four to six horses, acknowledging the bows of his subjects with great dignity.**

As noted above, the Canadian government had allocated the fifteen acres per Doukhobor family and enforced the regulations of the Homestead Act 'with the requirement of swearing allegiance to the Crown' (Kootnekoff in *S.M.*, 137). Then in 1907, under pressure of public opinion, the government

---

11 At the start of this book Van Paassen's imaginary uncle Kees was quoted, stating that Russians tend to interpret everything literally. In 1953 arson was thought to be a means to get to Russia, be it through revolving prison doors. Doukhobors try to come to an understanding of these acts among others by interpreting, citing from and comparing with the bible. Savinkoff (*S.M.*, 189) compares the Doukhobor burnings with the acts of "self-exalted" leaders who caused the Romans to storm their city, to raze their temple and concludes that apart from the said leaders to people "who, not having proper enlightenment and wisdom" that allowed themselves to believe false leaders were responsible as well. Savinkoff also cites the lines of St. John, "dried up branches were collected and thorn into the fire."

In a comment Popoff (*S.M.*, 190-191) rejects Savinkoff's condoning the burnings and argues that St. John's text should be understood as people who do not love whither away as dry branches and should be thrown away.

The anonymous woman on the CBC tape (see also page 96) states that nobody ever explained to her what their [Doukhobor] faith in non-materialism means and that it was why they burned their houses and disrobed - to remind to our addiction to our possessions. "I was embarrassed by those women [that disrobed], by their photographs in newspapers and books. But recently I read in the bible (Prov. 23:4): 'Don't work hard to gather wealth, be wise enough to resist this.'" Again the bible is interpreted, this time in hindsight serving as a justification.

issued one last call; the Doukhobors had to swear an Oath of Allegiance to the Crown immediately. Many considered swearing oaths sinful, so they refused: no oath to a second Lord, while they already had Jesus as the first and only Lord. 'As a consequence, in 1907 Verigin-Lordly instructed his followers to travel to British Columbia.'

Eyewitnesses: John and his grandmother

In 1908 the followers of Verigin-Lordly left behind a quarter of a million acres of ploughed fields, haystacks, and barns bursting with Saskatchewan grain. According to the 5 December 1943 Doukhobor Resolution, these acres had a value of $10,000,000. Others estimate seven or eight million dollars. The government presented these lands for sale to whoever was interested.

This whole affair raised questions: not only in Doukhobor circles, but also for a descendant of someone who had purchased one of these abandoned Doukhobor lots. John X from Ontario crossed my path electronically for entirely other reasons. He happened to mention that he had been tracing his grandparents' history and had come across some highly intriguing documents. He sent me a copy of a letter addressed to the Department of the Interior dated 8 September 1906. He wondered what this letter was all about. The letter reads:

> I beg to inform you that the recent inspection of the Doukhobor colonies has shown that certain lands are being held but that the entrants are absent and cannot be located. Among them appears the name of W. Salarcoff who has entered for the N.W. 1/4 of Section 23, Township 31, Range 1, West Second Meridian. You are hereby authorized to carry out cancellation and dispose of the land on the usual terms. There appears to be no improvement.
>
> Agent for Dominion Lands,
> Yorkton, Saskatchewan

After having received this letter from the Agent for Dominion Lands, John had noted in his diary, which he also sent me and follows hereunder:

> I have no idea what this letter means. Puzzled, I checked the land description to ensure it is correct. It is. Still puzzled, I look at the next document. This is a letter addressed to the Department of the Interior, dated September 5, 1907, and reads:
>
> 'I beg to acknowledge our letter of the 27th ultimo, file 1264784, and in reply have to advise you that the entry of Trophim Machortoff for the N.W. 1/4 of 23-31-1 W.

> 2nd. M. was cancelled under the instructions received from the Commissioner for investigating Doukhobor affairs. The list of these entries was forwarded to you at the time.'

This letter is signed by the Agent of Dominion Lands, at Yorkton, Saskatchewan.

I looked at the next two documents in the file. One is entitled 'Application for a Homestead Entry.'

> This documents indicates that Trophim Machortoff of Veregin, Saskatchewan applied for a Homestead Entry for this land dated 1 October 1906 at the Yorkton Dominion Lands Office. 'Number in family including entrant, 4; Nationality, Doukhobor; Where From, Russia, 7 years in Canada; Previous Occupation, farmer.'

The second document concerns Trophim Machortoff and is dated 1 October 1906. It indicates this individual had obtained homestead entry on 27 April 1904, for land NE 24-28-32 1W, but had forfeited this entry, and as such he is permitted to make application for and receive another Homestead entry.

John's diary continues:

> I sit back in my chair, trying to understand this. It appears this Trophim Machortoff had had a Homestead Entry in 1906 to a separate piece of land, which he forfeited. This same Trophim Machortoff then made Entry to this land, later to belong to my grandfather. Trophim Machortoff had for some reason, then, in August 1907, had his entry cancelled 'under the instructions received from the Commissioner for investigation of Doukhobor affairs'.
>
> To complicate matters a W. Salaroff entered for this same land but had his entry cancelled at an unknown date. Somewhat puzzled, but satisfied, knowing I have a great deal of information to consider, I put away the file. It's lunch-time.

John also sent me diary notes, in English, by his grandmother Marie, an immigrant from Belgium. In 1912 she came as a young bride to the town of Verigin, where she assisted her new husband in his shop. Upon her arrival in Canada she and her husband:

> Disembarked in Montreal, and spent the day there. It was Sunday, and we went to a Protestant Church, which I had never seen in my life. And I told my husband we are not in the right place, we are Roman Catholics. Let's go, and off we went. We went to a restaurant where we got a nice dinner for twenty-five cents. Then (that night) we took the immigrant train. It was much cheaper. I think that's why my husband took it. There were no sleepers or diners on that train, just day coaches. We took enough food to last us until we arrived at some city. And they came around with sandwiches in the train. We'd buy buns and bologna, we couldn't cook on the train [...]. When we arrived in Winnipeg we went right away to St. Boniface. Here there were some three thousand Belgian people. I felt at home right away. Those people made us very welcome and I said, 'People are making a living. Why go any further?' Dad [Marie's husband John] said, 'All my family are around Verigin and they expect me to build a store there. I already bought a lot there and I'm a month later than I expected [...].
>
> (As we approached Verigin), I was looking through the windows in the train and I really saw bush, beautiful country with a river running through the bush. When we got to Runnymede I said, 'I'd better get dressed to meet your people.' I went into the washroom and got out my best dress. Those days they were very long dresses, with boots buttoning half way up your legs. My husband did up the buttons and I put on my big hat, a great big white hat with a brim and two big black feathers. (When we arrived at the station) I asked my husband, 'Are all stations in Canada out in the country?' And he said, 'Oh, this is the town. This is Verigin.'
>
> There were very few buildings, maybe six houses, one store, [and] no hotel. This was my homecoming. I thought it must be the country and the station was in the country.
>
> [When we arrived at the station,] here was my husband's brother with a Democrat. Already they'd gotten past

the buggy state [...] And there I was with my fancy black wedding gown and my white hat with the black feathers and a big white handbag [...] and trying to get into that Democrat in those days in long dresses. And my hat. It was as windy country as could be. And I hung on with two hands. It was about 7 miles to his father's farm.

My husband's family were on the road (at the homestead). Usually the train was on time those days and they were looking for their brother and his bride to arrive, and, oh, waving their hands as I arrived near the gate, and they helped me down ...

Once we had the store, half of our customers were Doukhobors. We had two [Doukhobor] clerks because we couldn't speak the language. One was a Russian girl who came from Yorkton to work for us and the other was a Doukhobor who lived in town and was looking for work. Our customers were all Independent [Doukhobor] farmers. And they were quite nice people. We soon gave them credit. They didn't have any money or they came with eggs or milk to barter for food. They wouldn't eat meat; they were vegetarians. And peanuts. We'd buy them by the hundred pounds. They always had to have a pound of peanuts. And when fall came, and they were able to sell some grain, they came and paid us. We lost very little on those Doukhobors and their charge accounts. They were quite honest, faithful people. They all dressed alike. When we sold material for a skit, everybody took five yards. It would be wide and fully gathered with a long shirt on top of it. And head kerchiefs. We bought them by the hundreds. They were made of wool, rather warm things. At the time they were about a dollar apiece, but now they don't wear them any more.

Grandmother Marie about social life in the village of Verigin:

When I arrived (1912) there was no town of Verigin. There was only a post office, a little grocery store next to the post office. There was a station and a station agent. When we built the store a general store was (also) built at the same time. A hotel was built in 1912. Verigin started booming [...]

The Doukhobors were here [...] but they were settled in their own communities. The Doukhobors I liked very much. They were nice people to deal with; lots came to the store. By the time I was there, they were all independent farmers because the community had broken up. Those buildings across the way were empty.

The town was named Verigin because Peter Verigin was the ruler across the station. The Doukhobors lost their rights to their homesteads because they wouldn't take out naturalization papers or send their children to school. They gave the Doukhobors fifteen acres of land for each family and the rest was thrown open to homesteaders. Ontario people got here first and then they came from England and Europe. My husband got a homestead too because he was on the railway laying steel [...].

As soon as people got cars the population of Verigin went down because they started to drive to Kamsack for goods. The English people all moved to Ontario after the children began growing up. They thought, who would they meet here? They didn't want them to marry a Doukhobor or Galacian [Marie, 1974 and 1976].

Grandmother Marie was also interviewed by a member of a historical society, the tone of the interviewer reminding one of a KGB-agent. Hereunder grandmother Marie's eye-witness account of the split in the Doukhobor community:

Question: Was the (Doukhobor) community building where the prayer house in Verigin is now?

Marie: Much closer. Just, maybe a few steps across the rail yard.

Q: You would see them all the time?

M: Sure, and they all had a bathhouse. Saturday they heated fires for steam baths. They let some of our English-speaking people come and take a bath there. This Mike Kazakoff would let his English friends come.

Q: Did Peter Verigin live there?

M: No, he was in that house they burned down. They said it was too big for one man. Sons of Freedom in opposition to Peter Verigin burned it down. (They said) he should live in such style when they (had) burned all their own clothes and had nothing.

And the day that they burned Peter Verigin's house, they threw all their clothes into the blaze and they came marching into Verigin, naked. And my husband came in so excited, running up the stairs, and he said, 'Look behind the curtain, don't go outside. All these Doukhobors are bare-naked here in town. The police are rounding them up and we're helping the Mounted Police get them off the street and into the livery stables.'

And they formed a committee, the Overseer with his councillors. They went to different women and asked them to sew housecoats for the women. And the men, they put in overalls. And within two days they were on the train to Regina and put in jail. When they came to our store, they gave each one a bag of peanuts for the train.

Q: Were they looking for Jesus?

M: Yes, and they [were] caught before they got far enough to find Jesus. Another time, maybe two or three years later, maybe 1916, they started off from Verigin, and they got as far as Kamsack. A naked parade and singing, and the police, let them get far enough into town, and they got the people off the streets, so they could turn the fire-hose on them with cold, cold water.

Q: Why were they marching?

M: Oh, they were going to come around town, protesting that they didn't have to send their children to school, and that they shouldn't have to go to war, the war was on at that time. And it wasn't long until they got them all into jail also. They were marching and saying, 'we're going to go and go until we find Jesus. He'll do what He can for us.'

They believed that Jesus was a prophet and that he was still alive. The Doukhobors figured that Peter Verigin [-Lordly] was their god, that he was their prophet. He did the preaching. They went from one jail to another. They burned down the schools. They put them in jail and sent them to a larger centre. Our jails only held about four people. I think they rented some part of the school, where they herded them until they could get them on the train and on to Regina. Gradually, they all left for B.C. And life became organized and quiet for the Doukhobors who stayed here and who were farmers. They got well-to-do and they had cars and built themselves nicer homes.

Q: What about the incident with the corpse?

M: I remember that well. One of the Sons of Freedom had been preaching about quitting the community and not believing in Peter Verigin[-Lordly] and he must have burned a school or something because he was in jail. And in jail he went on a hunger strike and when he got out of jail he (went) home and within a few days he died. And they loaded him on a sleigh and put a blanket over him and they brought him to Verigin from wherever he lived, around Peter Verigin[-Lordly]'s house, I think he lived. And they brought him to Mr. Kazakoff's house and they knocked on the door and said, 'We brought you something,' and he said, 'What is it?' And they said 'Well, we brought you some fish for your Christmas dinner.' He didn't believe them. Finally he went and looked and lifted up the blanket and there was a pair of feet and then he stared in the face of this dead man who had been sent to jail through Peter Verigin[-Lordly] and they said, 'You killed him, and you can have him', and off they went back home leaving that body there.[12]

---

12   The story of the Doukhobors lives on at the National Doukhobor Heritage Village. Also see: http://www.ndhv.ca (Last accessed April 2013.)

To and in British Columbia

As Marie said, 'gradually they moved to B. C.' That is, around 1908 about 5000 Doukhobors moved on to British Columbia: the moderate members of the Christian Community of Universal Brotherhood (CCUB), the radical Sons of Freedom, and Peter Verigin-Lordly. There, they bought 15,000 acres of land. Swearing an oath was not necessary since the purchase was a private transaction and not homesteading. People settled along the Kootenay River; built houses, a bridge, and a sawmill - altogether, a brand new existence. The first settlement was called Ootisheniye, meaning Valley of Consolation. A brick factory and a jam factory followed. Communal life generally allows for speedy settlement or resettlement (sometimes to the distress of the neighbours).

In 1924 the Doukhobor assets already amounted to seven million dollars. But in that same year, on 29 October, a train in which Peter Verigin-Lordly was travelling was blown up. Until today it is not clear what caused the explosion. According to the government it was somehow organized by someone who wanted to succeed Verigin-Lordly. According to Tregubov (*S.M.*, 541), it was done by fascists. Another explanation is that some explosives where left behind from the time that the railway was being built - surely that would have been a peculiar coincidence since the railway was already forty years old.[13] The Doukhobor community, writes Tregubov:

> feeling that the English Canadian government was in one way or another indirectly involved in this killing because of their general persecution and pressures against everything that [Verigin-Lordly] and the Doukhobors were doing, were at a loss as to how they would be able to preserve their identity without their leader. While they were grieving, they decided to take their children out of the [B.C.] English schools and educate them at home in their own way.

The government urged the parents to return their children to school. The parents, who refused, were fined, and subsequently refused to pay the fines. Consequently, supplies from

---

13 Also see: http://www.doukhobor.org/Hannant.htm (Last accessed April 2013.)

the Doukhobor warehouses were confiscated and the guards lashed by the police.

A delegation of Doukhobors went to Russia to look for Peter Petrovitch Verigin (1881-1939), Verigin-Lordly's son. In Russia, Peter P. Verigin advised them to send the children to school as he had always been in favour of children attending school to learn grammar and arithmetic. But, he was against schools practicing militia training and singing patriotic songs: schools that prepared students for militarism. Just as his father, Peter Verigin-Lordly, had been released from jail after the 1902 Saskatchewan upheaval, Peter P. Verigin was released from Russian jail in 1927 and arrived in British Columbia in 1928 with his spouse Anna Markova and grandson, John Verigin.

Upon arrival Peter P. Verigin was not happy to see how the interim leaders had taken care of their financial affairs by speculating and taking out loans against a 'blanco mortgage.' He started straightening things out, and also wondered about the communal housing style. But, according to Popoff (*S.M.*, 328), the elders expected to go back to Russia, and thus were not inclined to change their structures dramatically for Peter P. Verigin.

In the meantime the warehouse confiscations had led to arson and more nude demonstrations. Though Peter P. Verigin did not approve, part of the populace nevertheless went through with it.

Olson in *The Doukhobor Centenary* lists some of the tribulations of the Doukhobors:

1. About 104 people ended up in jail for six months and, in 1929 about 250 zealots were exiled to unoccupied lands of the Christian Community of Universal Brotherhood (being the new name) in British Columbia.
2. In 1932 Peter P. Verigin himself was incarcerated, due to land fraud. There were rumours that he would not serve time, but would be deported to Russia. Consequently some 330 Sons of Freedom became very agitated, and started mass nude demonstrations in the hope of being arrested and sent back to Russia as well.

3 In 1932 another 600 were incarcerated because they refused to pay land tax and to register births and marriages. However, while they were arrested and incarcerated, they were never sent back to Russia as expected by their leaders. At that time some 365 children became 'wards of the crown,' and ended up in orphanages or industrial schools. Footnote 10 in Olson's article notes that 'it was reported that some of the children died and that certainly many were traumatized for life.'[14]

---

14 When I asked Mike about these events, he handed me a copy of an anonymous document that described the treatment of some of these wards of the Crown: the babies of the Babakaeff, Shlakoff, and Postnikoff families. In it the anonymous author states that:

> It's is 18 years today that I am keeping this secret, not telling anyone, fearing the recollection of the past, although it has been difficult to do this, as the picture still remains impressed in my heart and thought to this day. Now it seems is the time and place to bring this matter before you ... I was called upon the witness box to give evidence upon cross-examination. I was asked if I was one of them that was at Piers Island, I've answered yes. When further questioned, I was unable to answer questions, as the recollection of it has stunned me to the core. In the year 1932, as one of the numbers arrested for disrobing in protest to our eviction from our abodes at that time by our fellowmen of the Christian Community Universal Brotherhood with the help of the local police later transferred to Oakalla, from where we were taken to Piers Island. While at Oakalla two matrons appeared before me and the other woman who also had a nursing child, saying, 'Further you are not allowed to nurse your babies while you are in jail,' and forcibly took a ten week old baby boy from my hands. Although handicapped as I was by all surroundings, nevertheless, the baby was spry and healthy as can be ...[after a week or two] ... Upon entering the ward where our babies were, we found four little beds with babies in them. At the first glance we were unable to tell the babies apart, as they appear not flesh but bones to what they were a few days ago, their eyes saying, Yes mothers, we have been expecting you. At the time the matron was talking to our husbands, I took the courage by taking the baby in my hands, relieving the baby of its wet diaper, which was drenched to the last fold of its dryness. It appeared to me that they weren't changed for a long time. OH GOD, What do you think I have found out? They were neglected, their underarms rotten, behind their ears there were deep running sores ...[about two or three days later]... the matron came again, saying, I have bad news for you, your babies are dead [...] Their little feet were held together by a white ribbon. We asked the undertaker to remove the ribbon but he refused to do so. Upon closer examination, we found their little feet pricked with unknown instruments [...] Such mockery displayed upon our innocent babies, their unheard suffering and crying for their mothers, are the fruits of your educated people. We are uneducated, but we can say, One Slave Cannot Serve Two Masters. We are the servants of JESUS CHRIST and are not servants of man-made laws.

This document, mentioning the names of the deceased baby's parents, is not signed. I asked Mike about it; on September 10, 2000 he wrote,

4 In 1938 the Doukhobor assets were estimated at six million dollars and another $200,000 in public property. Despite all damage due to arson there was only a debt of $500,000. Insurance companies quickly took refuge in foreclosures or simply expelled people from their homes - this led to more arson. Even an insurance office went up in flames.
5 In 1940 the order to prepare for mobilization and a general registration was given. In the same year Peter P. Verigin's seven-teen-year old grandson, John Verigin, became the Honorary Chairman of the CCUB. Also, ninety-two men preferred to go to prison rather than to war. Another seventy-two were sent to work camps.
6 In 1943 the jam factory burnt down. Bombings and arson escalated in 1947 - the Sunshine Valley Co-operative was destroyed.
7 In 1950 John J. Verigin Sr.'s home was destroyed, and 'more than 400 zealots are jailed for arson and nude demonstrations.' Olson adds in brackets: '(mostly on the basis of false confessions).'
8 From 1950 to 1952: The Hawthorn Commission recommended that the Doukhobor voting rights [that the B.C. government had deprived them of in the 1930's] be re-established, and that their marriages should be (retro-actively) recognized. The commission also recommended that Russian language studies be included in their curriculum, that zealots be re-located, and that the penalty for public nudity be lowered.
9 However, in 1953, the violence escalated in the West Kootenays. The zealots, writes Olson, burned 400 of their houses in Krestova [which is were Mike lives]. Olson goes on that 'left without shelter, they create a tent-town at Perry's Siding in the Slocan Valley. Following mass arrests and a trial held in Vancouver, 148 adults are sent to prison.'
10 There was more unrest in 1959 where 170 children of zealots are removed from their families and incarcerated in New Denver as part of the provincial government's hard-line policy.

The document was [illegible] many times by all mothers [...] The brother of one of the infants just passed away last week. They wanted the truth out all these years and they weren't afraid of signing any documents. So I don't know why that specific document wasn't signed.

Perceptions of martyrdom, persecution, and repression are thereby reinforced - the zealots also perpetuated many myths.

Olson's chronology goes on until 1987, but from 1959 on we will leave her and switch to Mike Chernenkoff's account, which begins in 1953. His version is, of course, a one-sided account, but still an eyewitness account. Under the title *The Very Truth surfacing,* Mike argues,

> Thank God, The Truth is surfacing. My hope, in time all the facts will come to the surface for everyone to see who was behind the Sons of Freedom perpetrations.
>
> We all know, from day one, that the intention of the Canadian authorities was to assimilate the Doukhobors, at any cost. However, the methods used for this assimilation were, in some cases, so camouflaged that, not only the general public, but the majority of the Doukhobors themselves were not aware of the culprit. In time, we did learn of the policy of 'divide and conquer,' which also was very effective in dividing the Doukhobors and getting them to fight against one another, this is where terrorism came in.
>
> I am not capable of exposing all the facts, even though I was involved in many depredations, but one that bothered me most was the abduction of the children to New Denver, in 1953. I, by instruction of the lady who was heading the group at the Tent village, did go to 4 families and asked them to burn their homes. After my question and my convincing them that it was from the leaders, as the lady convinced me, they did burn there homes and came to the Tent Village from where we were to go straight to Motherland, Russia.
>
> I am not proud of this, but I have a strong desire to clear myself of this sin. And the only way I know how is to expose the facts that finally are at my disposal. The lady and her husband, Mike Malakoff, were doing all this believing they were doing it under the advice and instruction of the leader, even though he was in Uruguay at that time.[15] But his prominent man, close associate, was around to give

---

15 The leader at that time, Stefan Sebastianovitch Sorokin, is said to be a displaced person from Russia. Through a Doukhobor elder from Blaine Lake, Saskatchewan, he made a visit to that district [Saskatchewan]. Someone

↑ Mike at the premises of the former Tent Village, photo Mary E.M.

bought him a ticket to B.C. because there were many more Doukhobors that he could also visit and share his beliefs.

instructions, of burning the homes of people with school age children, in preparation or abducting them to New Denver for forced education and thus assimilation.[16]

This prominent man, Anton Kolesnikoff, whom every one trusted to be a true follower of Mr. Sorokin, was a true friend of Emmet Gulley, an official advisor of the government. No one would possibly believe that this Anton Kolesnikoff was a paid agent, at that time when the homes were burning for the purpose of preventing the public from uprising for such an inhuman act of abducting innocent children.

I was at the Tent Village when the children were abducted. The police also had this Anton there for the purpose of him counselling the people not to resist the abduction saying: 'Do not resist because they will take the children anyway, but if you resist too forcefully you could only hurt the children maybe, damage them.' I would never want to see anything like that again, how the children were clinging to their mothers and the police trying to tear them away. Everyone was crying, including many of the police.

At the beginning of our acquaintance, Mike told me similar stories that I had not understood. Reading the contents of his pamphlet still did not fully clear up matters. Fortunately, Mike had published his viewpoint once more as he had some misgivings about a film crew active in his community. He feared that they would be 'distorting the facts.' He reiterated the account this time in his 2000 monthly newsletter as follows:

Premeditated Conspiracy over The Sons of Freedom

Circumstances compels me to write this truth, due to what the film crew, is liable to distort the facts, to justify the atrocities committed over the Sons of freedom by governments.

Since I am about the only live witness left who was involved in the 'Three Strong Blows,' that Bonner used, 'to break the backs of the Doukhobors, once and for all,' I

---

16 'New Denver' was a one-time sanatorium on the northern shore of Lake Slocan.

decided to explain just how it happened to the best of my ability.

However, it was the problem of all the Doukhobors that Bonner broke the backs of (got them assimilated), not just the Sons of Freedom, but they got the brunt of his evil, so we must all unite to get the truth out the public and to the Doukhobors.

The first strong blow that Bonner used, was the burning of the community multi-dwellings of Shoreacres, B.C., in 1947. These were multi-dwellings of both the Sons of Freedom and the Orthodox [Doukhobors]. Bonner was capable of hiring a specialist for the job (a Quaker) Emmet Gulley, who intern hired a SOF [Sons of Freedom] leader, John Lebedoff, who was able to use these illiterate people, under the name of religion; burning these dwellings as protest to the 'third world war,' and moving back to Russia, etc.

I was of the orthodox community at that time but had a feeling toward the Sons of Freedom, so I was at the Shoreacres Orthodox meeting when they sent a delegation to the police in Nelson, for help. The delegation comes back with the words of the inspector: 'The sooner they burn you out the better.' So the orthodox barricaded the road to prevent the SOF from going to the next building, but the RCMP told them that, 'it was a public road and they [don't] have a right to stop anyone from passing.' So, the SOF given the right of way, went and burned the rest of the multi-dwellings.

I had an uncle in Krestova where I visited and saw how the officer, Moose Martin, would take a carload of women every morning from Krestova to Shoreacres to help burn the dwellings. They did not go to extremes to hide the gas that they took with them. The RCMP were watching and enjoying the fires and I saw one giving women matches. When the last multi-dwelling was destroyed, (to save face) the police arrested 12 people. Bonner's first blow was accomplished. All the communal dwellings, in Shoracres, were destroyed, so each one had to build to accommodate his personal family.

The community homes were all destroyed, therefore the Orthodox were to never say *Hello* to the Sons of Freedom.

The Second Strong Blow was to educate the children of the SOF. Since commissioner Judge Sullivan ruled, 'There is no quick solution for the Doukhobor problem, we have to close all the rural schools. Unite their children with ours, in central schools, then in time the Doukhobor children will become ashamed of their ways and will become ours.' The other Doukhobor children were assimilated, before, so it was only the SOF children left, which required an evil strategy. The Attorney General, Bonner's specialist for that, had other than John Lebedoff, who was able to get a Sons of Freedom leader, whom the people trusted, was a sincere advocate of Sorokin - Anton Kolesnikoff - later proved to be a paid agent and traitor [to] Sorokin. Who in turn had the SOF: under the name religion, burn the homes of SOF who, had school children, and later gave an order to go to Perry's Siding and settle in tents.[17]

In the tents all went fine. We had a large tent for all to gather with children for prayer. In 1953, early Sept., we see an army of RCMP marching towards us, with clubs and rubber hoses about 3 feet long. Upon entering the prayer tent, they went wild and started swatting everybody in sight. The children screaming ran to hide anywhere they could. Men and women bruised and crying could not figure what was happening? RCMP arrested two men and literally dragged them to their car and took off.

Next day the same gang came marching, only with a big van, this time to arrest the adult[s] and take the children to New Denver. I saw the children clinging to their mothers while the police are trying to take them away. Every one was crying, including some of the police.

Adults were taken in the van to wait for the train to arrive shortly. Then we were all loaded on the train and everyone thought right straight to the boat for Motherland, as promised. But we were taken to Okalla, of course just to register, then to the boat. We were sentenced for 2 and 3 years, for parading in the nude on the public highway and around a school in front of non-Doukhobor children.

---

17 Olson notes in *The Doukhobor Centenary* that in 1953, 400 houses were burnt and 148 prisoners sent to prison.

↑ Former railway tracks in Slocan Valley, photo Mary E.M.

↑ Non-Doukhobor school facing public highway, photo Mary E.M.

I must expose the inhuman act of abducting the children and sentences of parading in the nude, on the public highway and around the school, that never happened. No one, no one, has left the compound of the tent village. In the tent village, yes, even I stripped with a couple [of] boys to accommodate a couple of women, news reporters. But no one, absolutely, no one paraded on the highway or around the school that we were charged with. The NEWS MEDIA: 'Bonner had no intention of bothering the people at the tent village, but they sprung their own trap. They paraded unto the public highway, in the nude, and around a school with Non Doukhobor children, to protest the education of their children.' So, all the hundred and forty, or so people, with two and three year sentences, were held absolutely illegally.[18]

Anton Kolesnikoff made a confession in 1956 of working with Emmet Gulley and betraying Mr. Sorokin. His letters to Emmet Gulley and Bonner, speak about this, very plainly. These letters are in another document: 'Assimilating the Doukhobors. Bonner's method.'

The Third Strong Blow: to get all SOF arrested, sentenced with long terms, and dispersed on easy paroles throughout Canada. Threatening and enticing the women to burn all their homes and marching to the coast, Vancouver, so as to go with the men, all together, to Motherland, as promised by the D Squad, police.

Attorney General Robert Bonner was all set for that, third strong blow? The special prison was built. Agents, to get the SOF bombing and burning and confessing to all their perpetrations to get into jails, by the prophesy, and go to Motherland Russia. SOF head over heals, rushed into prison, guilty or not and tried to get their friends and relatives in jail, because this is the time, 'we all waited for.' The D Squad went to extremes to get all the committee member[s] into prison and Mr. Sorokin. 'You have to make statement against Sorokin otherwise you will be there

---

18 Even if they had paraded in the nude in front of the school, the children could not have seen them as the windows of that one classroom school look out to the river, not to the highway. At least, that was the situation in the '90's when I saw the school.

without a leader.' So a bunch of people made false statements against Sorokin.

But, being incarcerated for a time the men started thinking differently. There was no boat, as we were promised, but long sentences. Houses all burned and the women with the children in Vancouver just living anywhere. Something is wrong. Nothing is panning out the way we were promised. So we started thinking seriously and decide to go on a hunger strike, demanding a public hearing to learn what the matter was. We wanted Lebedoff to come and answer a few questions, when he came, he denied everything that he and the police promised us.

No way should [. . .] the fast or the hunger strike [have] lasted for so long, if the government wasn't behind all the atrocities of Bonner's 'Three Strong Blows, to Break the Backs of the Doukhobors Once and For All.' But, no way could the government allow the public to know the truth, so they stooped to murder, puncturing stomachs and causing pneumonia's.

No doubt, the government feels that their evil power was above that of God, but the game isn't over yet. They will have to answer before God for mistreating HIS, illiterate, sincere followers.

Much more should be exposed, but I am incapable of putting it all down on paper in the proper order, but still have a strong hope of someone doing it even from my documents for I have much in the documents, only no ability to put all in order.

Mike E. Chernenkoff.

Mike is not so illiterate after all.[19] But, how reliable is his view? Mike sent me a 1959 article by J.J. Perepelkin that deals with the same occurrences, but sheds light from another angle. It features a photograph of a twelve-year-old looking through a wire fence at the reader with accusing eyes. This photograph is captioned with: 'Canada's happy "freedom."'

---

19   Cf. Mike's letter: *An Open Letter-Appeal to the Society of Friends (Quakers) Living in Canada and in the United States of America from the Members of the Christian Community and Brotherhood of the Reformed Doukhobors in British Columbia, Canada.* Crescent Valley, B.C. (Krestova). May 24th, 1954.

Hereunder Perepelkin contemptuous take on Canada's national song, *Oh Canada*:

> How strange that I should learn this song
> Thou land of hope' so 'strong and free,'
> I have no hope I want my pretty home,
> My dearest parents. All my childhood gone
> And I have not been free, not for one hour
> In these long years. Oh God, what have I done
> That I should suffer so each day, each year?
> Perhaps there is no God? Or else He cannot hear
> Because I weep so much each time I pray?
> I do not know.
> Yet I remember at my mother's knee
> She told me of a loving God above.
> Oh Canada! Someday I'll look for God
> And find Him. Sure.
> But I will never stand 'on guard for thee!'
> **C A N A D A A W A K E**

Perepelkin continues his text with Leviticus 19:33:

And if a stranger sojourn with thee in your land, ye shall not vex him. But the stranger that dwelleth with you shall be unto you as one born among you, and thou shalt love him as thyself; for ye were strangers in the land of Egypt: I am the Lord your God. Ye shall do no unrighteousness in judgment.

He goes on to announce that he will compare the fate of the Hebrews in Egypt with that of the Doukhobors in Canada 'on the basis of God's word as written in the Holy Bible.'[20] Summarized it comes down to the following:

> Doukhobors share the belief of Christians and Jews that God Himself was responsible for saving His people from famine by sending them to Egypt and led them out of that country because they were not in the condition to liberate themselves - due to the extreme craftiness of the godless pharaohs.

---

20 Mike, asked why Perepelkin compares with the Bible, while Doukhobors don't adhere to the Bible, replied that it makes writing easier.

The Jews became mightier than the Egypt people just as the Doukhobors flourished in Canada. Now it is the Canadian pharaohs that are hardliners: Assets were confiscated, people crawled to another province like ants. But the children got schooling to the liking of the pharaohs, so they were kept at home. And then the leader died in a bomb explosion - more attacks followed and one group, the Sons of Freedom, was blamed. The general Doukhobor community also blamed the Sons of Freedom. [It was as Mike had written: one did not say *Hello* to the other any more].

The difference between the Orthodox group and that of the so-called 'Sons of Freedom' Doukhobors is that the Orthodox made no commotion, and allowed their children to attend government schools.

Perepelkin subsequently wonders why the Canadian rulers did not compromise on the issues that made that these people want to leave the country. His answer to his own question is that 'God Himself wants it that way.' And, he assumes that 'had the government left the Doukhobors alone, they would have become assimilated of their own accord.' He illustrates his article with pictures of people being taken away from the tent village. One of these pictures is taken from the *Vancouver Sun* of 12 September 1953, and has as a caption: 'Long planned trap sprung by Douks.'

From Perepelkin's next lines we learn that Sorokin, the leader of the Doukhobors, moved to Uruguay in the midst of all the burnings. Sorokin was not impressed with the goings on, condemned the burnings and the bombings, and had left under the pretence that he would look for a new land for the Sons. Simma Holt, a Canadian journalist, having checked on Sorokin in Uruguay, reported on his luxurious lifestyle in her 1964 *Terror in the Name of God*. Perepelkin argues that her provocation only strengthened the Doukhobor faith in Sorokin. What I heard is that some people like to see their spiritual leaders live in luxury, it makes the leader look like one of a serious religion, such as the Pope in Rome.*

Perepelkin's article goes on pleading for Sorokin's return. He notes that in the town of Brilliant, B.C., Verigin's house burnt down: Sorokin had found out that Lebedoff had told

* When I read this, I wondered why people always ask "What would Jesus do?", never "How did Jesus live?"

people to burn their houses, that Lebedoff had told people that Sorokin 'did not know enough', and that Lebedoff had told people that Sorokin 'could not otherwise' then tell people *not* to burn down their houses. Sorokin then found out why Lebedoff told people to commit arson: Lebedoff had said that according to prophecy, Doukhobors would leave Canada and that not a splinter would be left behind. Therefore, as soon as all of their houses were burned, they would return to Russia.

Sorokin on the other hand, thought that this prophecy should be interpreted as 'people could take their assets along to Russia.' He tried to warn people about Lebedoff. Lebedoff reacted by trying to incriminate Sorokin. Perepelkin continues by telling how Lebedoff tried to tarnish Sorokin's reputation.

First, there was a plan to invite a few girls somewhere late at night, and to invite Sorokin as well as the police. But this plan was leaked. Subsequently Lebedoff told two girls that they should go to the Kaslo, B.C. hot springs [there are no hot springs is Kaslo, there are in nearby Ainsworth], and there marry Sorokin. The girls did not fall for this plan and complained to their mothers, who in turn asked Sorokin for an explanation: No, he did not know about his upcoming wedding at the Kasslo hot springs.

But, before Sorokin appeared on the Freedomite (another name for the Sons of Freedom) scene, many people had pleaded guilty of arson. One night Lebedoff had invited Sorokin to come to an old hut to have a chat with a number of die-hards. Sorokin asked them about blowing up the railway tracks. That attack was to take revenge on the government that they held accountable for the explosion that killed Verigin in 1924. Someone explained that 'a farmer does not keep a milk cow that always kicks.' Meaning that if the Doukhobors would not continue to kick back, they would be milked and bled by the government. The die-hards wanted to be kicked; kicked back to Russia.

Perepelkin goes on arguing that the police knew that Lebedoff was behind the attacks. True? It is time to interrupt Perepelkin here. Mrs. Fenya Konkin (in Popoff, *S.M.*, 443), one of Lebedoff's spouses, later Stefan S. Sorokin's wife, but currently a widow, 'gave a brief oral presentation about some of her life's experiences,' which Popoff (in *S.M.*, 443) summarized:

> During the first part of her life she was a devout follower of Michael, the Archangel, Verigin.[21] Later she was a follower of, and then the wife of, John L. Lebedoff. However, she soon left him and became a faithful follower of the more influential leader of the Sons of Freedom, Stefan S. Sorokin, and shortly thereafter became his wife. She spoke very candidly and unreservedly about her first husband, Lebedoff, whom she characterized as an unprincipled, secretive, and untrustworthy person who had caused her much suffering and pain in her life [...]
>
> [Further,] she related that Lebedoff had a close friendship with members of the Royal Canadian Mounted Police, who often came to visit their home . . . . According to her words, she left Lebedoff when she found out that he was receiving some sort of payments from the Government. Mrs. Fenya Konkin also explained that it was Lebedoff who presented Sorokin to the Sons of Freedom after [Sorokin] arrived in British Columbia, and she came to the conclusion that Sorokin was the one she would recognize as her spiritual leader.

---

21 Regarding this Archangel, Voykin tells us in *The Spirit Wrestlers' Voices* about her grandmother Berikoff who was leading a quiet life until the death of Peter P. Verigin in 1939. A distant relative of this Peter, Michael Verigin, was told by Peter P. Verigin that 'the Father wanted to see him.' At the time Michael did not understand it. But a few weeks after Peter P. Verigin had died, Michael walked in a street in Vancouver, felt a tap on his shoulder, saw his late friend and heard his voice say: 'The time is now. Come, the Father is ready to see you.' They then boarded a train, 'the two men sped away 'swiftly upward' to a place where 'the Father met with Michael', instructing him to come back to earth and deliver a message to the Doukhobor people.'

The message was that enough had been burned, that they had to live together and that women had to be freed of male domination. Six women and six men then started a new order, first in Krestova, later, in June 1946 in Hilliers, Vancouver Island. The group lived a communal lifestyle, not only regarding material possessions, but to the private family unit too. This idea, according to Popoff (*S.M.*, 302) went back to a purported remark of Peter Christjakoff, 'You must not make any differentiation that this is my son or daughter, and that is your son or daughter. They should be all considered as 'our' children and we would be equally concerned about each of their welfare as if they were really our own.'

Perepelkin continues his lengthy article with allegations that the police had planted pieces of rags, paper, and bits of wire in peoples houses which he would like to have made known to a court in The Hague. He denies that the Communists had anything to do with it, tells about a lawyer who talked in Calgary about the ruination and deprivation of the Doukhobors in Canada. Perepelkin advised Sir Thomas White, acting Prime Minister of Canada in 1919, to read the *Open Letter of Professor James Mavor* of the faculty of Political Science of the University of Toronto which says that what happened then, what is happening now etc., etc.

Perepelkin mentions the dispersal of the Consultative Committee that had been established by the government of B.C., of which only Emmet Gulley was left. Perepelkin's article drones on and on - it would make a good script for a movie that warns people for blindly following whatever leader.

According to Popoff (*S.M.*, 302) Gulley was a representative of the American Friends Service Committee, and, as we saw above, also a member of the Consultative Committee on Doukhobor Affairs. What else was he? I asked Mike about Gulley, the American Quaker. Mike on Gulley in a letter of 8 November 1999:

> if you can recall, at the end of World War II, after Hitler did away with lots of Jews, there was a commotion to give the Jews back their land, which they had lost years ago. History says that was because they crucified Christ. And [using] the words of Gulley himself, the powers that be, in order to give them back their sacred land, . . . had to evict 750,000 Arabs to place 250,00 Jews in that place. The Arabs were so upset about it that they were doing all kinds of things to pay back the injustice. This is where Gulley came in. The United States knew of Gulley's religious actions, so they hired him to quell the problem. These [are] Gulley's own words, told [to] us in prison: '[The Arabs] were so upset, that regardless of what we tried to do in their favour, they wouldn't accept. But in time with some favours and some pressure, we managed to quiet them down, so I feel we will do the same with you.' This I heard with my own ears in prison. There was more to his story:

like he came directly from god to help us. For he was a Quaker and god knew that he could.

On 15 August 2000, Mike wrote me again about Kolesnikoff and the lady that had told him to tell people to burn their houses:

> Everyone thought that she was getting all her instructions from Sorokin through Anton Kolesnikoff, for everyone thought he was a sincere servant of Sorokin. But he was sold out to Emmet Gulley and was paid by the government. He did ask the boys to participate in terrorism as Gulley wanted to end the Doukhobor problem, by getting all the Sons of Freedom in jail and dispersing them all over Canada and selling the lands from under them and thus ending the Doukhobor problem.

Sons (and daughters) of Freedom on CBC radio

Mike also sent me a taped 1990's CBC radio report in which a polished voice explains that the broadcast is a documentary about *Operation Snatch*, which occurred in the fifties. In 1953, according to the voice, about two hundred children were taken from their houses by the police and put in a special, high fenced, boarding school in New Denver until 1959.

The religion of the Doukhobors, the voice goes on, caused them, among other things, not to want to have anything to do with the modern state - only with the laws of God. One segment of the Doukhobors, the Sons of Freedom, pushed this religion unto the extremes: bombardments, nude demonstrations, and the refusal to send children to state schools. That is why police officers looked for children who were kept hidden by their parents and among others in a camp near the American border. One child was in a haystack that was being pierced with forks, and another child was hiding at the neighbours' because his mother was incarcerated for bothering a police officer (because he took her child from her), and his father had to work. The voice goes on that sending the children to New Denver was Premier Bonner's measure to solve the Doukhobor problem.

One of the then children is interviewed in this same broadcast. He explains that the problem was not that their parents were against grammar, or an education, but were against the indoctrination that comes with education in Canada - such as singing *Oh Canada* around the flag: 'In Russia we were not patriots and we don't want to be that in Canada either. There should not be any borders.'[22]

The radio voice takes over, and explains that Doukhobors are pacifists, and that as one often sees, pacifists are met with the most aggression. The microphone is then returned to more adults who as children had spent a number of years in New Denver. Their stories are a list of abuses: being pulled

---

22 James Kolesnikoff in *The Doukhobor Centenary in Canada* mentions Mary Ashworth (1979, 141-42) who noted that in 1910 the provincial Department of Education had signed an agreement with the Lord Strathcona Trust, which would provide money 'for the encouragement of physical training and military drill in public school.'

↑ New Denver boarding school, photo Mary E.M.

by their feet from under their bed by a police officer; being forced to get out of bed at 7:00 a.m. to work; meeting their parents only once every two weeks through a wire fence with armed police officers in the background; having to look on as the matrons ate the food the parents had shoved under the fence for them; having to clean the floors with much too heavy equipment; having to scrub laundry on a wash board; the first years not being able to understand English instructions; and finally back home, not being able to trust their parents. This had forced one of their mothers to say: 'I am your mother, I am not a matron.'

One of the interviewees stuttered her story. Her stuttering had began when she was forced to read in front of the class from a book in a language she could not understand. Towards the end of the tape Mike can be heard rasping a few remarks: 'the CBC is paid by the government to cover the dirty works of the government.' He then elaborates on what happened when the children were taken away - stories we already heard.

At the very end of the tape, about three hundred Sons of Freedom are recorded singing in the Krestova Prayer Hall. Through it sounds a clear female voice addressing the interviewer: 'Do you see this, they thought they could break the Doukhobor beliefs, but they could not.'

Among the documents Mike gave me was a 1956 letter by Stefan S. Sorokin in which he urges people to send their children to school. He asks them: 'What kind of a belief do you have, that would be endangered by sending your children to school?' On the other hand Sorokin contradicts himself with a Stalinist children's song training them for war:

> Stalin is our militant strength
> Stalin, the light of our youth
> Struggling, singing, conquering
> Our people are following Stalin.

As mentioned above, in the summer of 2000, I met with a few of Mike's friends at his place. One of them gave me a handwritten letter, dated 14 February 1961, addressed to his lawyer.

> Dear Mr. Dean, I would like to thank you from my whole heart for all your efforts to [prove] my innocence. I am sure that the judge alone would have no choice but to set me free.

From the rest of the letter it is obvious that at the time of his trial, jury members had been convinced that Mike's friend had committed arson, despite the three non-Orthodox witnesses confirming his alibi. When Mike's friend handed me this letter, he explained that in 1961 he had owned a little construction company. Eying Mike a bit shyly, he confessed that then he did not live among the Sons, but wanted to live his own life and just work for his wife and child. However, he was arrested and found guilty, 'because I belong to this religion,' as he stated in his letter. He also said that at the time, now 39 years ago, it 'had made him think.' It certainly made me think as well. 'The birth of a Son,' is what I thought.

Mike's friend continues his letter about how hard it had been for him to be jailed despite being innocent, and being separated from his wife and daughter. In it, he also mentions how difficult it must have been 'for his mother to give him up.' I asked him what he meant by that. 'Well, [at] eleven months old, I was one of the babies that had survived Piers Island.'

At the end of the letter he thanks his lawyer again, and then states that while he had been losing his [Doukhobor] faith, the false accusation awakened his belief. He added that he 'would lose it even more by paying my fine, [and falsely] admitting my guilt.'

So, not surprisingly, in the 1960s the burnings started again. According to James Kolenikoff, it was a wave of childhood resentment (or hate) 'that resurfaced between 1958 and 1963.' In the end, so many people were convicted that the government decided to build a fire resistant prison for these arsonists.

In *Spirit Wrestlers' Voices* Voykin relates how her grandmother, previously a member of Archangel Michael Verigin's community, also ended up in prison. From there grandmother had convinced Voykin to partake in the big trek of family members to her. In 1962 about 700 people marched from British Columbia, through Castlegar, Grand Forks, Princeton, and Hope to Vancouver where they built a tent-village beside the prison. They camped there for about ten years. The police could do nothing but watch and make sure that everything was orderly.

Back home in Calgary I asked Mike about these events. On 2 October 2000 he wrote me that his late wife, Laura, had been on the trek. As Mike had joined the second wave of arson, he was also in that fire-resistant prison. He continued:

> **Yes, hard to 'trek' with four children if you have no faith. But Laura did it so who was able to give her that faith or whatever (*sic*). There was about 700 [that] started [which] reached Vancouver, but from Vancouver about half got lost to [the] Mountain Prison gates.**

In this letter Mike also summarized his prison diary. Below is an unabridged English translation of his prison diary (**translated by JS**).

Mike's prison diary

Only God knows how we suffered, how they tortured us. Two of three of them would hold somebody and Jones would insert a tube in the nose until the nose and the mouth were bleeding. They would pour meat broth down the tube, take it out; wash it with cold water and go to feed another prisoner. They were swearing and shouting while visiting every prisoner. They were torturing us with the tube and it was very painful to vomit the broth because the meat they used was not good. They were torturing us like this until Pavel Ponomarev died and many had fever and bloody cough. When we were complaining about the pain to the doctor, he would say, 'Start drinking milk yourselves or it will be even worse'.

The morning Pavel died, Dr. Enns came for the last time. Nobody wanted to talk to him and he seemed to be very ashamed.[23] On Saturday, August 24, another doctor came and examined everybody. He came back on Sunday, August 25, examined everybody and asked for an ambulance. The ambulance came and three brothers were taken to the hospital. They were being taken away on stretchers when Carson and others came in and saw it. On Saturday they used the tube for the last time but did not stop the torture. They'd approach somebody swearing loudly, grab him and rip the shirt off. They'd try to make us drink pushing the cup into the mouth until the lips were bleeding or the nose was pressed in. And milk was poured on the clothes and the bed. Sometimes they didn't raise the prisoners. They'd bring a cup of milk and pour it on the face and then get another one and do the same thing. We had to wash our clothes and the linen so we could sleep on it. They were beating us and twisting our ears. Sometimes the

---

23 I asked Mike after Dr. Enns. In shaky handwriting Mike wrote on January 16, 2001, 'I am in the hospital [...] waiting for a bed in Vanc. by-passes [...] previous strokes, but my mind is clear [...]. I knew Enns in prison very well. At the fact and asked hem personally not to mistreat the boys. His comment was: 'have to follow orders of the prison.' When I asked him how does that coincide with your pledge as a Dr? He never answered. The boy that died, Dr. Enns pronounced him dead in prison, but in the news they said from malnutrition, that was a [de]finite lie and Enns did not appear at the prison anymore.'

guard would jerk your feet from under you and you would fall on concrete floor. They did anything their bloodthirsty hearts desired. One of the guards used to say 'We were told to make you drink like this and I'll do it! If they tell us to do it anally I'll do it too'. These animals, vampires and man-eaters were torturing us even after the 32nd day of the lent when we were just skin and bones.

Cell #4

On August 15, 1963, Superintendent Wilson and medical officer Jones (they had a third guard with them) came to Cell # 4. Jones said to Ivan Kuznetsov, 'The doctor told us to feed you. If you want to drink milk from the cup, do it. If not we will force-feed you with the meat broth through the tube'.

Ivan Kuznetsov, a young man of 22, bravely answered, 'I won't take the cup myself'.

Then one of the brothers approached them and said, 'When you force-feed us with the broth, it goes against our religion. We are vegetarians and our religion does not allow us to eat meat'.

Wilson said, 'You have to see the doctor and tell him this. I can't go against his orders'.

Ivan was force-fed through the tube.

August 16: Three brothers were given drinks from the cup and in Cell # 4 Ivan Kuznetsov was force-fed through the tube. In the evening he was given drink from a cup.

August 17: Fourteen brothers were weak in four cells and were given milk. Vladimir Lebedev was force fed with beef broth through the tube. In the evening all fourteen brothers were made to drink milk from the cup.

August 18: All fourteen brothers were made to drink milk from a cup for breakfast and dinner.

On August 19 commissioner McLeod, Warden Gall and Superintendent Wilson visited all four cells. At dinnertime commissioner McLeod and warden Gall visited only Cell #4 to see how the feeding was going on. At 8:00 p.m. Dr. Ewans came and examined everybody and told to some of the prisoners: 'You have to start eating tomorrow'.

To Pavel Ponomarev and others he said, 'You are still strong and you can continue fasting'.

When the doctor was leaving he said, 'You will have to drink milk from a cup. If not, you will be force-fed through the tube'.

August 20: Wilson said to us, 'If you don't drink milk from cups we will force-feed you with meat broth through a tube. We have enough tubes to do so'. We refused to take cups and were force-fed through a tube.

August 21: Wilson came with the guards and said, 'We will force-feed you with broth through a tube. If somebody wants to drink milk from a cup, take a cup and drink'.

When the guards were giving us milk from a cup, we didn't refuse but they wanted us to take cups and drink from them ourselves. They wanted to stop our Lent and from that day on the jail administration continued to force-feed us through the tube.

Sixteen guards came in with stretchers. Some of them were drunk and were swearing and trying to scare us. Two or three of them would hold somebody and the fourth would insert the tube in the nose. Some of the brothers were force-fed like this eight times. Some of them had the tube inserted two or three times because the tube wouldn't go in. You could hear the moans of tortured brothers and their prayers to God: 'Oh, Merciful Heavenly Father please divide my soul from my body'. Because of force-feeding through a plastic tube some of the brothers had severe pains in the chest and stomach. Every day was like that and during the night we couldn't sleep because of the pain. But despite all the torture we were relying on the will of God.

During force-feeding medical officer Jones said, 'We want at least six people to start drinking from cups'. We would like to remind that when we submitted out petition to Wilson, it said that our passive lent had nothing to do with the jail administration.

Wilson answered, 'We understand'.

We were surprised that the jail administration was torturing us like this. Pavel Ponomarev was force-fed through the tube four times and every time three guards would hold him and the fourth one, Jones, would insert the tube in the nose. He was jerking the tube back and forth trying to make Pavel suffer and then would ask him, 'Will you take the cup and drink yourself?'

Pavel, a young man of 23 years old, couldn't answer and was just shaking his head, because it was impossible to answer. Jones continued to insert the tube further into the stomach but the food was not going through and was coming back from the mouth. When the tube was taken out it was covered with blood. They were doing the same thing to many people.

Force-feeding made four people in Cell # 4 seriously sick: Ivan Kuznetsov, Mikhail Saprykin, Pavel Ponomarev and Vassily Stuchnov. Nurses gave them shots.

Pavel Ponomarev was fed for the last time in the afternoon. After this he never left his bed again. He was lying there breathing heavily and moaning. We told the guard that he was seriously ill. The guard checked the temperature. It was 103. He asked Pavel, 'how do you feel'. Pavel couldn't answer. The guard said, 'he'll be alright. Let him moan, this is just a nervous break down'. It was 9:00 p.m. After that Pavel was unconscious. He didn't say anything and didn't answer. One of the brothers was wetting his lips with water and massaging his back. Pavel looked at us with tears in his eyes and then looked at his chest showing us that it hurt. We started massaging his arms and his back. But we couldn't help him. We understood that it was his last goodbye.

Later a medical officer came again and asked Pavel, 'how do you feel?' Pavel didn't answer. After that guards and a nurse came and one of the guards started pressing Pavel's back trying to make him regain consciousness. Pavel was breathing heavily and moaning. The nurse gave him a shot and Pavel stopped moaning but the guard was still trying to resuscitate him. It was close to midnight when Dr. Enns came and gave Pavel two shots. We gathered around Pavel and stood on our knees. We prayed to God to let Pavel live.

Physically we were very weak. Then Dr. Enns said to the nurse, 'He is dead'. One of the young men that were taking care of Pavel all the time fainted. We took him to his bed; we had these fainting accidents several time during Lent.

When brothers heard that the doctor pronounced Pavel dead, we all stood on our knees and cried and prayed and said goodbye to our hero and fighter who suffered for the faith of our ancestors.

After midnight Pavel was taken away. Same night two brothers were taken to the hospital. They were in critical condition. The next day Wilson arrived and announced, 'Your friend Pavel died this morning at 5:45 a.m. in the Chilliwak hospital. Will you start eating or you want two or three of you to follow Pavel?'

We answered that we would continue the lent till we die and that we were ready to follow Pavel. The next day Dr. Enns came. He approached Vassily Stuchnov and asked him, 'How do you feel?'

Vasya answered, 'You can see for yourself'.

The doctor told him to get up but Vasya answered, 'I can't get up and I have chest pain'.

The doctor helped him to get up and examined him and then said, 'You have about twelve hours to live. If you don't start eating you will die'.

Vasya answered, 'I won't take the cup and I am not afraid of dying'.

The doctor said, 'You will follow your brother Pavel'.

Our Thoughts and Conversations with Visitors

August 25: The following people came to the camp: A commissioner from Ottawa, Mr. McLeod; Warden Gall; Superintendent Wilson; Mr. Winch, member of SSF from Victoria Parliament; Carson and his associate Hindu Vashapati (these two were representing the Civil Rights Association); lawyer Simons and two of our brothers, Fedor Cherenkov and Vassily Kalmykov.

They visited all four camps where our brothers were being held. The floors were dirty because nobody washed them for several days. Not only the floors but the people were dirty, their shirts and pants were torn. When they saw that we were so weak and some of us couldn't stand, they understood that the jail administration was not treating us well.

The visitors came to Cell # 4. Warden Gall introduced them and said, 'Mr. Carson received a telegram from your leader Sorokin from Uruguay and he will read it to you. But I have to tell you that neither Mr. Carson nor his associate has any power vested in them by the Federal or the Provincial Government. These people represent a small group of people from B.C., which is called the Civil Rights Association.

Carson read us the telegram that he received from Sorokin. In the telegram Sorokin asked the brothers and sisters, who were fasting in the Agassiz Camp, to stop fasting and to start eating. Carson's friend expressed his concern and told us that they'd try to help us. He said, 'From this day on I will work day and night to help you'.

Carson asked us what was our reaction to the telegram. Would we start eating? We answered that we wanted to get together and talk about it. We asked Warden Gall to let us get together and discuss it and then we could answer the telegram. We then asked everybody to come and hear our answer. Everybody agreed and Warden Gall said, 'I allow you to have a council'.

When the visitors, left we started discussing the telegram. After the discussion we decided that we wanted our leader S.S. Sorokin to come to the camp in person and settle our problem together with the Canadian Government and Carson's Committee. Sorokin was a part of the Consultation Committee when they were dealing with the problem of Doukhobors. For some reason they couldn't finish their work and we asked them to continue and resolve our difficult situation.

We were fasting to attract attention of the Canadian Government and the people of Canada. We wanted them to investigate the reason of our imprisonment in a just and humane way. Everything was described in our Declaration of Lent dated July 21.

When we gathered in Cell #2, many of us could not recognize each other. We were all very weak and thin. We learned that the same decision was reached in all cells.

We asked once more if somebody wanted to say anything regarding this issue but everybody supported our decision.

All the visitors came back, except Carson and his friend lawyer Simon and our brothers. We asked where the rest of them were, because we wanted them to be there to hear our decision. Warden Gall said that they went to visit our sisters. Through the window we saw that they were coming back. We asked everybody to wait for them.

Commissioner McLeod said, 'we don't have time! Don't test my patience. Tell us what you've got to say. Winch is here and he will let them know what you said.'

Harold Winch said, 'You probably heard about me before and some of you know about me. I always support the just. I'll let Carson and his people know what your decision is'.

We discussed whether it would be better to wait for Carson and other visitors and decided to tell our answer right away. We understood that the jail administration tricked us.

Our representative, Vassily Babakaev said, 'we know a committee was formed to investigate the reason of our imprisonment. We would be very thankful to this committee if they would investigate our difficult situation. Moreover, we would like the Canadian Government to recognize this committee. Thus it would show its willingness to help and investigate our case. It would be good to invite members of our Brotherhood Council and our leader Sorokin to join this Committee. Then we'll have hope. When members of our committee and our spiritual leader Sorokin tell us that the Government and the committee have started to deal with our issue, then we'll start eating. If not, we'll continue fasting, as it was said in our Declaration of July 21, 1963'. All the brothers expressed their support.

Winch said, 'I will raise this issue at the Parliament session in Ottawa. I understood that you did not pay attention to the telegram from your leader Sorokin. He asked you to start eating. I see that you do not believe him. How can I invite him here then and tell him where to go and what to do about your issue. This is between you and Sorokin. If he wants to come, he can do it anytime'.

Fedor Zhmarev said, 'Mr. Winch made a very 'good' political speech at the meeting'.

We think that Fedor Zhmarev made a very good remark about the political speech of Mr. Winch. We thought that Winch had prejudices against us. We understood that he plainly showed his hypocrisy.

Commissioner McLeod said, 'I'm a Commissioner from Ottawa for all penitentiaries in Canada. I know nothing about your case, I'm just trying to determine if the law is observed'.

That day and on his other visits Commissioner McLeod was drunk. Mr. Carson told all the truth about this Commissioner.

Apologies and movie men

In 1999 the provincial Ombudsman said that the former internees were entitled to an explanation, an apology and compensation.[24] Mike wrote on 6 April 2000:

> The boys of the New Denver bunch just got a letter from the government denying to do anything about the Ombudsman report. But at the same time they got several offers from lawyers to sue the government. And they are offering to do this without cost to the boys. Apparently they have enough information, to get big profit from the government.
>
> On the 13th of this month a couple of aboriginal lawyers are coming from Calgary, who are also very interested in this case. They feel that our problem is much the same as theirs, so they want to get in and see what they can do. They want [to be] here for a couple of days so they can get to the bottom of things. Things are looking up.
>
> The other lawyers are from Vancouver and seven firms are interested to get in. I enjoy about the amount of lawyers that are interested enough to take the job to sue the government.

In a following letter, June 25, 2000, Mike wrote that the lawyers had still not showed up:

> ... but the ones that are trying to make a movie out of our story will want to come and start getting us on film in a couple of weeks. We want to get together and discuss it a bit for we can't trust them all the way. We would like a TRUE story not just like stories that they used to put out about us or the Indians.
>
> We know that the lawyers are after money and the movie men are after the same DOLLAR, so [we] have to be very careful. The government has the money and they may have the say, but we know that the government have tried to suppress the truth even went as far as murder in

---

24 A Statement of Regret by the Government of British Columbia was only issued in 2004: see: http://www.llbc.leg.bc.ca/public/pubdocs/bcdocs/371785/bcaa_nr_oct_04_04.pdf (Last accessed in April 2013).

Mountain Prison when we wanted a Public Hearing to get to the bottom of why we were railroaded in to prison.

Movie Men

Upon visiting Mike later in the summer of 2000, he took me along to the backyard of his neighbour Sam, where Movie Men, as he called them, were busy shooting a documentary. We quietly sat down at a table served with tea, lemonade, and homemade goodies and watched Sam being interviewed. He was sweating visibly and struggling to answer a certain question. The interviewer once more repeated this question: 'Does the recollection of being force-fed in prison still bother you?' Sam started to cry. One moment later the cameraman shouted: 'Stop.'

The crew director, holding up a round silver screen, visibly irritated, shouted back: 'Just now he cries he has to stop!?'

The cameraman shouted back that he had only five seconds film left so would have had to interrupt the crying anyway. The director urged him to hurry up. The interviewer repeated: 'Does the recollection of being force-fed in prison still bother you?'

Sam, getting a hold of himself said: 'They put tubes in cold water, pushed them through your nose and punched holes with it in your stomach and blood was spurting out.' Sam cried again. Now the director himself shouted that the filming had to stop: not far from Sam's house children cycled by, happily whistling, shouting, and singing.

After the last of the cheerful sounds had faded, the interviewer asked Sam (a bit lamely): 'When again did you start to cry?'

Humming birds were flying on and off to the colourful humming bird feeders, squirrels ran over the roof, the flowers were in full bloom in splendid colours, the homemade cake tasted awfully good as did the homemade lemonade. The Garden of Eden could not have been a better place than Sam's back yard.

The crew decided to finish for the day, and sat down to enjoy the cherry lemonade and the cake. Sam, now relaxed, told a story about a seven-year old girl that was pulled to the ground by police-dogs before she was taken away to the New

↑ Getting ready for a break: movie men, Mike, and Sam, photo Mary E.M.

Denver school. The crew murmured, 'He tells us now this instead of when the camera still on!' Filming could not be started again because the equipment worked on generators.

Mike later sent me a copy of this documentary about the history of the Sons of Freedom in Canada. The opening scene shows on the foreground a lot of nude people blessed with bulky, white behinds against a black background lit by flaring red flames. Rows of nude people then start marching over the screen: others can be seen to disrobe and police officers can be heard volunteering to 'watch what is going on.' Sam can be heard and seen in his backyard telling how he got in prison: 'Back in 1953 he had not participated in anything,' he said, but he had 'boarded the train because he thought it would bring him to Russia.'

A few younger men can be heard and seen to accuse Sorokin of having committed sodomy with them.[25]

At the end of the documentary a woman states that everyone should have a religion, but 'not so strong. Children and life should come at the first place.' Her statement reminds of what Tolstoy wrote to his friend Chertkov in October 1897. Tolstoy (1978) complains about his daughter, saying:

> How many people are like that, whom you can't talk to at all because you know they are drunk. Some are drunk with greed, some with vanity, some with being in love, and some directly with drugs. God save us from these intoxications. Their intoxications put barriers between people just as much as religiosity, together, side by side, all your life, yet you live like strangers.

Barriers - what are they good for; life is already too short. On 3 November 2005 Marilyn, Sam's wife wrote:

---

25 In the December 1998 *Istina*, in a letter to the Editor of the *Nelson Daily News*, replying to a letter to the editor Mike makes some remarks about healing and goes on with, 'I also believe the boys. They say that there were always people in the main room when these acts were done. Surely some one would have heard it if there was anything out of the ordinary. From this I understand that what there was, was done on a mutual consent.' If these sentences refer to what these young man say in the documentary, all I can say about 'consent' that sexual relations between "leaders" and youngsters in hindsight often lack 'consent.'

↑ Sam being interviewed, photo Mary E.M.

Mike is presently in the Nelson hospital and will be getting CAT scans tomorrow. Nobody seems to be quite sure what is happening to him, but we are hoping they will do a thorough investigation and see if they can ease his health problems. The IHA has found a place in Nelson for him to live in a few months. Aging makes it more difficult to live independently way out here!

We are keeping very well. Sam is still dealing with the cancer, but has done amazingly well and has pleasantly surprised everyone. There is no hope for a cure, or to stop the progression [of] it, but they have assured us that they should be able to keep him relatively pain free. In May, a sudden progression of the MS has confined me to the wheelchair, but we are managing to get by very well. We enjoyed a beautiful summer watching the flowers budding and blossoming and laughing at the antics of the birds and squirrels!

A letter straight from the Garden of Eden. All this had started with a chat with Mike in which I wondered about Canada - about what it all meant: 'Van Paassen in a Mike's journal, a Tolstoy statue in a Castlegar backyard, the 'pacifist' Van Paassen orchestrating a Jewish army from New York, the Black Sea, Christian pacifism at a Gorcum fireplace, nudity and arson, and pacifists in prison.'

Fortunately, I thought, the ashes that once had drifted through British Columbia have not clouded the pacifist spirit that still lingers in British Columbia. During the Vietnam War thousands of draft dodgers found their way to the Doukhobor-Nelson area where they could start a life that would not require later reflections on state-sanctioned maiming and killing. According to an American refugees' website:[26] 'From 1965-1973, more than 100,000 draft-age Americans who refused to participate in the Vietnam War made their way to Canada. More than half of those who came remain in the country today.'[27] In July 2006 a *National Reunion Weekend*

26　See: www.ourwayhomereunion.com (Last accessed in April 2013).
27　This website also honours Pierre Trudeau, the Canadian prime-minister at the time who said: 'Those who make the conscientious judgment that they must not participate in this war ... have my complete sympathy, and indeed our

Event was held near Nelson. In 2007 a second *Our Way Home and Peace Reunion* was hold. The invitation reads:

WHY CASTLEGAR, BC FOR THIS PEACE EVENT?

We are pleased to hold this event at the Brilliant Cultural Centre, a beautiful performance hall in the community of Brilliant, part of the city of Castlegar, B.C. Canada. The Brilliant Cultural Centre was founded by the Doukhobor population of the region, whose ancestors fled Russia in 1899 after destroying their weapons as a demonstration of their refusal to fight in the Tsarist Army. Russian author Leo Tolstoy was responsible for helping pay for the Doukhobors travel as new immigrants to Canada.

The towns of Castlegar and nearby Nelson, BC and the surrounding region of the West Kootenays were a leading terminus in what was known as the 'Underground Railroad'. It is estimated that as many as 14,000 US war resisters came to the area at the height of US immigration to Canada during the Vietnam War. New arrivals were frequently welcomed and assisted by members of two resident pacifist groups, the Doukhobors and the Quakers, the latter having earlier settled in the area after fleeing the US during the McCarthy period.

---

political approach has been to give them access to Canada. Canada should be a refuge from militarism.'

Chapter 3
Hutterites

The first time I heard about Hutterites was during a History of Immigration class at the University of Calgary shortly after having immigrated to Canada. An older man, Mac, was always seated at the back of the classroom; his toes stuck through his runners, he was wearing a vague vest, and his scalp looked somewhat motley. If he had paid more attention to his appearance, he could have been a professor: the students said, 'since he knows everything.'

I believed them. The professor often asked Mac to help him out when the students were posing questions. One day the professor, lecturing about Hutterites, noted that they only baptize their children if they (the children) indicate that they *want* to be baptized and enter the church. This occurs generally when they are about eighteen years old. I asked the professor what would happen if someone chose not to be baptized. The professor prodded: 'Mac?'

Mac, having lived for months on a Hutterite colony, said that as far as he knew, that had happened only once.

'They don't have to be baptized,' said Mac, 'but then they cannot marry.'

'How free are they not to enter the church?' I wondered out loud: 'What does freedom mean to them?'

Mac: 'They have a concept of freedom of their own.'

Not long after, one of my Dutch friends called. She had to go to Edmonton for a conference and asked whether Calgary was a nice city.

'Come and find out for yourself,' I answered.

'I travel with two colleagues.'

'Why don't you bring them along?'

↑ Hutterite cows, photo Mary E.M.

So, at the start of February 1990 three Dutch medical sociologists came to Calgary. After having toured the environment of Calgary, the weather was unbelievably beautiful that day, we saw a sign at a Hutterite Colony: *Potatoes for Sale*. I turned the car into the colony's premises. A heavily built, somewhat older woman, accompanied by a much younger woman, approached us.

'Can I some *Kartoffeln kaufen,*' I asked in my best German. As it was about 6:00 p.m., I feared that maybe their potato shop was already closed. But no, I could buy them.

'*Meine Freunde haben niemals eine Hutterite colony gesehen,*' I went on. Without further ado my friends (in the course of the week the two colleagues had become my friends as well), were dragged out of my car and taken away by the older lady. The young woman jumped into the car, indicating that I drive on. Around the corner of a small building I saw glimpses of white flakes fluttering in the air against a background of a rapidly darkening Chinook sky. The white flakes spiralled around, but it certainly was not snowing. Beneath these clouds of flakes, women and children dressed in billowing skirts and scarves were bent over a few buckets. I was led into a potato cellar where I had to buy fifty kilograms of potatoes - the old man said that he did not sell potatoes in smaller portions.

'*Waß floh da durch die Luft?* (What was that flying through the air?)' I asked the young woman. She said that they had been slaughtering animals, boiled their fat, made sausages from the fat and had been shaving these sausages into soap flakes. That had been fluttering through the air: soap flakes.

Next question: '*Who sind meine Freunde?* (Do you know where my friends are?)' The young woman took me along to the house of the older woman, Anna, where I found them in a bedroom, sitting on a queen-size bed with their legs stretched out, fitting and now proudly showing off colourful knitted socks. I asked Anna whether they could buy them. They could. We then got coffee and were interrogated: what we did for a living, where we came from, whether we had kids, whether we had cows in the Netherlands, when and what we sowed. We did not come across as very knowledgeable. All we knew about cows was that 'yes, there are lots of cows in the

↑ Hutterite visitor, photo Mary E.M.

Netherlands, but we were not sure about sowing or planting, and what and when, etc. Only two of us had children. But no, when asked again, 'none of us had any cows.'

After that first time I have often returned to this and other colonies. The Hutterites visit me in turn when in Calgary. Time and time again, when I visit the colony with guests, the mutual interrogations lead to mutual astonishments. So far, none of my guests have ever had cows, they are all very uncertain about sowing or seeding, and have only the slightest of idea about the mowing or ploughing seasons. It is nothing to be proud off, but that is how it is.

One of my friends, Maarten Biesheuvel, a famous short story writer, did not even now whether the *Steuer* (taxes) in the Netherlands was *teuer* (high) or not. Anna then asked what he did for a living.

'I am a writer,' he said, which made Anna write some words on a piece of paper.

'I write too, as you can see. How do I make money with this? I don't!'

During the Biesheuvel visit Anna took me to the basement to show me fruit they had been canning while Biesheuvel stayed behind with a few granddaughters. A bit later I heard him sing, and not too softly. For a moment I thought myself back in an Arnhem theatre back in the Netherlands, where a few years earlier I had heard him sing the same German songs. A bit later Anna and I joined the small audience in the basement and listened along.

Later, walking through the night to the car accompanied by giggling granddaughters, they asked whether he would sing '*noch etwa* (a few more songs).' That is what he did.

On another occasion, I visited with an elderly lady-friend from Calgary. My Hutterite friends could not get over it; does this eighty-something, nearly ninety-year old lady, healthy and cheerful, live all by herself!? Does she clean her own apartment!? (With the help of a cleaning lady.) Cook her own food!? (Often her son or granddaughter invite her for dinner, or bring her food, but in general, yes.) 'And do you yourself close the door at night?' Living alone is not something that Hutterites would like to fathom.

↑ At a colony, photo Ludo Jongen.

Others guests I brought along, saying that they were teachers (actually they were professors), were asked what they were teaching.

'Chinese literature,' he answered. It was hilarious. There are so many Chinese people and they speak Chinese, why would a Dutch guy do anything like this?

Another friend asked them about teaching at the colony

'We have teachers here. All they do is drink coffee and read the newspapers.'

One more guest I brought, a member of the Euro Parliament, was asked what he did for a living.

'Politician,' he answered. Anna and her family could not stop laughing.

'He must really be stupid,' they said to me in the presence of my astonished guest. (I explained to him that the then recent antics of Stockwell Day had turned Canadian politicians into a laughing stock and not only for the Hutterites.)

Another question for the visitors was whether people in the Netherlands are allowed to marry their cousin. For Hutterites, finding a partner that is not at least a second cousin is difficult; their gene pool is small, which can cause problems such as decline in fertility and lower levels of cognitive functions caused by inbreeding. This is a direct consequence of them not actively proselytizing.* One of them told me that they do in fact proselytize, 'by dressing the way they do, which is dressing in the way people have done since, well, since a few hundreds of years.' Promoting the simple life, is one of their tenets.

* This is a high price to pay, but on the other hand proselytizing often leads to religious wars and loss of life.

Once I was invited to a 'shiveree.' When a girl marries, she will go to live at her husband's colony, which is preferably not the colony in which she lived. On the Friday night before the wedding a shiveree, a farewell party, is held for her. The entire colony, at that time about ninety people, gathered in the communal dining room. The chairs were all set with their backs against the wall. Upon entering the men sat at the wall to their left, and served beverages and snacks for the entire evening. Beside them were the teenage and young boys, with men of marrying age furthest from the door. Continuing around the room, next sat the women of marrying age, then, opposite to the entrance, the bride and groom flanked by their

↑ Childrens' dining room, photo Ludo Jongen.

parents and two ministers. The married and older women closed the ranks all the way back to the right of the entrance.

As soon as everyone was seated, praying and singing started. Hutterite singing is ear splitting. It was such a cacophony that I asked about it. 'The idea is to sing in order to honour the Lord. When someone sings harmoniously, there is always a chance that someone might remark: "You sing beautifully." As the singing's purpose supposedly is to honour God, and not to glamour oneself, harmonious singing is not done.'*

After the singing the men entered with jugs of beer mixed with tomato juice, followed by cheese sandwiches, apple pies, ice creams, chips, cans of Coke, quarters of heads of salad, cookies, more chips, more beer and tomato juice, and more apple pies. When I took a break from eating, my neighbour poked her finger solidly into my rib cage.

'*Essen,*' she hissed.

At the occasion of another wedding I was invited for a dinner at lunchtime. More than one or two glasses of beer were served. Thereafter the parents left to sleep through the afternoon and the teenagers ran around, eager to play, let's call it, hide-and-seek in the barns. The scene made me think of a Dutch proverb: *From a wedding comes a wedding.*

I was asked to go along with the remaining group of youngsters to take photographs. While most of the Hutterites visiting for the wedding had their own cameras with them, some colonies don't allow cameras, while some do. In many regards the first impression is that all colonies are the same, but as the schoolbook reads and as I discovered over time, they certainly are not.

Later on that same wedding day I ended up in a living room where a number of women were seated. After a while I asked my neighbour where she came from.

'Lloydminster,' she said, looking straight ahead. I asked another lady the same question: 'Drumheller.' She also kept looking straight ahead.

I got the impression that this was certainly not a chat-room, and as no one seemed to be interested where I came from, I shut up and started to look straight ahead of me as well. My hostess asked whether I was feeling well. Actually I started to

---

* A 2001 Hutterite schoolbook, written by Hutterite schoolchildren on music: No radios, televisions, or tape recorders are allowed on the colony. No [...] guitars, violins or pianos are allowed, but any other musical instruments are allowed [...] The colony leader doesn't mind the harmonica. Hutterite children sing Christmas songs in English and German in school. They sing a few verses in the morning. Hutterite music is very monotonous. It doesn't have high or low notes. It is very beautiful and has a unique sound.

↑ At a Hutterite wedding, photo Mary E.M.

wonder that myself, and she suggested that I would join the youngsters in the basement. We descended from my cross.

In the basement, groups of youngsters were seated on benches opposite to each other and singing. One bench would sing, and then the other bench would respond. I sat beside a young man.

'What do you think about marriage?' he hissed between his teeth, and then added, 'be honest.'[28]

'Marriage is what you make of it; everyone makes something else of it,' I hissed back. The young man snapped back that he was about to marry the following week and sang along, a bit terse. Only then I understood why the little girls had asked visitor-Biesheuvel to sing for them. Perhaps, we should have asked them to sing for us?

The schoolbook on weddings:

> To get married boys visit other colonies and meet girls. Once they meet the girl they like they start visiting more often and ask the girl to marry. They get married from 20 years of age and up. The boy and girl need to be baptized to get married. The boy comes to the girl's colony after he is baptized to set a date for the wedding with the girl, but they tell their parents and friends [...] When the wedding arrives the 1st and 2nd shiverees are at the girls' colony. They do a lot of singing, serve food and they view wedding gifts. The bride and groom goes to everyone's house to give drinks. At the shiveree they serve food, pop, sandwiches, chips, Twinkies, beer, and ice cream bars. The girls and boys sing German songs. The 3rd shiveree and wedding is at the boy's colony.

Next: how did these people end up being called Hutterites, and why do they live in colonies?

---

28 An interesting discussion on marriage from the women's view is in: http://library.ndsu.edu/grhc/articles/newspapers/news/hutterite16a.htm (Last accessed in April 2013.)

A brief Hutterite history*

After Luther had nailed a copy of his ninety-five theses to the door of the Castle Church in Wittenberg in 1517, Zwingli started to preach from the open Bible in the Grossmünster Cathedral of Zürich around 1519. Subsequently Zwingli removed the usual mediums of Catholic worship such as statues and paintings of saints, stained glass, and even the organ from the church. For Zwingli, nothing was to obstruct the direct access to the throne of grace to obtain forgiveness of sin.†

Zwingli also turned against Swiss military service in the armies of the Pope:

> though on social and economic rather than scriptural grounds. As an army chaplain among these mercenary troops he had had ample opportunity for observing the evil results of this foreign service, first upon the morals of the troops themselves, and later indirectly upon the Swiss communities to which they returned after service (*Smith's Story*).[29]

After having resigned from the Roman Catholic Church, Zwingli was reinstated by Zürich's council, the Council of Two Hundred. This meant, according to Dijck, that independence from the Roman Catholic Church was established and also that political authorities had obtained the right to name ministers. This gave great control to Zürich's council. For example, the council objected when Zwingli started to eliminate the said religious artifacts. Nevertheless, Zwingli attracted followers.

Three years later, in 1522, the priest Wilhelm Reublin carried the bible around in an annual procession, married one year later, and subsequently refused to have his baby baptized. He also went to the villages around Zürich preaching

---

* Based on Smith's *Story of the Mennonites*, Dijck's *Introduction to Mennonite History*, P. Wiebe in *Mennonite Memories*, D. Wiebe in *The History of the Hutterites* and Snyder's *Anabaptist History* the story is roughly as follows.

† As said above, perhaps this is the reason that (some?) Hutterites sing in such a cacophonous way, at least so it was explained to me: Praise God, and do not want to be praised yourself for your singing.

---

29 Certain things don't change. Cf. Lavigne in *Hell's Angels*, 'The bikers who choose the name Hell's Angels in 1948 are former pilots, bombardiers, navigators and gunners. They bring to earth a rebellious tradition bred in the cloudy battlefields of Europe, Africa and China.' And this comment in *The Globe & Mail* of October 21, 2005 about Canadians joining the Iraqi insurgence, 'Those foreigners flooding into Iraq who are learning those techniques 'are going to go somewhere else when that conflict ends.'"

against child baptism. According to *Smith's Story,* the next logical step after rejecting child baptism was taken by Conrad Grebel. During a meeting, Grebel baptized Georg Blaurock of Chur (of the House of Jacob, a monastic establishment), who then baptized the others present. 'It marked a complete break with the state church and inaugurated a new church based on the revolutionary principle of religious freedom and a church membership upon confession of faith and believer's baptism.'

Hutterites have their own history book, Bieglschmid's **Daſ Klein Geſchichtſbuch der Hutteriſchen Brüder**, typeset in a German Gothic font. Bieglschmid also discusses Ulrich Zwingli, Konrad Grebel, and Felix Manz' gatherings to discuss questions of the faith. Once they were joined by someone from Chur: 'der Georg vom Haus Jakob, den man sonst hat genennt Blaurock.' During one of their sessions Blaurock had asked Grebel to baptize him - the others then wanted to be baptized also.

Zwingli's followers called the people who had themselves baptized again *Wiedertäufer,* Anabaptists. *Ana* means *Again* in Greek, so Anabaptists are people that are baptized again. Re-baptizing was then dismissed, as the original baptism was no longer acknowledged. Thus, the Re/*wieder*/*ana*/again was dropped and these people became known simply as *Baptists.* In Smith's words 'a church of adults, sin-conscious, admitted into membership by baptism upon confession of faith was born.'

In the autumn of 1524 it was Conrad Grebel, who explained Reublin's ideas to dignitaries such as Luther, Carlstadt and Müntzer. The main issue between the Zürich council and pious men like Grebel and Reublin was child baptism. However, after a public debate the council decided that children should be baptized, that Bible study groups were forbidden, and that radical anti child-baptism leaders not from Zürich, had to be banned from the city. Also, early teachers, Reublin among them, had to leave the city.

However, it was not only the Zürich council that held grudges against the Anabaptists. D. Wiebe writes that both Catholics and Lutherans hated Anabaptists with a passion. By 1525 Grebel, Blaurock, and Manz were pursued by the Swiss authorities.

Grebel managed to flee to southern Switzerland, where he died of the plague.

Manz was drowned in the Limmat River that flows through Zürich. His hands were first tied over his knees, a stick was put through his knees and under his arms, and in that way he was pushed into the water.

Blaurock, according to Snyder, was also a notorious disturber of the peace; once he 'began banging on the pews with a stout stick, and shouted to the preaching pastor, "Not you, but I am sent to preach."' He managed to flee to Tyrol, Austria where, in 1529 he was caught, tortured, and burned at the stake. This was witnessed by Peter Walpot, an eighteen-year old boy, whom we will hear from below.

A few years previously though, a number of Moravian followers of Grebel, Blaurock, and Manz had fled their homes to the protection offered by the Lords of Liechtenstein, in particular by Leonhard Von Liechtenstein. Word of this new 'church' spread and by 1527 there were about 12,000 Anabaptists in the area (now in the Czech Republic).

At the time the spread of ideas had been greatly sped up by the invention of book printing and book peddling. When the government of Ferdinand I, Holy Roman Emperor (1503-1564) urged Leonhard Von Liechtenstein to get rid of the Anabaptists, it was already too late; Von Liechtenstein had already been re-baptized himself. But, he caused divisions when he called the *Wiedertaufer* together and 'demanded that all prepare and arm themselves to defend his castle.'

One group, Balthasar Hubmaier (c. 1480-1528) and his followers, wanted to defend themselves; they would live on under the name *Schwertler* (Sword-bearers).[30] Shortly afterwards Hans Hut, a fiery preacher, arrived on the *Schwertler* scene. He and Hubmaier started a dispute about swords and paying war taxes that did not lead to anything. Not long after

---

30 Snyder writes that Hubmaier was from a humble family, studied with the famous theologian Johannes Eck (1486-1543) and became a doctor of Theology in Ingolstadt in 1512. In 1516 he became cathedral preacher in the city of Regensburg 'where his sermons contributed to the anti-Semitic fervour that led, in 1519, to the destruction of the synagogue and the expulsion of the Jewish community from the city' and he 'encouraged devotion to the Blessed Virgin and fed the popular need for miraculous intervention.'

Hubmaier was burned at the stake and Hut was executed, and the *Schwertler* faded away.

The other group, the followers of Jacob Widemann (d. 1535), decided to leave the castle. They did so with staff in hand, and became known as the *Stäbler* (Staff-bearers). They settled in Bergen, Nikolsburg, Moravia.

But then the Holy Roman Empire came once more under pressure to fight the Turks and urged Von Liechtenstein again to pay war taxes. Von Liechtenstein replied that he would receive any state troops with canon balls. At that point the *Stäbler* decided to leave and look for a nobleman who would tolerate them and not urge them to armed resistance.

Two-hundred people in Nikolsburg sold or abandoned their goods, and left the city. The party stopped just outside the walls, elected a minister for their 'temporal needs,' and:

> **laid down their cloaks, and every man threw down on it, entirely of his own accord without compulsion, his earthly possessions according to the teachings of the prophets and apostles for the benefit of the needy (*Smith's Story*).**[31]

The group travelled on to Austerlitz, Moravia, where they were permitted to settle on the estate of Ulrich von Kaunitz. There they lived as one family in a group, called *Bruderhof*, and from there they urged their persecuted brethren in Palatinate, Swabia, Bavaria, Hesse, and especially Tyrol to join them. Consequently, more *Bruderhofs* were established. Conflicts arose around Wideman's enforcement of his rigid regulations. This forced some others, such as Reublin and Zaunring, to leave and settle in Auspitz, Moravia on lands given to them by the Abbess of Brün, while about 250 individuals remained with Widemann in Austerlitz.

Jacob Hutter, who had already been in Moravia in 1529, was asked to be an intermediary between the quarrelling leaders. (The story is much more complex than told here.) He came back to Auspitz 'to assume pastoral duties along with others.'

---

[31] This act was based on *Acts 2:44-45*: 'And all the believed were together and had all things in common. They sold their possessions and good parted them to all men, as every man had need.'

Hutter though not only disciplined the members of his congregation, but also his fellow-ministers:

- Reublin was accused of retaining twenty guilders for himself,
- Räbel was excommunicated because he had said that people worshipped Hutter,
- Zaunring (who must have returned as well) was expelled for taking back his wife who had been accused of adultery. All of this led to Hutter's election as the chief-elder.

In 1535 Emperor Ferdinand I finally got his wish; the lords expelled the Hutterites. From then on they wandered around in small groups carrying their belongings on their backs. Those who were caught by government forces were persecuted, executed, or put into dungeons. In 1535, Hutter and his wife returned to their native Tyrol, to be caught. Despite being subjected to whippings and torture on the rack, Hutter would not reveal the names of any of his fellow Brethren.* On his way to the pyre in 1536, Hutter is to have said: 'This fire damages my soul as little as the burning oven was hurting Shadrach, Meshach, and Abednego.† His wife was executed two years later.

The surviving group took on Hutter's name and lived on as the *Hutterian Brethren*. As the Wideman group suffered much persecution as well, the remaining members joined Hutter's group, now under the leadership of Hans Amon.

During Easter 1536 the *Hutterian Brethren* decided to split into smaller groups and quietly look for employ with noble men. It did not take long before they could settle in *Bruderhofs*.

During Amon's leadership many missionaries were sent out, with an eye that their converts, often from Germany, would join them in Moravia.

Peter Wiebe continues the Hutterite history by listing the tortures that the captured missionaries underwent: they were hung by their arms so that their feet could not reach the floor; they were incarcerated in such damp cells that clothes moulded on their bodies; they were chained, bound on racks, and fed wormy food. But somehow, while these stories went on and on, the body of Hutterites kept growing.

* Bieglschmid describes the tortures Hutter underwent before he was publicly burned in Innsbrück in 1536. He was bound, held in freezing water, taken to an overheated room, brandy was poured on his wounds, and then set on fire.

† 'The Three Young Men' from the Book of Daniel.

Peter Walpot, the eighteen-year old who had seen how Blaurock had been burned on the stake, was made bishop and served from 1565 to 1578.* As bishop, Walpot also organized schools. The Hutterite 'little schools' were in operation 270 years prior to the establishment of the first German *Kindergartens* in 1837. Children were taught 'the fear of God,' and 'the right way of living,' but higher education and worldly scholarship were (and are) disregarded.

> * Of all the preachers in the different Bruderhofs, one was chosen to be bishop.

In 1621 there were about 102 *Bruderhofs* with a total population of about 20,000 to 30,000 residents living in buildings around a village square.[32] The main floors of these buildings were used for workshops, dining rooms, churches, and schools. Married couples lived on the second floor, while infants and children were in nurseries and dormitories.

People engaged in more than just farming: they also brewed, worked wood, made books, shoes and wagons, nursed, made medicines, and much more. Their *faience*, pots, called after Faenza, an Italian town, are still around in museums. Professionals were ruled by *Ordnungen*, or ethical standards. For example, the people that crafted cutlery were instructed that 'blades that are seen to be defective shall not be sold.' Hutterite medical practices were widely in demand.

But as time went on, wars raged on - the Jesuits had joined several kings' armies, which persecuted the Hutterites. These new persecutions caused the Hutterites to move further eastwards to Transylvania, where they were joined by the Austrian Lutherans (the Hofers, Waldners, Kleinsassers, Glanzers and Würzs), which had been expelled by Queen Maria Theresa of Austria (1717-1780). From Transylvania some in turn moved on to Walachia, while others ended up in Romania.

Where are we? So far we have found that the Hutterites are named after Jacob Hutter, and that they live communally as per *Acts 2:44-45*: '... and had all things in common.' Next question: how did they come to live in Canada? The answer takes us first to South Russia, then to North America, and finally to the Canadian prairies.

---

32 For an overview of the colonies at the time see: http://www.feefhs.org/maplibrary/hutterites/chb-821.html (Last accessed in April 2013).

To South Russia

On April 10, 1770, sixty persons left Walachia for South Russia, where they were invited to settle on the estate of Rumiantsev's private estate at Vishenka, 192 kilometres northeast of Kiev. Rumiantsev died in 1796. Thereafter they established a Bruderhof at Radichev. There they were joined by Hungarian Hutterites with surnames of Walter, Wollman, Tschetter and Mändel. After Rumiantsev died, his two sons tried to enslave the Hutterites. The community complained, and got permission from Russian Emperor Paul I (1754-1891) to move away from the Rumiantsev estate. They then settled thirteen kilometres northeast of the Desna River. But somehow things went wrong: communal living was abandoned and an appeal to the emperor for more land was denied.*

* How the Mennonites ended up in South Russia is dealt with in Chapter 4 below.

In 1862 the about sixty families moved again, this time to the Molotschna, where Cornies' son urged them to model their community after the Mennonite pattern: homes on both sides of a wide street and barns, storage bins and fields at the rear. The Hutterites, here in touch with Mennonites, subsequently thrived and established a second community, Johannasruh, named after Cornies.

According to Bieglschmidt, communal living was no longer practised after Jörg (George) Waldner's death in 1855, and the Hutterites found themselves in great material and spiritual need. In 1859 a meeting was held to choose new leaders, which subsequently led to the forming of three different sects.

In 1859 the Schmiedeleut sect was formed by Waldner's grandson Michael Waldner (1834-1889). As Waldner was a blacksmith, the group that followed him was from then on called *Schmiedeleut* (the Blacksmith's People). The 2001 Hutterite schoolbook comments on this sect:

> The Schmiedleut sect uses a lot of technology and it is very important to them. It is very advance on their colonies. Their dress is very liberal and not like the more traditional Hutterite sect. The girls shawls are draped on their head and pinned in place. They also wear a jumper instead of the two piece dresses of the other Mentioned Hutterites. Education is very important to them and most students

finish Grade 12. There is light industry on their colonies like manufacturing (i.e. building tanks, making brooms).

In 1860 the Dariusleut sect formed under Darius Walther (1839-1903) at the more secluded end of the village of Hutterdorp. The 2001 schoolbook on them:

> The Dariusleut sect is named after a man called Darius. Dariusleut are more liberal in their behaviors and beliefs. Each colony differs from the other. They use technology in farming. They earn money in many different ways. Their children start school at 6 years of age.

In 1864 the Lehrerleut formed under guidance of David and Peter Hofer, Samuel Kleinsasser, Jakob Wipf and Martin Waldner. Waldner was a teacher, so his group lived on under the name *Lehrerleut* (the Teacher's People). The 2001 schoolbook notes on the Lehrerleut:

> The Lehrerleut sect is fundamentalists. The word *Lehr* means teacher. They are very strict and live by stricter rules for behavior and religion. There is no selling of crafts as there is no personal profit. Their houses are very simple with no decorations in them. There is no technology allowed on the colonies. Any money they make is put into a central colony account. They do dress differently in that the girls wear starched shawls and the boys wear hats with no brim. Their language is of Bavarian origin and not as affected by the English language because they are more isolated. Children do not start school until they are seven years old and have had one year of German school. There are no field trips allowed for the children. All Leherleut colonies are consistent in their following of the rules and do not differ from each other.

To North America

After 1871 alternative military service was made mandatory in South Russia for all pacifist communities. Hutterites (and Mennonites) began the process of leaving. A few men were sent across the ocean, to the Americas, to scout for a place to settle.* The following, translated from German, is a summary of Joseph W. Tschetter's 1873 travel account in Bieglschmid.

Tschetter's diary starts on April 14, 1873, on a Sunday night, right after he said goodbye 'with a heavy and sad heart' to his dear wife and children, and all his Brethren and Sisters.† After this ordeal he travelled from his Molotschna residence to Odessa, and from there by train to Berlin, where he changed his money from Rubels to American dollars.

From Berlin they went by train to Hamburg, where he and his fellow-travellers heard someone shout: 'Klaasen, Töws, Tschetter, come with me.' The delegation (the journey had been undertaken together with a few Mennonites) was taken to an inn. To their wonderment, the people they met there, seemed to take a liking to dancing. And, these would also sail to America on the 24th of April. Additionally, about five hundred Mecklenburgers boarded. On the ship, the four Hutterites had a cabin with six beds, so they had to allow in two strangers. One would think that perhaps these were the Mennonites, but, Tschetter never mentions these two again. The description of the journey across the sea sounds familiar: rain, storm, seasickness, and at a late-night burial at sea so nobody could see it (although money was collected for the four children of the deceased).

Finally, in New York Tschetter exchanged $300 in gold pieces for $350 in paper money. The delegation went on to Elkhart, Indiana by train - a journey of 46 hours. Here they met with John Funk, an Old Order Mennonite, and had to see a circus trekking through town. Tschetter thought this entire happening to be sinful.

The morning service in the Old Order Mennonite church was held in German and in English. Praying was done on the knees. Men were wearing short jackets with buttons; the boys had green or blue bands around their necks, and their hair parted in the middle. Some women were wearing white caps, so thin that their hair could be seen - though there were also

* After 1868 only the Schmiedeleut still lived communally, the other two had sold their belongings.

† Bieglschmid explains that Tschetter adhered to the Julian calendar and that according to the Gregorian calender, introduced in 1582 by Pope Gregorius XIII, it was already the 26th of April.

those that wore black hats. The young girls wore straw hats and were dressed in bright colours, some even in red or blue. At 3:00 p.m. another church service was held.

Tschetter learned that the Mennonite community had had to pay $300 as contribution for the American civil war. In peacetime however, nothing had to be paid, and people did not have to vote. Two Mennonites still in Russia sent a telegram, announcing that they would soon arrive in New York. They advised the Hutterites to wait and to cooperate with them and the authorities. In the mean time other Brothers arrived from Pennsylvania.

The delegation was then brought to the Amish Mennonites. They dressed simpler, were housed simpler, carried no buttons and the split in the men's trousers was at the side, not in the center of their pants. Tschetter was not allowed to preach in their church because the Amish did not allow foreign preachers. Tschetter thought the Amish sinful people because they smoked - the women, and the preacher as well. The people looked pale: they had food, but it was too sweet, and too much. When Tschetter heard shots coming from the woods, and then learned that a preacher had been shooting, he *ergrimmerte sich*, in his mind - his soul hardened.*

Upon returning to the Old Order Mennonites, Tschetter attended a meeting that had to reconcile two men that had had a fight. From there he went on to an Evangelical church service. People there were quite relaxed about the practice of child baptism: they could baptize their children or not, either was equally fine. The preacher, Tschetter dryly noted, became insane during his preaching as he was screaming and slapping his hands. 'He preached the truth, but in an outrageous way.'†

On 21 May, Tschetter went to a mill to see how paper was manufactured. Next he had a small falling-out with an Old Order Mennonite about allowing music in church: 'Doesn't the Apostle say, sing and play in your heart for the Lord?' The next day Tschetter noted that he would not wait for the Brothers who were on their way from Russia and travelled on to Chicago, 102 miles west from Elkhart. Seeing a tunnel under a waterway, he could hardly grasp what people are capable of. He feared God's wrath.

* The diary does not elaborate on what had been shot, and as Hutterites are certainly not vegetarians, the reason for his soul's hardening is not clear.

† This preaching style can be seen currently in many U.S. churches.

On the 23 May, he went on to St. Paul, 408 miles further on from Chicago, where he learned about the types of land available for purchase. *Eisenbahnland, Schulland,* and *Regierungsland* were available. One could buy land from the railway company, one could buy land with the obligation to establish a school on it, or one could buy land from the government. They were joined in St. Paul by a delegation from Bergthal, South Russia, which included Jacob Peters, Heindrich Wiebe, and Cornelius Boer. They had been surveying land in Texas, but had not found a proper homestead there.

Subsequently, they all waited for a delegation from Molotschna. 'Important business is going on,' noted Tschetter, 'because we have to find land and obtain complete freedom from military service.' Preacher Wiebe reflected on the American commitment in this regard; the United States would not grant complete freedom, but the English [Canada] would give better privileges.'

On the 26th of May the delegation then moved on to Duluth. From there, they went by train further southwest as it was considered too cold in the north; fruit could only be picked late and there were still much wooded areas. They came across miserable huts inhabited by Indians, passed through Bremont, which had been established for two years, then saw more forests, and went on to Glyndon. There, in a Lutheran church, they heard a sermon in English, which they could not understand.

By May 29 they came across the Red River, and the James River. Here the editor makes a footnote, saying that in 1874 a number of Hutterites would settle there and that the latter is currently (1947) called the Jim River.

On 31 May Tschetter wrote a few letters home and composed twelve songs.*

On 4 June the delegation came across nicely dressed American troops and 'also many cannons.'

On 5 June they arrived in Winnipeg from where they surveyed the land. They met with Métis, and with someone who had a three-legged stand with something glass on top, who wanted to take their 'photographs.' Tschetter did not want his likeness be sent around the world, commenting, 'but what

* Tschetter's editor remarks in a footnote that he did not include the songs in the account 'since they are as good as worthless from a literary viewpoint.'

can you do with the world? The world is the world and will remain the world, until the Lord terminates it.' Underway they met with a woman who was alone at home; she was already two years in Canada and told the delegation that she would like to have some neighbours.

Back in Winnipeg, Tschetter recorded that the city was located forty-five *werst ab von dem Lande,* that the road to Winnipeg was very bad, that half-blood Indians would be the neighbours, that cattle and business was cheaper in the United States, and that import duties had to be paid to export cattle. Because of all this, he did not like the Manitoba lands, and the delegation moved on to Fargo, North Dakota. Here they saw flat river shores that would be good for their cattle. Some one hundred *werst* from Pembina they disembarked to have a closer look at the land. They spent the night in the house of an absent half-Indian, being hosted by his wife and his servants. It was a nice house, rugs on the floors, people were friendly, and gave them supper. Tschetter mused, 'They must be rich,' as he counted forty heads of horned cattle.

After disembarking in Grand Forks they went twenty *werst* this way, ten *werst* that way. Some eighty or one hundred miles from Fargo they asked a women whether it was cold in winter.

A railway agent joined the delegation and they travelled on: in both McCaulenville and Douglas the land was inspected but was found not to be good enough to establish a village.*

So, on to St. Paul, Willmar, Litchfield, Minnetonka, Delano, Manzata and Neapel. The delegation saw a hanging bridge, a saw machine that could saw 22000 square foot per day, a furniture plant, and a textile plant. 'My brains nearly came to a standstill,' Tschetter wailed. By the end of June they met with a governor in St. Paul and asked him about land and about conscription. The governor told them that he had no authority in these matters.

On and on they went, this time in a sleeping car, again in the company of a railway agent, to Worthington, Lake Huron, Windom, Sioux City, and Giblen where another railway agent was awaiting them.

* Bieglschmid adds here an editorial footnote: Tschetter was a landowner in Molotschna, that he himself had established the village of Neuhuttertal and was looking for a place to establish a village, not a communal Brüderhof.

Trouble arose in Kearney: Tschetter found out that he had left his papers somewhere, including his passport, but the journey went on. Lowell, Little Blue River, Red Cloud River, Nebraska, Hastings, Gatton, Fairmont, Krete, Lincoln, and Plattsmouth where they found a steamship on the Missouri. From here, a few members of the delegation went back to Elkhart; the others went to Malanka, Salesbury, Mendota, Aurora, and Chicago where another railway agent brought them to a German guesthouse. From there they went to Elkhart again, where one stayed with Joseph Holdeman (more about him in the Mennonite section below).

Some of the Brothers then wanted to go to Canada. The others, Tschetter among them, left for Philadelphia. This trip took them through Cleveland, Akron, and Pittsburgh where they did not know how to continue on. Fortunately, they met with a German who showed them the train station. Upon their arrival in Philadelphia, Tschetter learned that Klaasen, Cornelius Tschetter, and three Brothers from Bergthal were in New York. He telegraphed them and asked them to wait so he could travel back with them to South Russia.

Tschetter knew by now that land would cost him 3.50 Taler [per acre?], and that he only wanted to pay three Taler. Therefore, he wrote a petition to President Grant (1822-1885),* drank two bottles of wine with J. Cooke, a trustee of the railway company, and received from him a letter of recommendation. Tschetter also met with a few Hernhutters, with whom he got engaged in a conversation about the tenets of faith: whether Hutterite women could be preachers. They were answered with: 'No, they could not.' The Hernhutters did not like that, but according to Tschetter, 'the man is the head of the women, and we would rather take the head than the feet [as preacher].'

By 19th July, Tschetter found himself on a steamship from Philadelphia to New York. In New York, he had another long meeting with trustee Cooke about the price of land. Four days later he was *en route* to Washington where he finally got his way: land for three Taler. This caused him to rewrite his petition to President Grant. Grant replied to his newly phrased petition that he did not have to worry about conscription: there

* Ulysses S. Grant was the US President from March 4, 1869, to March 4, 1877.

would not be any war in the next fifty years.[33] The delegation decided it was time to return to South Russia.

Upon their return, Tschetter and his fellow travellers assured their communities that America, specifically South Dakota, was the country of the future. The South Dakota documents where the Hutterites settled contain phrases about the Hutterites' 'purposes of promoting, engaging in and carrying on the Christian religion,' and them 'having all things in common,' but don't contain one word on exemption of military service.[34]

Thus ends Tschetters diary. Bieglschmid comments that it looks as if the promises of cheap land and a mild climate took over from any solid agreement about exemption from military service. Bieglschmid continues that from May 1874 to 1879 about 1265 Hutterites immigrated to America:

1. in 1874 the Schmiedeleut at the Bon Homme Colony,
2. in 1875 the Dariusleut settled Wolf Creek Colony near James River,
3. in 1876/77 the Lehrerleut founded the Elmspring Colony in Hutchinson Country, all three in South Dakotah, The others became known as *Prairieleut*, and gradually joined the Mennonite congregation.

Bieglschmid sketches how their lives in South Dakota unfolded with ups and downs, but that (in the end) they did quite well.

---

33 This assurance is in a letter of the US Dept. of State (Domestic Letters, Vol. 100, S. 114) which Bieglschmid summarizes in a footnote: personal military services, the customary duty of citizens, jury duty and school matters are matters of the state where they would settle and that in case of war, which was not expected to occur in the next fifty years, the president did not think that Congress would exempt them from military duty.

34 Cf. the Canadian conditions in 'a report of a committee on the Honourable, the Privy Council, approved by His Excellency the Governor General in Council, of September 25, 1872, quoting Section 17 of the Act 31 Victoria, chapter 40. "Any person bearing a certificate from the Society of Quakers, Mennonites or Tunkers, or any inhabitant of Canada, of any religious denomination, otherwise subject to military duty, but who, from the doctrines of his religion, is averse to bearing arms and refuses personal military service shall be exempt from such service when balloted in time of peace, or war, upon such conditions and under such regulations as the Governor in Council may, from time to time, prescribe' (Bieglschmid).

History tells us that President Grant was too optimistic: it took not fifty, but only forty years for war to break out. In 1917 Tschetter's choice for cheap land and a mild climate caused a number of young Hutterites to face the consequences of being forcibly conscripted, which consequences in the end led to Hutterite influx in Canada. One of these conscripts, David Hofer, wrote down what happened to him and his brothers.

Hereunder follows an account of how I obtained his dairy, and permission to publish it.

On a rainy day, Anna's husband gave me a diary written by David Hofer, a Hutterite, who had been incarcerated in Alcatraz for objecting to military service in 1917. 'Perhaps I would find it interesting.' I found it so interesting that I decided to choose Hofer's account as a contribution to the anthology of literary translations. I needed permission to publish it along with a Dutch translation. Therefore, I had to go to one colony where the diary had been stencil-duplicated, and another colony to get permission from Hofer's oldest living daughter. Both of these colonies are in the very south of Alberta, one nearly along the American border along the Milk River.

The colony where Hofer's diary was once stencilled looked very affluent: shiny metal grain elevators, shiny new trucks, leaves and gravel paths raked, trees trimmed, and grass mowed. Upon my knock on the door of the house, the one with the yellow bench in front, an elderly woman opened the door, saying that she had dreamed that night that someone from the twilight would come to visit them.

'Are you from the twilight?' she asked me.

'Well, no, I am from Calgary.'

'I dreamed that today someone would come from the twilight,' she murmured, 'would the twilight be there?'*

The living room had a voluminous three-seat couch and a modest bookcase containing, apart from the usual bibles, some other books as well. It was the first time I had seen 'other books' in a Hutterite household.

An entertaining chat followed about who I was and what I did, about the activities of the colony, and the usefulness of translators and translations. The old boss signed the paper that authorized me to publish my translation. Upon asking how to get in touch with the oldest living daughter of David Hofer, the old boss went to the kitchen, phoned the oldest living daughter, returned to the living room, and said that I was expected there the following day. He and his wife subsequently invited me to their kitchen were we enjoyed coffee, cheese, cucumber, and crackers.

The next morning, upon arrival at the other colony somewhere along the Milk River, I came across a young boy, who brought me to an older man, who brought me to a very old

---

* Only much later I found that 'The Twilight' is a Hutterite colony in Manitoba. But, back then I thought this lady had a point with this twilight thing – being around communities where 20th century technology is competing with 16th century living patterns does have its twilight moments!

lady. She was heavily seated in her rocking chair and had a very friendly face, with a bit of a naughty twinkle in her eyes.

She asked why I had come visit her. I explained to her that her father had written an account about his time spent in Alcatraz; that people who take the pains to write in general want others to read it; and, that I wanted to translate her father's story to reach even more people. She nodded, bent forward, leaned backward and inquired whether I wanted more coffee. While a granddaughter poured coffee, a jovial guy of about forty or fifty years old walked into her living room. He was the old woman's son. I had to tell the whole story again. To him, publication of his grandfather's story seemed an excellent idea.

'Mom, how is it? Are you signing this form or what?' he urged his mother. His mother nodded benignly, pointed her finger to some knitting work on the table and started to discuss it.

'She may think,' I thought, 'that I will leave as soon as she has signed. How often will she have a visitor?'

We drank more coffee, ate more cookies and chatted along. At noon her granddaughter brought us a hot lunch.* After lunch, I helped out with the dishes and looked at more handicrafts. By the time the old lady seemed to tire, she asked where again she had to sign. I left, but not before promising to be back in six months to give her a copy of the literary anthology.

Six months later, having set aside the entire day for handing out copies of my translation, I first dropped off a copy with the boss of the colony which had the old stencil-duplicator machine. Once more, a pleasant visit! I could stay overnight with friends in Coaldale, and headed the next day again towards the American border colony. There, after several cups of coffee and a nice, warm lunch, the same old lady suggested her granddaughter show me the colony. The girl led me around and also brought me to the school where nine children aged between six and fifteen years old were attending.

In Canada it is mandatory to attend school until age sixteen, but Hutterite children only have to attend school until the age of fifteen. After that the boys go to work on the land,

* In general Hutterites eat together, men and women at separate tables in one room, children in another room. However, those who have trouble walking, are sick, or have visitors, get served at home.

help maintain equipment, and learn a trade by participating on the job in the many cow, calf, pig, duck, and chicken barns.

Someone once told me that if you were trained to work with the cows, you would remain for the rest of your life in the cow barn. 'If you are good with pigs, why bother with cows?' one young man replied when I asked whether he would not like to rotate or so. I am not sure if it is like that at every Hutterite colony. The 2001 Hutterite schoolbook:

> **Hutterites have a pig barn boss and seven other people that look after the pigs and feed them. They also have a cow boss that milks 91 cows twice a day, with the help of five other people. There is a chicken boss that feeds the chickens and grades all the eggs. He has two helpers. The people who are helpers are other men, young and old, on the colony.**

Hutterite schools are always on the premises of the colony where every morning an English teacher (meaning: the teacher speaks English) comes in. If there are not enough children, about twenty-one or so, the colony has to pay the government for the number of children they are short. The same schoolbook on schools:

> **Hutterites have a German teacher that looks after the kids and teaches them to read and write German. He is responsible for the children's behavior on the colony. He also preaches at church. The German teacher also looks after the garden. He is the gardener for the colony.**

The English teacher I met with that afternoon seemed happy at some distraction, and his students seemed happy with him being distracted. They quietly convened and chatted in a corner of the classroom.

'The government has just started a health program,' the teacher told me.

'All of the children got information about brushing teeth from a nurse; after three months a dentist came here and inspected their mouths. Little Paul was the first one to be checked and he left the examination room beaming. I asked him, 'Paul, did not you have any cavities?'

Paul still beaming, grinned: 'I have three!'

'That is what they learn,' the teacher went on. 'Those who do not brush get cavities, and those that have cavities have to go to Lethbridge to have them filled. They like outings.'

Subsequently I was shown the cow barn. As in the other colonies I have seen, everything was fully automated and extremely clean. Close by, at an entrance to the colony, a young man seemed to be practicing how to operate a backhoe. He was shovelling garbage from one hole in the ground to another.

'He is only eighteen years old, and he can already handle such heavy trucks,' my young female guide said admiringly.

Keeping youngsters busy and giving them a sense of pride is one of the things Hutterites are good at; at the same time, putting young men in a position that evokes the admiration of young women will surely benefit their survival.

So, this is the story how Hofer's diary ended up in an anthology of literary translations. Hereunder the diary, that was previously translated from Low German to English by Karl and Franziska Peter, which I subsequently translated from English into Dutch.

The Hutterian Brothers in the Military Prison on the Island of Alcatraz in the Bay of San Francisco by David Hofer (1917)

The following memorable events were reported by the Hutterite Brother David Hofer, who was released from the military prison after two of his brothers, Joseph and Michael, lost their lives in prison under terrible circumstances.

A fourth Hutterite Brother by the name of Jakob Wipf, a brother-in-law of the aforementioned, testified to the truth of this heartbreaking event. The stand the Hutterites took towards military service was just as strong as it was found under the Mennonite. That is the reason the treatment they received during their internment at the military camp was so gruesome. When the four brothers left their homes in South Dakota for the military camp their sufferings began already because of their beards, just like other believers like the Mennonites. The other young men on the train started to cut the beards and hair of the Hutterites, and of course this was not done in a very gentle way. The Hutterites cried over this mistreatment, which was like a bad omen for the things to come.

> When they arrived in Camp Lewis, Washington, a paper was placed before them, on which they had to promise to follow all military commands and obey. As conscientious objectors towards all military service they refused to do any work inside the military camp. They were ordered to stand in a row and to march with the others to the drill fields. They refused this also and refused to wear uniforms. (The Hutterites have their own homemade clothes). The four men were placed right away in the guardhouse. The most painful thing for them was the constant swearing and scolding they had to endure. After two months in the guardhouse they were convicted before a war tribunal to 37 years in prison. This was reduced by the Commanding General to 20 years.
>
> The prison they were going to was the military prison on the Island of Alcatraz in the Bay of San Francisco. They were chained two by two on hands and feet and, under the protection of four armed guards, brought there. During the

day the chains on their legs were removed, but never the ones on their hands. During the night two men, chained together, had to lie on the floor. There was not much sleep during the two nights they travelled, but only crying and sighing.

When they arrived at Alcatraz, their own clothes were forcefully removed and they were told to put on military uniforms. They refused just as before. After that they were brought into the lower parts of the prison, into dark cells full of dirt and foul smells, the uniforms were thrown beside them with the warning, 'If you do not conform you will stay here until you die, just as the other four we dragged out of here yesterday.' So they were locked in there in their light underclothing. In the first 4 1/2 days they did not get anything to eat, only 1/2 a glass of water every 24 hours. During the night they had to sleep on the wet and cold cement floor without blankets. The prison of Alcatraz lies below the surface of the sea and so the seawater seeps through the walls.

The next 1 1/2 days they had to stand with their hands over their heads crosswise chained so high to the iron bars that they could barely touch the floor with their feet. This was such an ordeal that David Hofer, even after his release, told his people at home how much he still suffered from pains in his hips. He told them that sometimes, just to ease the pain, he tried to move the pail, which was used for a toilet under great strain towards him, so that he could rest his feet and the strain in his arms was eased. They could not talk to each other during this time since they were separated from each other. Just once he heard Jakob Wipf cry out, 'Oh, Almighty God!'

After five days the four men were brought out of the lower part of the prison into the prison yard where more prisoners were standing. Some of those were overcome with compassion when they saw the Hutterians. One commented with tears in his eyes, 'Is it not a shame to treat human beings in such a way.' the men were covered with boils, bitten by insects and their arms were swollen so badly that they were unable to slip the sleeves of their jackets over them. They had been beaten with sticks.

Michael Hofer was beaten so badly that he, on one occasion, became unconscious, and fell over.

After the five days they still did not get any food until the evening meal. After that they were put back into their cells [during both the] days and nights. Only on Sundays were they allowed to walk in the prison yard for one hour, but only under strict supervision. After a while they were transferred to Fort Leavenworth, guarded by six armed sergeants, chained together two by two again. They travelled through Texas for four days and five nights. They arrived in fort Leavenworth at 11 o'clock at night. They were herded into the middle of the street with loud shouting and urged on with bayonets, as if they were a herd of swine.

Chained by their arms, they carried their bag in one hand and their bible and a second pair of shoes under their arms. Also they were driven on in increasing haste, up the hill where the military prison was located. When they arrived at the gate they were bathed in sweat, even the hair on their heads was wet. In this condition in the rough cold air of winter they had to take off their own clothes and when after two hours their prison clothes were brought it was around 1 o'clock at night and they were almost frozen. Early in the morning at 5 o'clock they had to stand again outside in the cold wind by the door and wait.

Josef and Michael Hofer were unable to endure this day more and their pain became so severe that they had to be brought to the hospital. Jakob Wipf and David Hofer were brought down to the solitary prison cells since they again refused to do prison work under military control. They had to stretch their hands through the prison bars where they were chained together. They had to stand on their feet all day for nine ours and only were given bread and water.

This was continued for 14 days; after that they were given their regular meals for the next 14 days, and in this way it alternated. When the two brothers got very ill, Jakob Wipf sent a telegram home to the wives of the two men. The women left the children at home and left the same night in the company of a relative. The whole thing became very confusing when the railway agent insisted that the telegram had been sent from Fort Riley and not from Fort Leavenworth. He sold them a ticket to the wrong station and they lost a whole day because they first went to Fort Riley. They arrived at Fort Leavenworth at 11 o'clock in the evening and found their husbands so close to death that they were barely able to talk to them.

When they were let into the prison the next morning, Joseph Hofer was already dead and his body had been put into a coffin. They were told that they could not see him anymore. But his wife, Maria, forced her way through the guards and doors until she was able to see the colonel, whom she begged for permission to see her husband once more. She was led to her husband's coffin and she was in tears when she saw him. To her horror she saw that they had dressed her beloved husband in a soldier's uniform, which in his life he had so much rejected in order to be true to his religion.

When his brother Michael died a few days later, he was dressed in his own clothes, since his father who had arrived in the meantime had strongly insisted on it. When Michael died, his wife, his father and also his brother David, were present. He once more stretched out his and said, 'Come Lord Jesus, in your hands I command my spirit.'

After the relatives had left with his body, David Hofer was sent back to his lonely cell in chains. He said, 'I stood there all day and cried; but I could not even wipe my tears away, since my hands were chained to the bars of my prison cell.'

No one seemed to have compassion with him. But on the next day in the morning a guard declared himself willing to bring a message from David to the colonel, in which he asked for permission to be put in a cell closer to his friend, Jakob Wipf, so that he would be able to at least see him even if he could not talk to him. The guard took the message to the colonel and an hour later he returned and said Hofer should pack his belongings, he would be released. This was too much a surprise for him and he could not believe it. The guard took him along to the colonel, who repeated the same and signed David Hofer's release papers. Although he pleaded for permission to go and see his friend, it was not given. So then he left through the gate. Once outside he hesitated and doubts entered his mind.

Was this reality or a dream? While he was still standing there a guard came towards him and asked him why he was still standing there. He replied that he was told he was released, but could not believe it. The guard then told him that he could be sure that he was, since no one would get out of there who was not released. David Hofer told the guard that he would like to send a goodbye to his friend, Jakob Wipf.

He was told by the guard to write a few words on paper and he would give it to Jakob Wipf the same day. He kept his promise, because in his next letter to his wife Jacob Wipf wrote, 'Kathrine, ask David, he will tell you himself everything much better than I can write.' From this it was clear that he already knew about David's homecoming.

The heartbreaking funeral service and the great compassion, which was shown by the people in the surrounding area is indescribable. They had been away from their home and their loved ones for six months and spent most of the time in solitary confinement under the most gruesome treatment, coming home in their coffins. There is more than one can say with a pen. They march as soldiers of Christ into the arms of their Lord and went to their eternal rest.

On December 6th the Secretary of War released an order whereby the chaining of military prisoners and other corporal punishment was forbidden. But when five days later two Hutterite brothers went to Fort Leavenworth to visit Jakob Wipf, they found him still in solitary confinement, his hands chained to the prison bars, standing for nine hours a day. At seven in the morning he was given bread and water for breakfast. Around noon he was released for 30 minutes so that he could drink his water and eat his bread. And at 5.30 p.m. he got some water and bread again, when he was released from his chains for the night. He was given four blankets in this place, but he had to sleep on the cement floor and there were cockroaches, too many to count.

When the visitors left, Jakob Wipf sent the following message home: 'Sometimes I envy the three who are delivered from their suffering. Then I think, why does the Lord's hand rest so heavy upon me? I tried to be true and industrious and did not trouble my brothers too much. Why do I have to suffer now by myself? But then I feel happy again and I could cry for joy when I realize that the Lord finds me worthy to suffer for him. And I have to confess that I feel that my life here, after our former experiences, is like living in a palace.[35]

---

[35] The account from the Congressional Record of March 4, 1919, page 5280 reads:
"Mr. —— speaker. I insert here the following memorandum in refutation of the charge that conscientious objectors have been treated with leniency, furnished me by the National Civil Liberty Bureau, of 41 Union Square, New York.
The matter referred to is as follows:
The charge has been made that conscientious objectors in this country have been treated with undue leniency. What are the facts? Actually there are authentic, undenied statements of cases on record where conscientious objectors have been beaten, prodded with bayonets, immersed in filthy latrines, held for periods of from 15 to 45 minutes under cold shower baths, fed only bread and water, and placed for long periods in solitary confinement.
At the United States Disciplinary Barracks at Alcatraz Island, California, four religious objectors - three Hofer brothers and Jacob Wipf - were placed in a perfectly dark dungeon where water seeped in from the sea, their outer clothing removed, and where they were fed only small amounts of bread and water. At the end of the fifth day they were removed by the recommendation of the medical examiner and placed in isolation. Later they were transferred to Fort Leavenworth. Two of the brothers died of pneumonia within ten days of their arrival. The body of one of these men was sent home dressed in military uniform of the United States Army, although he had gone to prison because of refusal to wear the uniform (Murphy Ed. 1996).'

Hutterites to and in Canada

Christian Tschetter (1882-1962) wrote the following verses,
in German, about this move (translation by Mary E.M.):

Da reisen die Hutterischen Brüder zwar	The Hutterian Brothers traveled all the way
Nach dem Canada zu.	To Canada.
Im neunzehn-hundert und achtzehnten Jahr,	In the nineteen hundred and eight,
Um frei zu sein von Krieg in der Zeit	To be in the future free from war
Welches geschieht durch Gottes Geleit	Which will happen by God's guidance
Das Dreschen blieb halbfertig stehn	Half way the flair was left alone
Als wir sollten registrieren gehn	Because we had to go register
Ein Dienst zum Krieg zu tun.	For wartime services.
Von Jahren 20 mehr der Zahl	From the age of twenty
Bis dreiundvierzig, das ist wahr ...	To forty-three, that's true ...

The poem is longer and I can't get the translation to rhyme as nicely as the German version, but hopefully it conveys the reasons the Hutterites left America for Canada.

Before the Hutterites travelled from the U.S. to Canada some problems had to be dealt with. Canadian public opinion had soured against people with different lifestyles.

Bieglschmid quotes J.A. Calder, the 1919 Canadian Minister of Immigration and Colonization's reply to Joseph Kleinsasser's request for 'the removal of the remaining members of your community [from the U.S.] to Canada.' The minister argues that he can appreciate Kleinsasser's wishes, but writes:

However, I must advise you that after the most careful consideration of all the facts and circumstances, the government concluded that it would be inadvisable, owing to the general feeling prevailing throughout Canada, to continue to permit certain persons to enter Canada because their custom, mode of life, habits, etc., were such as to prevent them becoming readily assimilated. These persons included Coukhobors [sic], Mennonites and Hutterites. We have had so much trouble in Canada in connection with school and other matters in the colonies and communities of these people that their neighbours and people generally insist that no more should be permitted to come. Unless they are prepared to become Canadian citizens in the truest and best sense of the term, and unless they are ready to assume all the obligations of citizenship including military service if called upon, it is extremely doubtful if any government in Canada would be prepared to admit them.

I trust I have made the situation quite clear. Should you desire any further information, or in case you wish to place any further facts before me, I shall be pleased to hear from you.

A letter by L.S. Turcotte, Barrister of Lethbridge, Alberta, Counsel for the Hutterian Brothers, implies that the government's concerns were put to rest. After having voiced a concern that the Hutterites would overrun the available agrarian lands, Turcotte wrote in 1934 (Bieglschmid):

All Hutterites have entered Canada by legal means through the Department of Immigration [...] When they were admitted to Canada, both the Dominion Government and the Alberta Government knew that the Hutterites were conscientious objectors, knew that they lived a communal life in colonies, knew that they wore beards, [and] knew that they wore the same clothes. There was no secret about any of these things. Furthermore both Governments knew that the Hutterites engaged in only one means of livelihood and that was farming.

But then, dire poverty was awaiting them in Canada. Tschetter put his feeling down in a poem:

Nord Rockyford	***North Rockyford***
Ach Brüder, was ist hier zu sehn,	Oh Brother, what is here to see,
Auf unsern Platz, da wir jetzt stehn?	From the place where we now be?
Bei tausend Gophers grau	Where one thousand gophers gray
Die haben ihre Hauslein doch,	Do have their little house,
Und wir haben kein Oberdach.	While we have no roof above our heads.
Jetzt auf Kanadische Platz und Land	While now on the Canadian prairies and flats
Kein Haus, Bett, Stuhl ist nicht zu sehn	No house, no bed, no chair where we could go
Da wir nur konnten hinein gehn.	Is to be seen.
Kein Huhel, Herd noch Pferd,	No *Huhel*, hearth, or horse,
Kein Schüssel, Löffel, alles fehlt	No key, no spoon, no nothing
Wie blos sind wir auf dieser Veld.	How naked are we on this field.

    These were the days. Things are much better now, most Hutterite colonies in Canada do well, and are not lacking keys, spoons, chairs, or beds.

    All follow a daily routine: breakfast in the communal dinner room; the men then do their things in the barns, mow and plough the land, maintain equipment, make window frames, oil drums, coal burners, or other such small manufacture, lunch in the communal dinner room, go back to work, go to church (unless the minister is combining, harvesting, or otherwise working in the garden), have the evening meal in the communal dinner room, go back to work or rest, and finally go to sleep.

As for the women, each week a different group do the cooking for the entire colony. Elderly women take care of the children up to three years of age; meanwhile teaching them to sing hymns in their own language, Low German. Other women's chores are sewing, painting, caring for elderly, and garden work. Sometimes work from outside is brought in: for example, folding hospital linen, processing wild meat, or charity work for poor people in Ukraine.

After 3 PM the mothers come home. At the end of the afternoon, a church service is held. The women's evenings are free and spent at home, though during summertime they often work on the land well into the evening. Women often spend their spare time knitting, sewing for their flock of children, making their own clothes, and even sewing their husband's shirts and costumes.

A *Globe & Mail* article of 8 January 2003 reports that Hutterite colonies have no Internet, no Channel surfing on TV, no flipping through fashion magazines, no radios, no make-up, nor Harry Potter books.* Children are quoted, saying that they look forward to work in the kitchen or the laundry building, that they find school boring while experiencing something new every day while working at the colony. Teachers quoted in this article express their relief on coming to the colony: no broken families, no students going through their parents' divorce, and no hungry or poorly dressed children.

Adding to this sketch, married daughters leave to live at the colony of the new husband. When a woman gives birth, her mother or sister visits and helps her out for an entire month. When an aunt or uncle is sick, even though he or she may live in a US colony, they can still expect a visit and a helping hand from a far off family member. Hutterites in nursing or seniors' homes are unheard of. Weddings and funerals are often attended by hundreds of family members and friends.

My impression of the Hutterites so far is that the colonies are big, extended families,† thriving through their agricultural and manufacturing efficiently. It seems though, I have heard that not all colonies are thriving; there are those that need help from the more successful. Sometimes they do get help; but sometimes they have to split up and the people scatter into other colonies.

---

* Since 2012 cell phones and cameras have infiltrated daily life.

† ... and more extended than you would think; the Hutterites are very generous with donating blood. In a Red Cross centre in the north of Calgary, I was told that they give about 70% of the total supply.

In general, when a colony reaches about 120 to 140 people, the ministers and the heads of the families draw straws. The outcome determines which families will move on, and with which minister, to a new colony. According to the Canadian law, a new colony cannot be established on adjacent land – in order to prevent the amalgamation of over-large Hutterite areas.

Still, Hutterites are people and where people are, things happen: for example, abuses of power. In principle, such is dealt with by the system of elected bosses, and the ability of individuals to complain to a minister or the bishop of the Lehrerleut, Schmiedleut and Dariusleut. These authorities have the power to curb spouses', colony leaders', or even ministers' misbehaviour or abuse of power. The culprits have to admit their guilt, whereupon they are excluded from church services while they repent their sins. Subsequently, the offenders must confess in public before being allowed to participate again in the community.

And, just as in any community, some people are happy and some aren't. They may have a fight with their spouse, an argument with a boss of a barn, or not agree with some colony rule. Sometimes these disputes spill over into the Canadian newspapers. For example, an article in *The Globe & Mail* of 20 January 2003, was about a married couple that sit in their living room for the entire day, watching their fellow colony members walking by.

'"We just sit in the house and look out the window, more or less," said Mrs. Waldner, 57, describing their days.'

The article went on to explain that this couple was shunned by their colony because they took a dispute to the public courthouse, 'an act frowned upon in Hutterite culture, but increasingly common in the sect's North American colonies.' The dispute is said to have started with the German teacher slapping Mr. Waldner's grandson, who (the grandfather) had won the vote to become colony boss. The colony elders did not act, whereupon the boy's father enlisted the help of the police and provincial child-welfare, was subsequently shunned for calling on outside agencies. Later, he and his wife were expelled. At this, they asked a court to declare, 'that they were improperly expelled, and [to] order them reinstated, or award damages of $500,000 apiece.'

Their colony in turn declared that this couple failed to comply with the teachings, rules, and beliefs of the colony: the situation was deadlocked, the family could not survive on their own because they didn't have more than a grade eight education, few skills, and no savings.

Apart from family feuds, other issues, such as morality and substance abuse are brewing in the Hutterite colonies, just as everywhere else.

Once I was handed a list of grievances that was faxed to a number of colonies:

- Some preachers don't believe what they preach.
- Jesus has to live in your heart or you will not be saved.
- **There are those that despite confessing that Jesus lives in them, are physically and mentally abused by leaders, 'people,' and unbelievers in general: they are driven out of their house. Matthew 10:23: if they persecute you in this city, flee into another.**
- How come Lehrer, Darius, and even Schmiedleut persecute Christians?
- 'If a man in the colony is converted by outside influences, or preachers, well shame on us!'
- God does not tolerate 'adultery, fornication, whoredom - there are many illegitimate children born every year'.
- The God of alcohol is worshipped, which leads to stealing and fornication, and the consequences will be everlasting fire, pain, weeping, and gnashing of teeth.
- Young people living in the Christian Community, that is supposed to be holy, live in sin and wickedness.
- In the colony you can be saved, but not if you sin.

The list sounds as if we have to do with 'real people.' The rest of the list elaborates on the difficulties between the three branches of Hutterites on issues such as paying taxes ('blood money'), and differences. For example, whether people that leave should have to leave empty handed (after all, doesn't *Timothy 5:18* say, 'For the scripture saith, Thou shalt not muzzle the ox that treadeth out the corn. And, the labourer is worthy of his reward'). The author goes on to strengthen his arguments with many more bible quotations, but this is the gist of the message.[36]

Another issue is photo ID on driving licenses. In May 2003 the Alberta government passed legislation requiring photo identification for all drivers. On 24 July 2009 *The Lethbridge Herald* reported that for nearly 30 years, Hutterian Brethren were issued licences without photos and that the requirement of (a photo on) a passport to cross the American border will land them in court again. However, Hutterites believe the Bible's second commandment, which bans 'graven images,' prohibits them from willingly having their photo taken. The Lethbridge Herald:

> **The Alberta government took the case to the Supreme Court of Canada in a final bid to overturn the exemption, arguing advances in technology designed to enhance the security of driver's licences and help prevent fraud, identity theft and terrorism, have made it necessary for photos to be used on licences. The government further contends too many people would take advantage of a religious exception to the photo ID rule.**

Again, not all Hutterites think alike. The people I know don't agree with protesting this law and see photo ID's as one of the necessities of modern life.

Sometimes people do leave because they want to find out if they really want to spend their whole life at the colony. Discussing 'running away' with a young Hutterite, and his parents during a breakfast at my place, I asked him why he stayed in the colony.

'It is my faith to live in this way,' he replied.

Another young man told me that he had left several times. The first time he had spent time at the house of a rude, grumpy farmer. The second time was not much better, and he had returned permanently, recognizing that life was better at the colony.

There are also those that try for the big city. For example, members of the Schmiedleut seem to have a network in Calgary that houses and employs the new runaways. Life in

---

36 Fax in the author's possession.

that boarding house, as one of my guests described it, does resemble that of the colony. The girls, who are employed as chambermaids in hotels, cook and do laundry, while the boys, employed at construction sites, take turns shopping for groceries.

My guest went on to tell me about the parents' heartbreak, and the insecurities that run-away Hutterites face outside the colonies. They find out that freedom entails having to pay rent, having to pay for a car, having to pay for food and drinks; and when all these things have been paid for, there is not much money or time left to enjoy freedom. Further, some marry and have children outside the colony, divorce, and then have to pay alimony and child support.

This same Schmiedleut member pointed out one of the hardships of living outside a colony: you have to pay for your own funeral. I joked that it was not going to be a big deal for me, but for my family - I would not be around to have to pay any bills. But, I added something about responsibility, putting some money aside, or buying insurance for the big day. Also, I pointed that when I die, not hundreds of people will show up, and that certainly helps in defraying the costs.

Sometimes the family cuts off relationships with the runaways: if they come to the colony in a nice car and dressed in nice clothes, it might give the colony youth some ideas. Some can visit, but then just with their parents - they are not allowed to show off by running around with a crate of beer. People that want to return to the colony are generally most welcome - although sometimes only after a mandatory check-up and a subsequent clean bill of health.

All in all, my impression is that Hutterites are as happy or unhappy as the general population. In the case of unhappiness with being in the colony, it is very difficult to move to the outside world due to lack of education, a bank account, social networks, or employable skills.

One 'success' story of stepping out is Samuel Hofer's *Born Hutterite*. He is also author of humorous books on colony life. Another book, *I am a Hutterite* by Mary-Ann Kirby centers on a family where the father married into the colony from the outside. After numerous disagreements the whole family left the colony under the thrall of some evangelists. This family is now free to do what their new spiritual leaders tell them to do.*

> * Nowadays Hutterites text each other and blog.

The best book about colony life I have read is *Das Vergessene Volk* (*The Forgotten People*) by Michael Holzach. Holzach was a good-looking Hamburg German who spent a full year in the early 1980's in a colony in southern Alberta. After he had split from his then girlfriend, Holzach wanted to 'find himself,' and withdraw from the world for a while. Holzach states that he liked colony life: physical work, good food, and peace and quiet. Well, not always. Holzach was invited to stay, but thought that he would end up feeling like he was buried alive. So instead he went back to his previous life in Hamburg where, he later drowned in an accident. The colony where he stayed can be contacted via the Internet for tours, so you can see for yourself:

> **Group tours of the Pincher Creek Hutterite Colony are available, for a reasonable fee, every day except Sunday and usually include lunch or dinner with colony members. Tours must be booked in advance. Phone Rosa.**[†]

> † Or, go to www.billcorbett.ca/files/PincherCreekHutteriteColony.pdf (Accessed April 2013.)

About the organization these days; in 1950 the three groups making up the Hutterites (the Darius, the Lehrer, and the Schmiedleut) united under the banner of the Hutterian Brethren Church (HBC). A smaller, separate group is led by Jake Kleinsasser.[37]

---

[37] For a 2009 overview of Hutterite colonies on the North American continent, Japan, and Nigeria, see Janzen & Stanton in their excellent study *The Hutterites in North America*.

Chapter 4

Mennonites

As said at the start of this book, in 1988 I had not yet lived two years in what I guessed to be pristine oil, gas, cows and grass Canada, when I met Hannah at a coffee party. She introduced herself saying that she had recently moved from Winnipeg to Calgary, but had lived in Paraguay until the age of eleven. When asked whether she was born in Paraguay, she said 'no,' adding that she was born in Germany and that she was a Mennonite. She went on with a bizarre story about her Russian-born mother who, while pregnant with her, had fled Russia with her six children. Her mother went to Westphalia - the very west of Germany - and there Hannah was born in March 1945.

Her mother had fled for Germany from Russia and had ended up in Paraguay in 1948 with seven children? We were sipping coffee. Hannah casually related her background as if her story was not in the least mind-boggling. I wondered aloud what impact such a family background could have on someone's mindset. Hannah cheerfully supplied me the answer.

'Mary, when you say garden, you mean your backyard. When I say garden, I mean the Garden of Eden.'

I wondered what the Garden of Eden had to do with backyards? Despite the fact that her story and her words apparently had different connotations for us, I felt familiar with Hannah; the togetherness that people, being abroad, experience when they meet with people from their own country. Certain matters do not need explanation. In Hannah's case, I could not discuss Dutch matters such as Sinterklaas, the eternal talks about the WAO (allowances for sick people) and the AOW (seniors' allowance), governmental affairs in general, the contents of *Vrij Nederland* (a political weekly), or the weather (mostly rainy). However, when Hannah asked me if I wanted to try some Huttekäse, I answered: 'What the farmer does not know, the farmer does not like (Wat de boer niet kent, de boer niet lust).'

Hannah was surprised, and replied, 'My mother used to say that.'

There were more examples: Hannah saw a little glass with teaspoons in it on my countertop. Canadians generally hide their teaspoons in a drawer in the kitchen block.

Hannah: 'My mother also used to keep her teaspoons that way, in a small glass.'

Halfway through the sixteenth century Menno Simons, a former priest, had become a Baptist. At the time he and his followers, many of them from Flanders, were driven from Frisia. Hundreds of years later, despite language connotations altered by their ancestors' flights and fights through the tribulations of the troubled times, after having lived in Poland, Prussia, Russia, and Paraguay, Hannah and her family still hold to teaspoon glasses, Dutch proverbs, *kaantjes* (titbits of fried bacon), and *oliebollen* with icing sugar.

In 1990 the Mennonite World Conference was held in Winnipeg. Hannah and I went there together and stayed for ten days at her sister's. Every morning we went for breakfast to the seniors' home where her mother lived. One day, after having slept in, we decided to have a big breakfast so we could skip lunch: big, but how big?

I suggested a fried egg. Hannah made it happen: butter, sunny side up and down eggs, and what else? All that time her mother stood right behind her, breathing heavily down her neck, rolling her eyes to me, and providing much unwelcome advice. Fortunately Hannah could not see her mothers' eyes, but she did feel the panting behind her, and heard the ongoing counseling.

'I raised two kids,' she sighed later, 'and she still can't leave me alone when I fry an egg. On the other hand, John [her husband] said that when another war breaks out, he wants to hide under my mother's wings. She fled with six children, did it all alone, but now she can't let me alone when I fry an egg.'

A short while later my university course, History of Immigration, required me to write a paper about some group of immigrants, and interview members of that same group. I asked Hannah and John whether they would be interested. They were. Here follows a transcript of this interview with Hannah.

Hannah

Hannah's Mennonite mother and first husband grew up in Russia, married around 1934, and lived in the Molotschna colony. Early in the war, Hannah's mother lost her husband. Her second husband, Hannah's father, was a non-Mennonite German. Upon the Germans 1941 invasion of Russia, Germans living in Russia were forcibly enlisted in the German army. Suddenly, their wives and children were perceived as being wives and children of traitors, what caused many to flee to Germany. Hannah:

> My father ended up as a prisoner of war and my mother, highly pregnant, fled with six children. She crossed the Russian border through barbed wire fences, and had to ford rivers with three- and four-year-old children on her shoulders. While many other children were sent to group homes and their parents had to work, she fought to keep her family together. My oldest sister was lost for eight months. Later she was found at the Red Cross. Three months before the end of the war, I was born as number seven, in a farmhouse which was bombed that very same night. That was somewhere in what is now West Germany. My mother's friends, who stayed in the Eastern part of Germany, were all sent back to Russia, and ended up in Siberia. We stayed two years in that farmhouse. In 1947 we went, for several reasons, to Paraguay. Canada was closing its borders and Paraguay was the only place that took refugees. My mother was happy to go as far as possible from the Russians.
>
> In Paraguay we settled in Steinfeld and later in Gnadental. We lived with Mennonites who went there in the 1920's. They built a six to eight foot clay hut for us with a straw roof. After a year we got a bigger house. Due to the sandstorms all the kids soon got eye sickness, which was cured with cow urine. Mother planted her own food: peanuts, melons, and cotton. Cotton could be harvested and sold in the village ten miles away. It took a day by horse and wagon to go there. Our food was often chicken, and every month we got a ration of twenty pounds of white flour. Further we ate beans, kafier (a sort of whole

wheat), griddle cakes, beef, and pork. The whole village shared the beef or pork. One animal was slaughtered at the time. There was nothing to keep it cold, no electricity. There were Indians over there, who lived off the land. One of them became a hired help. We stayed altogether seven years in Paraguay. It meant fighting ants, storms, droughts, and locusts all the time and spending hours to get some water from the well. Still I can talk of a happy childhood. For my mother it meant no fear of a government. She worked all day for the food, but she also valued education. My father, her husband, had been a teacher. All her work still meant not much hope, no future. On the other hand she knew that material things could be taken any time.

My mother's sister got us to Canada. In Canada my mother worked in a sewing factory. We, her children, went to school. I went to a Mennonite high school, a Bible College, and a University teachers' college. Around 1966 I taught in junior high: language, arts, and physical education. After two years I married, [and] took care of my husband and the two kids. In 1984 I got a bachelor's in History by way of night school and summer courses at the University of Winnipeg. In July 1988 we arrived in Calgary.

So, the Mennonites also came from South Russia to Canada - when and how did they come to live in South Russia in the first place?

We already saw how the early dissenters such as Luther, Zwingli, and Grebel had to flee their towns and countries, and that many of their followers died at the hands of their fellow Christians. While these pursuers often succeeded in capturing those fleeing on foot or horseback, the invention of the printed book enabled reformist ideas to spread faster - out beyond the persecutors' pyres and prisons.

Already in 1522 Emperor Charles V issued a decree against Luther, which he declared to be enforceable in his lands, the Low Countries included. However, this decree and the ensuing persecutions did not stop people engaging in bible studies, or doubting the Church tenets such as the transubstantiation of the water and bread into Jesus' body.

In the northern parts of the Low Countries, people came under the influence of Melchior Hoffman's exalting preaching. He was a Swabian tanner. Smith writes that Zwingli referred to him in 1523 as 'that good-for-nothing fellow who dresses hides.' Despite his profane profession, Hoffmann was 'unusually familiar with the bible's contents.' Hoffman had started as a Lutheran, had been evangelizing in Stockholm. According to Decavele in *De Dageraad van de Reformatie in Vlaanderen (1520-1565)*, from 1527 on he had been the king's court preacher in Schleswig-Holstein, then Denmark.

Decavele writes that after his sojourn in Denmark, Hoffman travelled around the northern parts of Holland and the east of Frisia, where he managed to turn 'thousands of down-and-outers (armoedzaaiers)' into 'Melchiorites'; people who did not want their children baptized, and who initially turned towards violence. Decavele also mentions attacks on a monastery in Bolsward and on the city hall of Amsterdam - significant forebodings of the terror, trials, and tribulations yet to come in Münster, Germany.

Snyder notes in *Anabaptist History and Theology* that Hoffman had a falling out with the Lutheran clergy. He denied 'a real presence of Christ in the Lord's Supper,' and was banned in 1529. 'Following a brief work in East Frisia in the spring of 1529, he moved south to Strassburg.' According to *Smith's Story*, Strassbourg was a free haven for dissenters until the late 1520's.

In 1534, Jan Mattijsz, a Haarlem baker and one of Hoffman's students, aggravated the situation. In order to hasten the coming of some new kingdom, he took control of the Baptist movement. For starters he re-baptized all those who had already been baptized. He subsequently invited people to come to Münster 'to await the ushering in of the New Jerusalem' (*Smith's Story*). Snyder, using a different spelling, argues that Jan Matthijs 'interpreted Anabaptist baptizing in the sense of the TAU, following *Revelation* 7:3: a mark of the 144,000 elect.'*

Snyder in *Anabaptist History and Theology* provides an example of Hoffmann's persuading power:

* Tau is the last letter of the Hebrew alphabet. The Latin Bible version of the Vulgate [also] reads in Ezekiel 9:4 and Ezekiel 6, that a part of the people of Jerusalem were marked with the 'sign of tau' on their foreheads, and that these thus marked would be saved in the coming great tribulation. See: www.gameo.org/encyclopedia/contents/T536.html (Last accessed April 2013).

167

He (Hoffmann) carried on with much emotion and terrifying alarm, and with great and desperate curses cast all into hell and to the devils to eternity who would not hear his voice and who would not recognize and accept him as the true Enoch.

Apparently it was this proselytizing that caused the Prince Bishop Franz von Waldeck of Münster (1491-1553), who had been driven out of the city, to gather together a small army in 1534 and lay siege to the city. On Easter Sunday, Matthijsz was killed, and a Jan van Leyden grabbed the reins. For a year he ruled the city and indulged in 'horrible excesses and bloody orgies.' While the city was under siege, escape resulted in execution and people had to stay and took to eating horses, dogs, and cats. Upon the successful ending of the siege, Van Leyden's rule came to a torturous end. His remains were put into a cage where they were bleached for many years in the sun. His and his fellow dissenters' cages are still suspended at the St. Lambert church in Münster.

After the Münster episode many ex-Münsterites fled to Antwerp, Brussels, Gent, and other Flemish cities or towns. From then they wisely opted for a quiet life. Still, after what had happened in Münster, the Flemish government did not trust them at all, and badly persecuted them - forcing many of them to flee, back again to the north.

In *De Dageraad van de Reformatie in Vlaanderen* (*The Reformation's Dawn in Flanders*) Decavele sums up the reasons why the government might not have been enthralled with the newcomers: 'their asocial attitude and the fact that they turned away from the 'sinful" world caused them to be seen as dangers to the state.'

In Flanders, two thirds of the people murdered for their beliefs were Baptists (that is, not Lutherans or Calvinists). Most of the men died in the flames, while the women often met their 'saviour' after having being drowned.

In 1556 Philips II (1527-1598, king from 1556 on) issued a general edict, which forbade all laymen to discuss or teach the Holy Scriptures on the penalty of death. Dijck writes in *Introduction to Mennonite History* that this edict did not keep a missionary by the name of Bouwens from baptizing over 10,000 people - of which 592 in Flanders

Flanders' Mennonites were not only Münsterites. Bakhuizen van den Brink explains in *Documenta reformatoria* why, despite everything, (Ana)baptism still fell on fertile Flanders' soil. Many of those in Flanders already lived there in concealment. These were the Waldensians: followers of the lifestyle initiated by Jean Valois, a rich Lyonnais merchant. Inspired by the song of a minstrel, he handed out all of his worldly possessions, and started to live as the apostles did. That was already in 1170. He went around preaching, armed only with a few bibles and texts by Augustine and other church fathers. At the fourth Lateran Council of 1215 the Waldensian movement was declared heretical; persecutions, trials, and tribulations had followed (and Jews and Saracens had to wear distinctive clothes).[38] A number of Waldensians subsequently ended up in Flanders where as early as 1421 a great number of them were burned in Donau, a Flemish village.

Perhaps Waldensians were susceptible to Anabaptism - for starters it is said that they were against baptizing children. Van Braght citing Jacob Merning's 14 January 1400 notes: I have a very old confession of a few Waldensian brothers in Bohemia, printed in German language. In it they explicitly state that at the start of Christianity no children were baptized.

Pierre Van Paassen also mentions Waldensians. After listing all the foreigners in his hometown Gorkum in *Earth could be Fair,* he comments: 'Huguenot families, ... and the descendants of Waldensian and Savoyard refugees - the Peverellis, Antoniolis, Ravellis, Sinoos and Sizoos - do you ever think of them as strangers?[39]

---

38 This council also ordered Jews and Saracens to wear distinctive clothes.
39 Earlier on I mentioned that Van Paassen never overtly mentions the name of his maternal grandfather, or his wife's name, in his publications. However, he obliquely references their history when he writes pages later in the same book: 'my mother's people came from Italy. They were Waldensians. Persecuted for their faith in the Piedmont valley, they found refuge in Holland.'

Van Paassen's biographer, David Kirk reveals in his 2002 publication the reason why Van Paassen never mentioned the name Sizoo, his mother's name. Van Paassen worked as an assistant Methodist preacher in Canada, had to marry a local girl pregnant with his child, married, enlisted in 1917 in the French army, as an interpreter. Back in Toronto he found that his wife had

Among the many books about the fate of the first Protestants in Flanders, there is also one by Van Paassen. In *Days of our Lives* he notes:

> In the second half of the sixteenth century the Spanish armies occupied Holland and Flanders and the glare of the Inquisition's *autos-da-fé* lit up the market squares of the cities great and small. After a long vigil in prayer, the silent man with the cruel eyes [Phillip II] in the Escorial had decreed the extermination of the new religion in the Netherlands. In less than a decade there perished by his will in the torture chambers, on the gallows and on the pyres, two hundred and fifty thousand men and women of the Dutch race. Nobles and burghers, old and young, rich and poor, all were dragged from their homes, frequently on secret denunciation, to face the grand Inquisitor - the monk Titelman - and his helpers, who knew no mercy. From Amsterdam to Lille, and from Maastricht to Ypres, the bells were tolling for the dead each morning and a procession of priests, halberdiers, and archers could be seen conducting the heretics to the place of execution. Before the victims were at the stake, their skin was cut off their feet so that they could not run away and their tongues were pulled out or twisted into a knot so that they could not blaspheme God and his Son in the midst of the flames. Then the torch was applied to the faggots and the priests sang:
>
> *Si de coelo descenderes*
> *O sancta Maria.*

Van Paassen continues, after details about the sickening smell of the burning men and women's flesh, with the story of Klaes, a coal burner from Damme, and his wife Soetken. After Klaes was tortured, his wife and son had to look on, while Klaes,

---

left and had left his five year old daughter with his parents. These then 'had sent for their 22-year old niece, Coralie Sizoo, from Gorkum.' A divorce did not happen; Van Paassen lived the rest of his life with this cousin, passing her as his wife.

> ... was burnt by slow fire in the market square of Damme [...] Soetken could not see her husband twist his body in pain, for a white cloud of smoke enveloped the martyr [...] Later at home Soetken took a piece of red silk and a piece of the black silk and she made a sachet of them. She sewed two strings to the ends and placed the ashes in the sachet and fastened it around Thyl's neck and she said: 'My son these ashes are the heart of Flanders.'

The story of Klaes and Soetje is not in Van Braght's *Martyr's Mirror*, in which he compiled stories about penalties such as being burned alive, being put in a bag and thrown in the water, being stretched at a rack or having body parts pierced, etcetera - all for daring to stray from Catholicism. Van Paassen borrowed this story on Charles de Coster's *The Legend of Thyl Ulenspiegel and Lamme Goedzak (1867)*, a 16th-century romance.[40]

Thus far we have seen travelling preachers causing disturbances and distresses, and people fleeing to and from Flanders. Up in the north of the Low Countries (in Amsterdam), Hoffman converted Jan Volkertz Trypmaker. Trypmaker in turn converted the tailor Sicke Freerks. 'It was the beheading of Freerks that drew the attention of the priest Menno Simons, who, subsequently started to study the bible on the subject of child baptism' (*Smith's Story*).

Simons knew firsthand about people that had fled Münster and had hid in a cloister. Most of them had been put to the sword by the local governor, among them Simon's brother. This had contributed to Simons' conversion. He decided though that he was going to represent a pacifist brand of Baptism.

Simons quit priesthood in 1536, married and became the foreman of the Low Countries' Baptists. He issued *The Foundation of the Christian Doctrine*, which became the guide for Baptists as Calvin's *Institution* was the guide for the Calvinists. Also, Simons believed that a church is made up of believers, believers obey God's commands, believers have to acknowledge that they are sinners, children can not repent,

---

40 Thanks to Eleanore Aukes who pointed this out to me.

therefore not be a member of a church. The conviction that people are sinners is the base tenet for being against child baptism. This is about the gist of what Lee (2007: 29) writes about Simon's tenets.

Simons subsequently became not only a foreman, but also became a wandering Baptist preacher: in 1542 Emperor Charles V issued an edict, promising 500 guilders for the person who caught Menno Simons,

> No one was to receive 'Minne Symonsz' in his house or on his property; to give him shelter, food, or drink; or speak with him; or to read any of his books, under penalty of loss of property and life as a heretic.

Menno complained that:

> for eighteen years now I, my poor feeble wife, and little children have endured extreme anxiety, oppression, affliction, misery and persecution (*Smith's Story*).

Back to Flanders: many Flemish Baptists escaped, if they could afford it, to Frisia, but not to Amsterdam, which at that time was known as *Moorddam* ('Murderdam'). The Baptist refugees settled in four Frisian towns: Harlingen, Franeker, Leeuwarden, and Dokkum. Together they formed the 1567 *Ordinance of the Four Cities*, which prescribed that preachers also had to preach in the three other cities, and that quarrels had to be sorted out by the preachers of all four cities. This *Ordinance* violated the independence of each individual church; which started to be a concern because of the sake of independence of the community by the Spirit of God. After all, had this 'sake' not been one of the points they had disagreed about with Zwingli?

However, the more affluent Frisian residences irritated the Flemish, while the Frisians were irritated in turn by the rich dressing styles of Flemish. The Flemish tended to look down on people that had not suffered as much as they had: for example, having to leave everything behind for their faith. At the same time they managed to serve visitors a good glass of good wine. Baptist Bishop Bouwens had noticed the good wine and enjoyed visiting them.

↑ 'For no one can lay any foundation other than the one that has been laid; that foundation is Jesus Christ.' 1 Cor. 3:11, device Menno Simons.

Soon the Frisian community discovered that the bishop visited the Flemish too often, and that he should ask Frisian permission before doing so. Bouwens found that it was his own business: whom he chose to visit. Suspicions arose that perhaps Bouwens thought that he could just do whatever he wanted to do.

Unsurprisingly, the *Ordinance* caused discontent. Van der Zijpp notes that the spiritual leaders, called teachers, did not agree that Jeroen Tinnegieter, one of the Franeker teachers, also had to serve the towns of Harlingen, Leeuwarden, and Dokkum. An attempt to mediate led the Frisians to ban the Flemish, who responded by banning the Frisians.

After a disagreeable meeting, a certain Ebbe Pieters took the boat to Leeuwarden. On board, a fellow brother told him what had happened; that people had been banning each other. Ebbe then called a church meeting in Leeuwarden, which caused everyone to know soon of the then secret proposal to ban. It was secret since the Flemish wanted to conceal the 'Ban the Frisians verdict' until the decision had more people behind it. Ebbe was accused of then saying that the Flemish had banned six members of the Frisian church council - this proved to be not true, since only suspension had been considered.

Van der Zijpp elaborates on the conflict in *Geschiedenis der Nederlandsche Doopsgezinden in de Zestiende Eeuw (History of the Dutch Baptists in the 16th century Netherlands)*. Ebbe was held accountable for his actions, and was discharged. However, Tinnegieter, the scorned Franeker teacher, made sure that Ebbe had to also give a public account of his actions. During this occasion, the Harlingen brothers 'de-brothered' brother Ebbe. Dirk Philips (1504-1568), who had become the unofficial leader of the Baptists after Simons' death, subsequently wrote a reconciliatory letter that also showed that he no longer supported the *Ordinance of the Four Cities* by comparing the Frisians with the *Amalekieten*.

Philips was on the right track: people should control their own community. Unfortunately, the Frisians were not interested in Philip's reconciliatory efforts, and called in the help of two young teachers from Hoorn, a small city forty kilometres north of Amsterdam, named John Willems and

Lubbert Gerrits (1534-1612). Leaving Philips out, Willems and Gerrits then asked ten co-judges to reach a verdict.

The ensuing verdict of 1 February 1567 held both the Flemish and the Frisians guilty. Both parties had to kneel down, confess, and promise that in the future they would get along on a brotherly basis. First, the Frisians knelt down and then jumped back onto their feet. The Flemish then knelt down, but once they went to get back up, they were told to stand up only when the Frisians told them to do so: because, in the end, it had been their fault. The Flemish then indignantly sprung up and withdrew their confession. The result was that most Baptists spoke out for the Flemish, and caused an Old-Flemish and a Young- (or Soft-) Flemish Church split.[41]

Around 1567 Philips requested a number of teachers and judges to come to Embden - at that time the 'Rome of the Baptists'. As soon as Philips had gathered enough like-minded people, he suspended all Elders and Deacons of the province of North-Holland. Kuiper reacted by saying that it was 'impossible for him to stay brother with Philips,' so Philips solved this problem by banning Kuiper as well.

Dijck has this same story, and concludes that 'the tragic, and in a way almost comic, point was reached in Embden, where minister Jan van Ophoorn finally banned everyone in the congregation except himself and his wife.' *

Apart from the skirmishes around Brother Ebbe's statements, the unfortunate manipulation of the verdict by the Frisians, and the combination of jealousies, narrow-mindedness, and anxieties, there were also substantial differences between the two groups. The Flemish did not agree on the *Incarnation doctrine* that Menno Simons had taken from Hoffman. The Flemish also struggled with the question of the 'sleep of the soul:' are those waiting for the Last Judgment in their grave or in heaven? assuming that the Lord would then awaken them from their graves.

* Such splits also spread amongst the Frisians. However, for the church in Zierikzee, in the province of Zeeland, it was different. These Zeeland Anabaptists were subsequently called the Standing Still and banned by the Frisian and Flemish brethren alike 'The Flemish were less rigid in the use of the ban and less autocratic in their ministerial elections and practices' (*Smith's Story*).

---

41 Cf. Epp in *Mennonites in Canada*: 'The Flemish and Frisian [...] each developed left and right wings, thus, the former party sprouted an 'Old Flemish' offshoot, and the offshoot was later subdivided into 'Groninger' Old Flemish and 'Dantzig' Old Flemish wings. The Frisians in turn expanded into a 'Hard' and a 'Loose' or 'Young' Frisian party.'*

These, and other vicissitudes meant that the Frisian and the Flemish Baptists were not allowed to marry one another until 1878. The division into the two churches was not purely geographic: rather, the notion of the Flemish Church indicated a spiritual trend. Indeed, in 1672 the last members of the Old Frisians joined the Flemish church.

The Mennonite's path toward Canada is roiled with stories, each one more entertaining than the next. Unfortunately though, a complete overview of every Mennonite upheaval is far beyond the scope of this book. However, we will return to more differences in the last chapter while cruising in 2001 with 155 Mennonites through Ukraine.[42]

Many other Baptists fled to England. The story of England as a place of refuge for the Anabaptists is left out in this chapter as the focus is mainly on emigration to the North American continent. From England many went on to Germany and settled in the archbishopric of Cologne and to Crefeld.[43&*]

* Those that went to Crefeld, later established Germantown in Pennsylvania.

Other Baptists had already heeded the 1534 invitation of the Council of Danzig, 'to board the ships to [Poland].' More followed. The Flemish and Frisians alike were welcomed, as Smith remarks, because they had won 'recognition as industrious workers who converted the swamps into pastures or grain fields.'

---

42 For example, the Flemish read their sermons while seated, but the Frisians preach standing up. People that wanted to be baptized into the Flemish congregation had to call in two character witnesses, and were baptized by water being poured over them. Conversely, the Frisians baptize by sprinkling water. While Flemish churchgoers had their Bread handed out while they stayed seated in the pews, the Frisians filed past the pastor who gave the Bread into their hands.

43 The story of England as a place of refuge for the Anabaptists is left out in this chapter as the focus is mainly on emigration to the North American continent.

To Poland and on to South Russia

Having settled on the banks of the Vistula River, it turned out that the Frisian/Flemish divisions had moved along with them, this despite Menno Simons himself had spent time there, in 1549, 'admonishing them to brotherly love and unity.' Unfortunately, Poland itself did not prove to be a place of brotherly love and unity.

From 1506 to 1548 Poland had resided under King Sigismund I, who was succeeded by Sigismund II (1548 -1572). Two-hundred years later, in 1772, when a large area of Poland became Prussia.[44] Poland and its population, Baptists among them, could look back on attacks by Muslims, Russians, and Swedes; the serfs had become like slaves; the Cossacks had united with the Tatars. The Jesuits had taken over education; laws were issued that bereaved all non-Catholics of a vote; and the population was soon to be decimated by disease and war. In many ways, Poland must have been more of a hell than a heaven on earth.

In 1772, the Vistula Delta, where many Mennonites had settled, was absorbed by Prussia under the rule of Prince Frederick II, who disliked the Mennonite objection to conscription. However, he agreed that Mennonites would be exempted by paying 5000 *Thalers* annually for the maintenance of the military academy in Kulm. Furthermore they had to accept that they were no longer entitled to buy land and had to contribute to a medical fund. Haxthausen notes in *The Russian Empire* that existing farms could not be split as one wished; people did not want to be separated from each other, and the population was growing fast. These developments poised the Mennonites to move again.

So, when the Russian empress Catharine II invited them in 1786 to settle in her empire, with the guarantee of all the privileges one once enjoyed in Poland, many eagerly accepted. Her invitation went through the Russian colonization officer, George von Trappe, who was of German descent, as was Catharine. Von Trappe advised the Mennonite communities

---

44 The first partition took place in 1768 when areas of Poland went to Russia. This alarmed Austria, and in order to pacify the region, Russia, Prussia, and Austria signed a treaty that partitioned Poland once more, causing it to lose half of its population and one third of its land area (*Encyclopaedia Britannica*, VIII, 74).

to first send a few agents to the designated areas 'to see what it was all about.'

In that same year of 1786, Jakob Höppner and Johann Bartsch left to look for a suitable location near Berislav, along the Dnieper river. Despite Bartsch's frozen toes and Höppner's broken leg, they returned one year later with a favourable report. Meanwhile the Prussian authorities did not want to lose the Mennonites, and had advised the elders not to support the emigration efforts. This is why one Sunday, George von Trappe found himself, on the steps in front of a church in Prussia, handing out brochures that had to convince the Mennonites of the joys of living in Russia.

Settlement in Russia, both during and after the reign of Catharine II, brought each family 175 acres of free land, freedom to confess their religion, freedom from conscription or having to vow an oath, consent to teach the children in their own language (i.e., Low German), the right to prohibit the establishment of pubs in their villages, and the right to brew their own drinks, which in Russia at the time was reserved only for the nobility. Further, while the Mennonite orphan's care was legalized, they were banned from proselytizing. This prohibition may be seen as an infringement of their freedom to confess their religion, as it seems that proselytizing is in intrinsic part of the Mennonite religion. Nonetheless, this stipulation was accepted.

Prior to 1788, only four poor Flemish church families had gone to South Russia, but were then followed by another 228 families. Most of these members of the Flemish church spent the first winter in a camp in Dubrovna: this couldn't have been very easy. Also, as Smith phrases it, 'there was a certain measure of unrest as there was no spiritual leader.' They were deprived of someone who could baptize, marry or bury them. In the end they obtained consent to elect a minister from their own community.

When spring came the group could continue travelling. The 'haves' went in wagons, the 'have-nots' walked while boats floated their households downstream. Upon their arrival in 1789, Governor-General Potemkin (1739-1791) advised them not to settle in Berislav since it was too close to a Turkish war zone. Therefore they settled on an isle in the

Dnieper; a former *Hetmanat* where the Cossacks used to have their *Sich*. The Cossacks had since been removed (ethnically cleansed) because, according to Catharine II, they had been behaving too independently. The surviving Tartars had been banned to the southwest Caucasus's and to Kuban in the east.

The second winter was again not easy. Fabricated sod and mud huts proved to be insufficient in the constant downpours, and many goods that should have arrived by boat were stolen or damaged. Strangely enough though, the surveyors Höppner and Bartsch could afford to build proper houses. Inevitably, the question came up how they had gotten the money. It came out that their houses were built with the money that had been earmarked for the community - both were banned from the Flemish church. Further, Höppner was incarcerated and later became a member of the Frisian church; while Bartsch confessed his sins and was taken back into the fold.

When spring 1790 arrived, Bernard Penner was elected elder. He was about to conduct a service, only had *Bastelschuhe,* homemade sandals. It was thought 'not right' to conduct a service on such sandals. The well-to-do came across with a few boots, so the service was held on good footing. Smith writes, 'Loud were the sobs, it is said, that swept through the audience as the participants in this first communion service were reminded in their present miserable situation of the happy homes they had left behind in the Vistula Lowlands.'

Smith goes on to describe subsequent settlements; at first people settled per family in a farm, but later in villages of fifteen to thirty families. Later townships were established: such as Chortitza, Rosenthal, Einlage, Neuenburg, and etcetera. Farming was by now on dry land, but grasshoppers had to be dealt with.

In the meantime, back in Prussia the economic and religious situation had not improved for the remaining Mennonites. One of them, Cornelius Warkentin, having visited the Chortitza colony, discovered a large section of untilled land one hundred miles to the southeast at the Molotschna River. From 1804 on, more Mennonites left Prussia to settle there. By around 1840, about 46 villages had arisen, and counted about 10,000 inhabitants. These were named after West Prussian villages, and included Halbstadt, Tiegenhagen, Ladekopp, Alexanderwohl, Rosenort, Ohrloff.

The Molotschna group had a much better start than the Chortitza group. From the beginning they had spiritual leaders, and could sell their products in Taranrog, a city at the Sea of Azov. But, they were also closer to the border and often the displaced Tatars raided their settlements. After one of these raids resulted in the deaths of four Mennonites, the Russian government forbade the Tatar hillsmen to carry any weapons - which helped.

As said, farming in South Russia was not the same as in West Prussia, but the Mennonites became accustomed to the climate and the soil. An Agricultural Commission was established, which focused on the political and the economical interests of the Prussian colonists. President of this commission was the affluent Molotschna farmer Johann Cornies (1789-1848), we heard about above, a genius who did not restrict his efforts to improving people's lives to just his own people. Under the wings of his commission, the Mennonites, but also Doukhobors, Hutterites and Jews learned about dry-farming, fertilizing, and crop rotation.

In 1866, the Russian land reform and nationalization program started to affect the Mennonites. They became minorities inside shifted regional boundaries, Russian became the mandatory language for keeping records and in the school curricula, and, importantly, the problem of landless Mennonites arose. After a delegation of the landless had been to St. Petersburg to plead their case, the Russian government pressured the Molotschna colony to split 64,500 acres of communal land into parcels of 88 and 40 acre sections for the landless.

A turning point came in 1874 when Mennonite youngsters were no longer exempted from military service. The community still viewed alternative service as military service. From that year on, the Mennonites started to opt for the Americas, as had the Hutterites.

The 1874 wave: John's story

As we saw above, the privileged sojourn of the Mennonites in South Russia came under unfriendly fire. Education had to be in the Russian language, lands were forcibly split up, and alternative military service was required.

Smith provides an interesting overview of Mennonites' and other Protestants' immigration to America. He also points out that 1874 was not the first year Mennonites made the move to America. Germantown, Pennsylvania was the first permanent settlement, established in 1683 by people from Europe, from Crefeld and the Lower Rhine region. Germantown was later inhabited by a mix of Lutherans, Mennonites, and Mennonite Quakers.* Over the years North American Mennonite settlements had also been expanded by Mennonites from Hessen, Bavaria, and Amsterdam, and by Amish from the Alsace. The list is very long, and goes on and on stretching the Bible belt.

* Mennonite Quakers were Mennonites that had become Quakers.

Here we will restrict our attention to the 1874 immigration wave. From 1874 to 1880 about one third of the Russian Mennonites immigrated to North America. Although, compared to the later immigration from all over Europe, it was more of a ripple that took Hannah's husband's family from South Russia to Saskatchewan.

Smith writes that most Mennonites that settled in the prairie states of America were from the Molotschna, while 'the *Kleine Gemeinde*,' represented by David Klassen and Cornelius Toews' went to Manitoba. Earlier on we read the story of Hannah's mother who fled Russia in 1944. Hereunder follows the story of her husband John's family, who left in 1874:

> **Reimer and Toews are the only names I remember on my father's side. They were all in farming, back in the Ukraine. One reason was that they were highly principled people. They saw the direction Russia was going. Another reason was that they were poor; people who didn't have anything to loose. My family belonged to the *Kleine Gemeinde*.**[45]

---

45 About the *Kleine Gemeinde*: around 1812 Klaas Reimer and Cornelius Janzen and thirty five others found the Molotschna Mennonite church discipline not to be very effective. They split and formed the *Kleine Gemeinde*. From 1843

They settled in Steinbach in the East-Reserve in Manitoba. The first winter, it meant living in a sod house.

Soon after they arrived, my grandfather was born; he also became a farmer. My father was born in 1906, became a teacher, and later a businessman. It was the beginning of education. There was a high school in the West-Reserve, right on the American border.

My mother was nine years younger. When she went to school, there was a full high school in Steinbach. Her father was the principal. My maternal grand- and great grandparents came from the West-Reserve. My grandfather on that side was one of the first Mennonites to get a university education.

I went to high school in Steinbach and to the university of Manitoba. My residency in psychiatry took place in Hamilton. It is not an accident that I ended up in psychiatry. Mennonites have a very strong mental health interest because during the war the refusers were sent to mental hospitals, to work as orderlies. They came out discouraged by the conditions there. They argued that the church should improve this.

In 1982-1983 I spent a sabbatical in Barbados. That was a peculiar Mennonite experience as Mennonites put a strong emphasis on Christian service. For years my uncle was the principal of the Mennonite Central Committee (M.C.C.). He was the second large influence in my life. I regret not having done any service for M.C.C.

I got my chance in Barbados by trying essential psychiatric services in a mental hospital. It is a poor area of the world. Today, in my academic work, I continue to work with the Mennonite Mental Health Services.

---

on they were officially recognized as a Mennonite church. Having arrived in Canada, the *Kleine Gemeinde* expected to settle on the west side of the river, but that side had already been sold. Toews accepted this, but a Mr. Klassen objected because he thought that the land at the east way lay too low and was too far from Winnipeg. Forty-six families, John's family included, went to the East-Reserve; the other eighteen families stayed in Winnipeg. Life there was not easy: for example, the joy of finally having a well was shared by legions of mosquitoes.

Life for the Mennonites that had stayed in South Russia, moved on as well: large estates and factories were being passed on from father to son, people thrived, fulfilled alternative military service, and learned Russian in school. But that changed in 1914. It was ruled that all people of German descent had to sell their land. In 1917, after the Bolsheviks dethroned and murdered Tsar Nicolas II, foreigners were heavily taxed. Then the Red-Russians started to fight the White-Russians; the Mennonites sided with the Whites while the Reds won. And unfortunately, Nestor Makhno, one leader of the Reds held some grudges against the Mennonites.

The 1919 wave: Nestor Makhno

Russian Nestor Makhno, who had organized one of the Red-
Russian bands, fought in the winter of 1918 against the White Russian Army, who were in charge in the Mennonite area and with whom the Mennonites had sided. Subsequently his band forged an alliance with the Red Army, which took over in the area in 1919. So now Makhno ruled! And took revenge! Tales of destruction, robbery, murder, and rape follow. By 1919, life as the Mennonites knew it had gone completely down the drain. Smith quotes a survivor from the village of Sagradovska:

> Nearly everybody in our village was struck down or murdered - old men of eighty, as well as infants of a few weeks. This terror lasted from 7 [am] to 8 [pm] and during that time ninety-six persons were killed.

Would all of this have happened if the Mennonites had treated their farmhands better, or is there simply no hope for successful foreigners in a country hit by civil strife?

Makhno certainly knew how rich the Mennonites were. Dijck (1967) argues that wealth was not the sole motive for these murders. He points out that Makhno used to be a farmhand on a Mennonite estate, where,

> in his opinion they had underpaid him and he was now collecting his wages with the help of thousands of peasants. As result of this reign of terror hundreds of Mennonites were killed (240) alone in Zagradovka in November 1919 and countless villages completely destroyed.

Reimer writes in *My Harp is Tuned to Mourning* that Makhno started his raids in Ukraine, and that he went with his band of raiders to Jacob Loewen, contending to be a representative of the 'Union of Peasant of Gulai Polye,' saying:

> We have come to pay you a little visit - for old times sake, he [Machkno] added with a sly grin on his boyish face, 'It is a long time ago, but I can still feel your *nagaika* on my backside.'[46]

---

46 Also see: http://www.isreview.org/issues/53/makhno.shtml and: http://www.ditext.com/sysyn/makhno.html (last accessed in April 2013). There seems to be

↑ Nestor Makhno: http://en.wikipedia.org/wiki/Nestor_Makhno

much more to Makhno than is generally known.

The surviving Mennonites requested a petition from the Central Executive Committee of Ukraine Communist Party: could they leave, please? It was a dangerous undertaking since such requests could only implicate that they no longer appreciated living in Russia. Many stayed, did not want to leave their estates behind, but others left, and saw a chance to settle in Canada. Unfortunately, once in Canada, some, but not nearly all, felt forced to move again when in 1926, the Canadian government ruled that children had to be taught in English.

The 1926 wave: from Canada to Paraguay

Wiebe (1977) writes about his school years prior to 1926 in Friedensthal, a village near Steinbach on the East Reserve in Manitoba. The German-language school counted about forty Mennonite students, farmers' sons and daughters who started to attend classes as soon as the harvest was over. In school they learned to sing hymns and read the Bible. The culprit of the class always took the magazine *Der Nordwestern* to the classroom to put it in his trousers so it could soften the teacher's blows. The children were used to occasional visits by ministers coming to the school to check out if the catechism was instilled deeply enough into their heads.

But, this changed after the visit of one particular English school supervisor, a foreigner who had no authority with regard to heaven and hell. He just sat there and did not say anything. He also did not address the teacher, but, notes Wiebe, what use would it have had? Our teacher did not speak a word of English.

Strange rumours circulated. The children had to learn English in school. Questions started to circulate too: '*Best du uk en tratja* (Are you a trecker too)?' A new movement arose: 'leave and look for a location far away from the sands and the rocks of Canada.'

'I don't know why our fathers settled on this worthless ground; they should have left it to the Indians.'

Wiebe concludes that in the 1920's the question was 'to *tratj* or not to *tratj*.' The movement was about language and about land. With time the people realized that they would have to accept the new regulations or move once again. They again began to look for places to emigrate and found Paraguay to be a safe haven. There was Fernheim, the first Mennonite colony, established in 1921 by Mennonites that had fled Russia from around 1920. During 1926-1927, about a third of the 3000 people from the (Canadian) Chortitzer Mennonite church started the Menno colony in Paraguay.

Wiebe's cousin left for Paraguay from where he kept him posted about the trials and tribulations they faced there, but he assured him that at least they had preserved their language and their faith.

The 1945 wave: Bartel moves from Germany to Canada

As said above, in the 1880's Catharine II had invited the paci-fist Mennonites to settle on the lands she had secured from the Tatars. The Flemish Mennonites went first, though not all Mennonites had left Prussia at that time. Among those that chose to stay were the ancestors of Bartel, who ended up in Canada about 160 years later.

Bartel authored *Living with Conviction: German Army Captain Turns to Cultivating Peace* on the Mennonites that had stayed on in Prussia in the 1870's, and had given a copy of his book to Mike Chernenkoff. During his time in jail in the Aggasiz prison near Vancouver, Mike had occasionally worked on Bartel's farm: 'A Mennonite, a friendly man. Every year he still pays me a visit.'

Bartel, born in 1915 in Reichsfelde, Prussia, describes how he spent his childhood on a beautiful estate with an abundance of personnel and horses. He had been home schooled, and had grown up in a rigid class system.

'Nothing lacked me,' writes Bartel, adding that by the time little Mennonite boys had grown up, the sons of the Prussian farmhands had to address them with *Junger Herr*. Bartel briefly summarizes his Mennonite background: by 1530 Mennonites arrived in Poland. When Poland was subdivided in 1772, they lived on under the Prussian crown. Three years later, despite hearing that they had to pay 5000 *Thaler* in order to support the military academy in Kulm, and that Catharine II enabled people to leave Prussia for South Russia, his family chose to hang on to their properties.

However, their choice meant that they had to grit their teeth when one of their privileges, exemption of military service, was withdrawn and their young men had to perform alternative military service. Bartel notes though that in the Great War many of them went into the army on a voluntary basis, perceiving it as a challenge - after all, doesn't *Romans* chapter 13 state that people have to obey the local authorities? In 1937, when Hitler introduced general conscription, Bartel himself went into the army, and dryly notes that he even killed a Polish man.

After the war Bartel became manager of an estate somewhere in Germany. One day a certain Mr. C.F. Klassen, a representative of the Mennonite Central Committee, rang the doorbell. He was looking for 'lost' Mennonites and asked him whether he was interested in moving to Canada. As it had proven not easy for Bartel - formerly the son of an estate owner - to cope with a subservient position, small living quarters, and a growing family, he certainly was interested. The rest of Bartel's book is like many immigrant books, narrating the arrival in Canada, the initial challenges, and the successes in the end.

The 1948 wave: from Germany via Paraguay to Canada

Klassen, looking for lost Mennonites, missed Hannah's mother and her seven children. However, by 1948 Hannah then three years old, her mother and six siblings were on a steam ship heading for South America. Queen Juliana of the Netherlands had left the *Volendam* at the disposal of displaced Mennonites in Germany. Hannah and her family were part of the contingent of displaced persons who were seen as Russians in Germany and as Germans in Russia. They were not welcome in America or in Canada, but were now about to be welcomed by Paraguay.

According to Fretz (1962), Paraguay was a country that depended on immigrants. While he mentions numerous groups whose settlements failed, there were some who were successful. For example, The Social Paradise founded in 1887 by Dr. Bernard Fourster (a brother-in-law of Friedrich Nietsche). Among the successful settlements, Fretz also lists the 'ethnological Dutch colonies,' mostly Mennonite. We saw the 1921 and the 1926 colonies, Fernheim and Menno.

Subsequently in 1947, the *Neuland* and the *Volendam* colonies were established; the *Volendam Colony* is still functioning.[47] I asked Hannah whether she had ended up in the *Volendam Colony* as well.

'Mmm,' she said, 'when we arrived in South America, there was civil unrest in Paraguay, so we were first housed in a refugee camp in Brazil. Terrible conditions there.'

That is what she could remember, but the *Volendam Colony*?

'That ship of your queen was named so.' And, that they lived about six hours drive from Fernheim.

'Six hours?'

'Yes, with horse and wagon. For the doctor or the hospital, people went to Halbstad; that was only three hours.'

A three-hour trip to a doctor is strange as there was a doctor in the Volendam. Rimland, a twelve-year old passenger at the Volendam, writes in *The Demon Doctor* about a Dr. Hans

---

47 Cf.: www.gameo.org/encyclopedia/contents/V6382.html (Last accessed April 2013.)

Joachim Fertsch, a doctor [?] who is said to have come along at the *Volendam* ship, specialized in appendicitis and not much else. Rimland suspected him, but did not succeed to prove, that Fertsch was Dr. Josef Mengele (who is said to have fled to Argentina in 1949).

When Hannah was eleven years old, her family was sponsored to come to Canada. The above story of her ancestors is how it came that her mother was born in Russia, that she looks Dutch with blond hair and blue eyes, but was born in Germany, raised in Paraguay, and ended up in Canada.

Chapter 5
Answers 1 and 2

As said before, Indians have lived from time immemorial on the North-American continent that also held and still holds oil, gas, cows and grass. But I saw that there was more to Canada, a new layer, so to speak.

Finding out about Van Paassen, a pacifist, who is said to have established an army in Israel, about Tolstoy's involvement with Russian immigrants, about Mike having spent many years in prison for nudity and arson, Anna in a Hutterite colony, Hannah being born in Germany and raised in Paraguay - it was puzzling to me and not only to me: in *Earth Could Be Fair,* Van Paassen posed similar questions:

> What became of the Doukhobors in America anyway? What became of all those sectarians who migrated there from here and other parts of Europe: Mennonites, Gerardists, Quakers, Hernhutters, Peculiar People, Anabaptists, Labadists? Do they still exist?

Van Paassen died apparently without finding out. Hereunder my answers:

> Dear Pierre,   Calgary, 2013.
>
> In a way I can say that reading a few pages in Mike's journal contributed to my search into to background of a few people I met shortly after arriving in Canada. It brought about my correspondence with Mike, which brought about awareness of the fact that just as Mennonites and Hutterites, Doukhobors also had lived and left South-Russia. A few of my other projects, *Montana 1911, a Professor and his Wife among the Blackfeet(2005), Missionaries among Miners (2007), and Gustave Aimard,*

Feiten, Fictie, Frictie (2009) caused some delay: not to mention family, friends, travel, and cats & dog affairs. I have only looked at said three groups of immigrants, as we (Hannah and I) and they had parts of their history in South Russia in common. Somehow it reminds me of Susan Boyle, a 2009 discovered Scottish singer. In front of the sceptical jury and audience of a TV show, *Britains Got Talent*, she wiggled her hips and said: 'I am forty-seven, and that is only one side of me.'

In the same vein, I can say: 'The three groups I looked into are only three sides of Canada. What else is there to say, than what a rich history these "Canadians" have!'

Back to our questions:

Dear Pierre, first about the Doukhobors.

There are about 40,000 Doukhobors thriving in Canada. They do fine, have their own journal (http://www.spirit-wrestlers.com/excerpts/Inquirer/), a genealogy website (http://www.doukhobor.org/New.htm) and of course there is more. As far as I can see, the approximately 130 Sons of Freedom also do very well, apart from their age-related health problems. What the woman said at the end of the British Columbia radio documentary (see p. 96) is a good sign: 'Children and life should come first.' Hopefully her remark is a stern warning for people to not blindly follow one or another leader. I hope that one of these days this documentary will be heard and seen by students of extremist Christian, Jewish and Muslim schools.

Before you say that I was bewitched by Mike or Nellie, the woman where I invited us for a Coke, see what Peacock had to say while collecting for his *Songs of the Doukhobors*:

I found little evidence of the extremist activities so luridly described by reporters and journalists in the popular press. It soon became evident that the views and activities of a few zealots had been blown up out of all proportion, and that the great mass of Doukhobors now live peacefully in all walks of life throughout Canada.

Demonstrating in the nude is now a worldwide phenomenon. It is not so much that these people want to parade their bums, but it is the last resort to get attention for their ends. The freedom of speech, or freedom of expression, is unfortunately not automatically matched by the right to be heard, to get adequate answers or actions, in short, by accountability. When two shoes were hurled at George Bush Junior's head, he commented 'that's what people do in a free society, draw attention to themselves' (*Globe & Mail,* December 15, 2008).

'Anabaptists'?

I take it that you mean the Hutterites, don't you Pierre? They also do fine. Hutterites are good farmers: a country with Hutterite colonies will never know famine. While regretting for them that it has consequences for their gene pool, I appreciate that they don't proselytize. Having said this, one of my Hutterite visitors said that they do in fact proselytize - 'by dressing simply, just as Jesus did.'

The Hutterites still hold on to quite a secluded lifestyle. But in the twenty-odd years that we have been visiting each other, I have been seeing changes: newspapers, cell phones, secular books, the Internet, and small private enterprises are on the rise. Many colonies quietly contribute to good causes. For example, Hutterites help keep the Canadian blood supply at a healthy level: indeed, many Canadians are not aware of the Hutterite blood running through their veins.

As we live across from a hospital, a good number of them regularly camp in our basement during sickness of their relatives. Generally they are a happy bunch: they are cheerful (depending on how sick the family member is), energetic (today the chickens are slaughtered, last week we were baking, and this week we have to take in the harvest and so on).

Despite seeming a bit aloof from the conceits of the modern world, in businesses they are much more proficient than they initially come across.

Pierre, I have to end this letter. My pleasure to have talked to you again - remember I said something about a grand scheme. Think of it: our ancestors' religion caused death and destruction in Europe, and currently wars are raging in the Middle East. Lots of people have not been born, and will not be born, because of all kinds of fights for freedom.

I wondered about looking back: are Mennonites' North American offspring as interested in their roots as African Americans who visit Africa? I asked Hannah whether she ever saw the site of her conception: 'Mary, why did I never think of this?'

Well, bye Pierre. Three days after 9/11 on 14 September 2001, we went off to cruise through South Russia, which since 1990 has been the Republic of Ukraine. As soon as we are back, I will send you my impression of how Mennonites are doing and a travelogue and then you can see how the Mennonites are doing.

Signing off,
Mary E. M.

Chapter 6
2001 (South Russia) Ukraine Travelogue

Preliminaries
Hannah and I booked for the 2001 cruise along the banks of the Dnieper River in Ukraine. With about 150 Mennonites we were going to follow the river flowing along their ancestors' stomping grounds.

It did not take long before we soon-to-be cruise passengers received an e-mail from a previous passenger. In it he explained the advantages of travelling to Ukraine as a seed-carrier. The letter suggested that we bring sachets with 'all kinds of seeds' to hand out to beggars.

I wondered whether the Ukraine homeless had backyards or Gardens of Eden. Just in case, I looked at seeds in garden centres. They are very expensive. No wonder beggars cannot afford to buy them. Fortunately my Hutterite friends gave me a few bags full of grain seeds, so that problem was solved.

Another suggestion came from travel-agent Walter:[48] 'bring along coloured pencils, batteries, and underwear.' These items would be handed out in Ukraine to the poor from whatever denomination. In April 2001, I found myself asking my friends to bring underwear, coloured pencils, and batteries to my birthday party. So, this request was also taken care of.

Next: I got a phone call from a Mennonite minister from Ukraine, who was visiting his daughter who lived near Calgary: 'Could he please put the old clothes his daughter would like to donate to his Ukraine parish in my suitcase?' My suitcase, donated by my friend Tom, being already stuffed

---
48 In this chapter all family names have been left out.

with brand new underwear, pencils, and batteries in all sizes, now nearly burst at the seams. Suddenly, there was a destination for my suitcase - it would go to his parish in Zaparozhye, a city south of Kiev. To his parish? I wondered whether the underwear would indeed make it to the bums of people of every denomination?

Next: travel-agent Walter e-mailed an article, titled 'Proselytizing in Ukraine: Positive or Negative?' by Tatiana Riazantseva, Ph.D., T. (n.d.).[49] In hindsight, this article gave a very good impression of things to come, and I have included it here as part of the preparatory phase of our trip:

THE FAITH THAT YOU HAVE, KEEP BETWEEN YOURSELF AND GOD; HAPPY IS HE WHO HAS NO REASON TO JUDGE HIMSELF FOR WHAT HE APPROVES' (ROMANS 14:22).

Introduction

It's always hard to write on religious matters for the fear of hurting somebody's feelings. But I think that some inside commentary on the present situation with the so-called 'new confessions' or 'non-traditional' Christian churches, introduced to Ukrainian believers by US, German, and other foreign missionaries, would be of a certain interest for the North American readers of 'Preservings'.

The first thing to say about the religious life in Ukraine is that it is many fold and vigorous. The freedom of conscience is guaranteed by the Constitution of Ukraine (Chapter II, article 35) and this time not only on paper as it had been during the Soviet period. For many people, old and young, perestroika and the further development towards democracy in independent Ukraine has become a period of real spiritual renaissance.

It's not a secret that many of our people coming to the meetings with the foreign proselytizers do not seek God directly, but some escape, some entertainment, some remedy against loneliness and indifference, that is to say, they are essentially looking for brotherly love and friendly support.

---

49 Published by the Shevchenko Institute of Literature, at the National Academy of Sciences of Ukraine, Kiev, Ukraine. Efforts to ask Mrs. Riazantseva for permission to reproduce her article failed.

This is especially true with our senior citizens, who in many cases obviously treat their 'new' churches as certain clubs. Many of them, like my 85-year-old neighbour, are perfectly happy just to be able to get together somewhere once or twice a week for a common prayer, Bible reading and singing followed by the community dinner and an occasional excursion, organized by their pastor and free for the community members. The last is very important, since many of them are simply poor getting pension equal to approximately $20 US a month.

The Youth

The young Ukrainian parish of the Western proselytizers looks mainly for the same. Still like in any other part of the world, the kids are eager to learn, they welcome any new experience be it the Old Testament and Gospel studies, choir singing, English classes or just making new friends. If charity is the main form of activity provided by the Western churches for the senior citizens of Ukraine, education is their basic way with the youth (Though charity is not, of course, excluded. There are special programs for disabled children, orphans and young delinquents, for example).

Many representatives of the US and UK Protestant churches successfully combine their parish work with teaching English at different language training courses in Kiev and around Ukraine. Some teach at universities and maintain different research programs. And many young people of Ukraine, attending the services of foreign proselytizers or taking the language and other courses like those above, hope this might make their way to some US or Canadian university much easier.

Mennonites

I am especially pleased to mention the fruitful activities of the Mennonites in this sphere. The members of this community are now well known in our country, above all in their once native region of Zaporozhye, for their deeds of charity and educational efforts. (To my knowledge, there are also some Mennonite professors teaching geography, English language/literature and history in

Lithuanian universities.) Many schools are thankful for the humanitarian aid coming every year, brought by the participants of The Mennonite Heritage Cruises.

The local Society for the Preservation of Monuments in cooperation with the Mennonite community of Zaporozhye, largely supported by the brothers and sisters from Canada and US, has started a big project aimed to restore the places connected with the Mennonite history in the region: temples, schools, etc. The international conference on the grounds of the Zaporozhye University, collecting Ukrainian, Russian, US, Canadian, and German academicians involving Mennonite studies of all trends was considered to be one of the most interesting scientific events of all 1999.

All in all it could be said that the activities of the Mennonite communities in Ukraine demonstrate their lively interest for the country which once used to be their home. Their care to find their own roots, to restore their own history by bringing back any possible recollection or displaying every treasured possession, by examining every discovered text and making it interesting and useful for the present generation sets a good example for everybody. All these efforts finally help us, the native Ukrainians, to make the big picture of the Ukrainian history complete, adding there some important and very interesting details.

The Negative

Much could be added about the positive aspects of the Western proselytizers activities in Ukraine. Many of them are really dedicated, sincere people, wishing to help those in need. Still, not everything is so ideal. In the Ukrainian newspapers recently a number of stories appeared informing about the negative cases within non-traditional communities like certain illegal manipulations with the real estate and other property of the community members, using the people's money for some private dealings of the leaders, even escaping with the community's money, etc.

For many Ukrainian families, one of the couple joining some 'new church' often means divorce. A proselyte husband or wife might become too absorbed by their new relationships and stop paying usual attention to their family or instead start trying to persuade them to follow this new way of life, which leads to frustration and other problems if all such efforts fail. The proselytized children might start ignoring their parents opinions and care, taking into consideration only their leaders and community mates views and instructions, this may lead as far as leaving home and school in some cases [...].

Riazantseva's article gave me a déjà-vue experience. It reminded me of the woman in the Doukhobor documentary who said: 'Children and your life should come first.' It also made me think of what Jaenen (1977) wrote about proselytizing among Indians:

> The intrusion of Christianity [and the subsequent] conversion inevitably destroyed the unity and homogeneity of native communities, set off conflicts within families, bands and tribes and finally threatened the authority of the *shaman*.

Would this not be the same for the Ukrainians?

The e-mails kept coming in. The participants on the cruise could indicate which town or village they wanted to visit along the Dnieper. Travel-agent Walter kept everyone posted on the places people wanted to visit. We got messages such as: 'Please drop me from the trip to Heuboden. As for the extra trip to Gruenfeld, Eleanor and myself want to be included in it.'

One e-mail to the Calgary passengers contained an invitation:

> Dear Mennonite Heritage Cruise passengers online
> Here is the schedule of upcoming appearances by Derek Fraser, Canadian Ambassador to Ukraine
> UCC Event: Thursday, March 8, 6:30, Calgary
> Assumption Church Hall 703-6th St. NE. Calgary.

That evening, Hannah and I found ourselves in the big basement of a Catholic Ukrainian church with cookies and coffee on flower-patterned plastic-table-cloth-covered tables.

Both ambassadors, one from Canada to Ukraine and the other from Ukraine to Canada, sat behind an empty table. The Canadian ambassador spoke for twenty minutes in (I assume) perfect Ukrainian. Thereafter his Ukrainian colleague briefly explained the economic situation in Ukraine in English and in (surely perfect) Ukrainian: the net national product of Ukraine was doing well, and had even increased. Any questions?

The audience turned out to be not just a few cruise passengers, but mostly enraged, recent immigrants from Ukraine. Enraged because their family members did not get visitor's visas and could not visit them. Their questions, rather remarks were a far cry from the smooth, polite Canadian way of speaking.

Still, Canadian Ambassador Fraser elegantly rebuffed: 'It is better to ask for an immigration visa, because forty percent of visitors stay illegally [in Canada] and that is why potential visitors have to show so much proof that they will return.'

It was not an easy evening for poor Fraser, being from a country that was doing so well, sitting beside a colleague representing a country from which people were so eager to leave.

The Ukrainian ambassador also got some questions: 'When visiting Ukraine, why do you need a stamp from the police in every city one visits?' 'Why does one have to take travel insurance [to travel from city to city] in Ukraine?'

'Shameful rules,' the Ukrainian ambassador admitted. 'They have to be changed.'

Time went on, our departure for Ukraine was looming. More e-mails gave elaborate ideas of what lay ahead of us. Friday, March 9, 2001, Edmonton

> From repeat passenger Peter ——
>
> Dear 2001 passengers. My name is Peter ——. I live in Southern Ontario, and you will be joining me this fall on my third trip to Ukraine on the Mennonite Heritage Cruise. I was born in a small village called Adelsheim (Dolinovka). This village is about 30 km north of Zaporozhye and 3 km west of the mighty Dnieper River. It is very close to Eichenfeld, scene of a terrible massacre.
>
> We dealt with many questions before booking our first trip on the Mennonite Heritage Cruise such as will we really be able to see our village? Do the cruise organizers know what they are doing? Let me say that we were

pleasantly surprised, in spite of having huge anxieties. The bus took us to our village and the tour guide was very helpful. To find our plot of land (our house was destroyed during Word War Two) was not easy. Things have changed a lot. All the roads entering our village have been changed so it is important to ask a lot of questions about old landmarks. The old school house in our village is still standing and we recognized it. A landmark of greater importance to us was the remains of the old dam, which, during our days, created a very large pond. This dam was in the back of our property.

We made certain that the people understood that we were only visiting and not expecting to get our land back. They then treated us as old friends. We expect to have a long visit with them again this fall and gain as much information as possible.

So, ask a lot of questions. Memories are long in the former Mennonite villages. There is an important thing to remember when on the bus tours. The bus can't stop too long for you, so we take the cruise bus one day, in order to share our experiences with new cruise passengers, and go on your own on a private trip the next day. This way we have plenty of time to visit and a little time to reminisce and shed a few tears. For me it is the place where our family suffered the tragedy of losing my father.

Please be advised that the cruise is very well organized but the [Mennonite travel guides] have not yet been able to control the weather. I look forward to meeting you on the Glushkov.

The next e-mail was from Cruise Director Galyna

You will be greeted in Ukraine and especially on the cruise with kindness and respect. This cruise has become a very special event for us who work in Ukraine travel industry. The ship's staff and our travel industry partners in various cities look forward eagerly to each September Mennonite cruise. It is like no other travel project in our country. We have tourists and Mennonites - but never enough Mennonites. You brighten our life.

Many of you will know that this cruise is known as the 'University of Glushkov,' our ship being called the Akademik Viktor Glushkov, named after a 20th century Ukrainian mathematician. Here in Ukraine we take great pains just now in rediscovering our history. It turns out that your history is also part of our history, which was distorted during Soviet times. The university idea, which has been growing with each cruise, allows us all to look at new historical research and debate its implications vigorously. It also allows us to study, respect and celebrate our different cultures and spiritual sensibilities. This combination of travel, study and reflection is unique for us and we find it as fascinating as you will.

You will be discovering an interesting new country with very ancient roots. Together we will have a great travel adventure with few anxieties, thanks to good planning and the comforts of a floating hotel with restaurants on the Black Sea and up the Dnieper River. Actually, I cannot claim that our cruise ship will match your ideas of Caribbean cruise comfort, but the food will be authentic! After all, it is part of your heritage too.

Most of all, I look forward once again to the singing. Please sing a lot!

One more e-mail of the many I received: this time from a Colorado repeat passenger:

Travelling the second time on the Mennonite Heritage Cruise was again a wonderful experience and also a different experience from the first time. This second trip allowed me to open my mind beyond my own family history to a wider understanding of the Mennonite experience. I began to understand more profoundly the great contribution our Mennonite peoples made to Ukraine as well as the great sacrifices they endured.

A moment outstanding in my mind was when Cruise Director Galyna Z. spoke poignantly of her feelings at the Memorial Service toward the end of the trip. She told us that when she first became involved with the Mennonite Heritage cruise and heard of all the hardships the Mennonites endured while living in Ukraine, she began to feel overwhelming guilt for what her people had done to our people. After wrestling with these feelings, she suddenly realized it wasn't her people's fault. In fact her people, the Ukrainians, themselves were also in bondage, suffering terribly under Soviet rule. Not until 1991 has Ukraine been independent and in control of its own destiny. I found it profound to hear her express these feelings . . . never having thought a Ukrainian could have internalized our Mennonite experience in that manner. Is there a chance that others have also felt as Galyna?

All Ukrainians I have met as we travelled in their country received us as precious gifts. What a privilege we have to travel in their land, to visit their villages, eat with them, laugh and cry with them, remember with them and extend the hand of peace and reconciliation. Healing for host and visitor can come in the most unexpected circumstances. All we need to do is respect them, as they too have sacrificed, and accept their beautiful hospitality.

While Ukraine gained its independence from the USSR in 1991, there still is economic failure everywhere. It is appropriate for us to take some of our bounty to share with them. A simple question to ask your self is 'what are my interests and likes?' If something pertaining to those interests is simple and travels well, take some of that (or a lot of that) along to give away. Someone there also will like it and find it interesting, remembering that batteries are hard to replace and their electricity is different. I like to draw so I take brand new crayons and drawing pads to give to village children. The schools are always in need of art supplies.

The next message from Walter provided details of one particular day during our trip:

Program: Public Meetings - Mennonite Centre in Ukraine

Date: Fri, 20 Apr 2001, 09:39:52 -0400

[...] Learn how the former Maedchenschule in Halbstadt, Molochna Colony, will become a development centre and beacon of hope for destitute Ukrainians in the region where Mennonites once lived [. . .].

Things are happening quite swiftly now on two continents. Renovation will begin shortly in Ukraine. The interim directors are busy in Halbstadt/Molochansk and will have a rented apartment shortly. We own one historic Maedchenschule, one pre-rusted new automobile, pilot medical aid projects are in place, we have a matching fund request in to the Canadian Government, we have a funded 8 month internship, and we have lots of strategic plans and goodwill.

Still at home and I already felt carried away! The next e-mail was a bit alarming:

Subject: Choral singers & Instrumentalists

Dear cruise passengers online,
   Marina and I trust your summer has gone well [. . .]. I have also been very busy recently as board chairman of the Friends of the Mennonite Centre in Ukraine:
   Friends of the Mennonite Centre in Ukraine will acquire and maintain a historic building in Molochansk as a vehicle of humanitarian services which are community-based, provided without discrimination, foster local initiative, and are sustainable, while interpreting and commemorating the Mennonite past.
   The new Co-Administrators, Al & Peggy will arrive in Ukraine in October. Alas, family events prevent them from arriving earlier. The pace of renovation of the Halbstadt/Molochansk schoolhouse has picked up recently. We have decided to schedule the opening September 24 coincident with the cruise. A recent photo of the site, taken by the supervising architect is attached. Plans for the gala opening are being refined as you read this. Toronto historian (creator of Khortitsa '99) Harvey is in charge and leaves for Ukraine in early September. Mayor Saenko has Molochansk buzzing with anticipation. The village band and choirs are rehearsing. The Chortitza Island equestrian troupe has offered to come down to Molochansk for a special performance for the event and to take part as much as possible. Artist and designer Paul has created a special logo and posters for the event.
   Here's what September 24 looks like

1 we dock at 8 am in Zaporozhye, having sailed up the Dnieper overnight from Kherson

2 the morning has us all rotating through nearby Chortitza/Rosenthal, the historic 1789 founding Mennonite sites.
3 after lunch on the ship we are all off to Halbstadt/Molochansk, two hours distant to the southeast
4 3 to 6:30 PM - Gala opening of the Mennonite Centre in Ukraine
5 the main ceremony will take place outside, at the schoolhouse entrance: dignitaries in three languages, local musicians, cruise choir, etc., (rain option - event takes place inside the former Halbstadt Zentralschule).
6 Command performance of Cossack equestrian show in nearby park
7 *Faspa* (Mennonite Tea) for 400 invited guests (including cruise passengers)

The decision to pick up the pace of renovation for the Sep 24 opening has its financial implications. If you would like to contribute to this historic project, you can do so and get a receipt for tax purposes. Please make your cheque payable to 'FOMCU' and mail it to:

FRIENDS OF THE MENNONITE CENTRE IN UKRAINE [...]

The next e-mail was as exciting:

Dear cruise passengers online,

With the Mennonite Centre opening gala now in preparation, plus other special occasions on the cruise, it would be very helpful to our musician/conductor Howard to know which of you can play portable instruments such as violin, flute, recorder. Howard will likely form a chamber choir plus a cruise choir. It would be helpful then to know which of you can read choral music and have had experience in ensembles.

Hopefully, one or two of you are soloists. We already have an SATB vocal quartet if we can find an alto. Please comment for friends and relatives not online.

Please respond to me.

Next, two planes flew into two buildings in New York, triggering Walter's 11 September 2001 e-mail:

Subject: US Tragedy & Impact

Date: Tue, 11 Sep 2001 23:08:21 -0400

Dear 2001 cruise passengers online.

Firstly, we mourn the tragic loss of life in New York and other sites. We will want to memorialize them in a special way on the cruise. Russian Mennonites surely know about tragedy and loss of life. We understand the concerns of passengers, especially Americans, about flying just now. Hopefully the skies will be cleared shortly and all will be well.

We fully hope and expect that the airlines will be resuming international flights shortly. At this time we expect the cruise to go forward as planned.

Next e-mail:

Subject: Travel Update

Date: Thu, 13 Sep 2001 12:59:41 -0400

Dear Mennonite cruise passengers online.
It is a time for prayer and patience.

1. Austrian Airlines has begun international flights to Canada. Marina and I expect to fly tonight.
2. Lufthansa will likely start flights to Canada on Friday. Lufthansa's planes are in the wrong places and it will likely take until Saturday for flights from Canada. Most of the passengers are on Lufthansa flights.
3. Domestic air traffic has begun in the US and international flights will follow shortly.
4. We are working on backup plans with our Ukrainian travel partners and therefore it will be important for Marina and I to be in Kyiv tomorrow. Our colleagues in Ukraine are extremely professional and flexible. I have been on the phone to both Kyiv and Zaporizhia today.
5. You will need to be in touch with the airlines on which you are ticketed. It may be that some of you may be delayed a day or so. If so, we can deal with it. The ship is ours. It goes when we want it to. And we can make plans to have you join the ship en route too.
6. We need to know if you are cancelling and you need to know that cancellation will not be covered by insurance since the cruise is not cancelled and flights are happening, even if delayed. It is very important to us to know if you are cancelling.

7   Here are some extra FAX numbers for you to communicate with us. These people do not make airline or ship decisions but will relay information from you and vice versa [...].

Trip to Ukraine

15 September 2001: off to Europe

Despite the Americans' paralyzing fears, the sun also rose on September 12, 13, 14 and 15. That last morning, at dawn, Hannah and I departed for Frankfurt. American anxiety had spread to the Calgary airport and led to custom officers' questions such as: 'Do you have a leg shaving razor and/or a nail clipper in your purse?' Once up in the air, the pilot, Captain Herr Braun, apologized for not having been able to get enough plastic cutleries, and begged us to 'please eat with metal knives and forks.'

The first night in Europe, Hannah and I overnighted in Florsheim, 25 kilometres from Frankfurt airport. The cab driver was not shy in showing his unhappiness with our six pieces of luggage. We each had a small suitcase for the night in Florsheim, a larger one for the fourteen days on the cruise ship, and one stuffed with underwear, batteries, and crayons.*

* The original idea was that the big suitcases were to be put in the plane to Kiev right away, but because of New York, we had to keep them all with us. Thank you Bin Laden!

From Florsheim we walked a few kilometres to the neighbouring village and checked out the five local pubs. But between 3:00 and 5:30 p.m. everything was closed. We imaged the Florsheimers lurking behind their layers of half-lowered shutters, closed windows, and drawn curtains; and if they were not lurking there, where on earth were they, and what were they up to? We ended up taking a break from walking on the terrace of a closed Chinese restaurant, with a soft rain gently falling on our heads.

Back in the hotel, and after a nap, Hannah and I went to the dining room where about twenty-five people had just finished their evening dinner. They turned out to be our fellow cruise passengers and fired numerous questions at us: had we been sleeping? Had we had ordered a cab for the next morning? We answered with: yes, we had slept, and yes we had already ordered a cab for the next morning. They advised us to de-order the cab, and instead join them on the bus that they would order. A young woman bent over me and started to translate the German menu for me. Having just woken up, I let her do that, but after realizing what she was doing, I told her that I could read German. 'But, thanks anyway.' The rest of the journey she did not bother to speak to me again.

One of the passengers walked around, wrote down everyone's names and ordered a bus so the next morning we could all go to the airport by bus. Someone cheerfully exclaimed: 'This is real Mennonite togetherness.' I guessed that I had to get used to 'togetherness.' After dinner we cancelled our cab.

16 September: learning a few lessons

5.30 a.m.: Taking a shower.

5.45 a.m.: A fellow-passenger knocked on our door. Hannah opened. Without further ado then 'shall I put your suitcases in the bus?' he dragged them from the room. Hannah and I, the last ones to board the bus, were told that we were number 25 and number 26, and that we each had to pay twenty Marks. This was fine with us, since the cab driver had us charged seventy Marks. I learned that 'togetherness saves money.' A few moments after the bus took off we were all singing *Happy Birthday*. I now learned that 'togetherness also comprises singing *Happy Birthday* without knowing whose birthday it is.'

At the airport we did a 'group-check in,' which meant a lot of time shuffling along with the entire group. Togetherness also includes shuffling along, without knowing where exactly one shuffles to.

The flight to Kiev, only a few hours, was pleasantly short. Upon disembarking we were welcomed in a hallway by Walter and Marina. Outside the airport hall a well-dressed man showed us a card: 'I am deaf, I am not starving, but I would like to have a good life.' Well, who doesn't? He sold ugly key hangers: now he has a good life, and I have an ugly key hanger.

Next we drove for seven hours in a bus through endless rolling plains of black earth, each plot lined with a double row of trees. Brightly lit stalls lined the road selling bottles holding colourful liquids: no roadside restaurants in this country.

Around 10 p.m. we arrived at the quay at Odessa where our ship was docked. Seamen dragged our suitcases inside. All suitcases intended for Zaporozhye had to go to the blue room, which is where my humanitarian contribution went. On the fourth floor of the ship, a late dinner was served in, and with, an old-fashioned chic ambiance: glass-bead chains everywhere, starched linen, and a host of staff serving in black and white formal outfits.

17 September: Odessa

Waking up on a plank bed with a flannel under-sheet by way of mattress: I had never slept so well. Violin music sounded through the intercom. Walter's sonorous voice sounded something about pilgrims, the program of the day, and the blue sky. After showering, getting dressed, leaning over the ships railing, I was finally eye-to-eye to the Black Sea, which really is black because of the surrounding rivers feeding in sulphurous hydrates. The sea's darkness is lightened occasionally by floating green and yellow jellyfish.

Beside me stood a man also staring into the water. He said: 'In 1919 this harbour was filled up with bodies.' He then stared straight ahead of him, seeing nothing. 'My parents moved here from Germany in 1919. They thought to find peace here. One year later they moved to Canada.' Without saying more he took off and walked inside the ship.

Breakfast was in another old-fashioned chic dining room. Instead of praying, people sang before eating. My tablemates said that they had not shown up in the Mennonite Church for thirty years and set to discuss the desirability of the Mennonite Brethren (MB) rejoining the General Conference (GC) or vice-versa. They said that the MB practice full immersion, while the GC only sprinkles them.

'They don't take risks, the MB's. They want you to get wet all over, so that you are really cleaned from the original sin.' (I felt like diving into the Black Sea.)

'The GC's,' the conversation went on, 'don't take it so literal.'

Later, aboard the ship, I asked other people about this immersion practice.

'What, do they [MB's] still believe in that?' was the reply.

After breakfast we boarded the bus for a tour through Odessa. The first stop was the top of the Potemkim Steps: wide stairs that lead from the harbour to the city above. Here is a statue of the Duke de Richelieu (1766-1822), a refugee from France, who was the first governor of this area and had done an excellent job.*

* Odessa was established in 1774 because Russia wanted an export harbour for its' grain. In order to establish the city, the Turks had to be chased off.

From the stairs we walked to an opera building that was being renovated, and went from there by bus to the National Museum. There we were told that Turks, Tatars, Mongols, Polish, Russians, and others form the Ukrainian national make-up. Someone from our group asked about Count Voronsky and told the local museum guide that without Voronsky, the Mennonites and the Hutterites could not have survived.[50]

The museum guide repeated, wondering, 'The Hutterites?' She shrugged. She had heard of neither Mennonites, nor Hutterites. A Mennonite woman beside me remarked that she found that we had spent too much time in the museum where 'they don't even know anything about Mennonites.'

It was apparent that the Mennonites did not have a niche in the local consciousness. The guide went on and on about the Italians, Polish, Albanians, and Chinese, who all lived in their own quarters. She pointed across the street, to the catholic St. Petrus Church and proudly stressed the current tolerance.

'We now have churches for the Catholics.' This remark also failed to cheer up the Mennonites' mood.

We left, boarded the bus again and de-boarded within five minutes in front of a light-blue cathedral that also had a worship area half under-ground: gold paint, icons, fresco's. Outside, old women were begging. Further down the street a few people slept under a blanket.

In the bus back to the ship, we saw another onion-dome church under construction.

'On this spot the old cathedral was blown up in 1934 by the Russians,' explained the guide. Later we learned that the World Bank lends money to rebuild all these blown up cathedrals, and there are not few of them!

---

50 Voronsky (Count Michael Woronzoff, 1782-1857) was also involved, as Governor-General of New Russia and Bassarabia, in the exile of the Doukhobors to the Caucasus. According to Haxthausen in *The Russian Empire*, he made sure that they could sell their property. Haxthausen also cites 'Woronzoff's' 26 January 1841 Doukhobor proclamation: 'Woronzoff goes to great lengths to explain why one is exiled and that one is entitled to compensation for land left behind (and that one is not exempt from service in the army), and to sell one's property, etc.'

↑ Light blue cathedral, photo Mary E.M.

Back on board the ship, people were not happy, one found that the museum guide should have given the floor to our accompanying Mennonite historian. Lunch was salad and soup, the table conversation was about borscht (beet soup). After lunch we had a get-together on the fourth floor of the ship: a saloon lustred by small glass-beaded lamps, a kind of gala party room with a dancing floor, now packed with rows of kitchen chairs.

Walter introduced us to the Mennonite ship conductor who right away started to conduct a river hymn. It was number twenty-four in the book we got. 'Together' we sang several hymns. Having not been raised with hymn singing, I tried lip-synching. After this, the historian spoke about the Peter Braun archives in Odessa. This brought about some audible relief: finally some Mennonite presence in this city.

After singing one more hymn, the restaurant group 1, that I was assigned to, was herded into the music room. Here, an Odessa archivist had displayed the Peter Braun documents: long lists of names, drawings of inventions and houses, street plans. I also spotted many notes by Cornies about the Doukhobors and one document revealed that once a few Mennonites had refused to bow to a representative of the Tsar because they considered themselves his equals.*

*Later efforts to order copies from these papers failed.

In the afternoon, we went downtown, or rather up-town, as we had to climb the Potemkin-stairs again. In the shops we saw the latest fashions, such as Benetton, etc.. Everywhere old women were selling their handicrafts. One such little old lady, selling necklaces, told us in splendid French that she had been a surgeon until her retirement.

18 September: history lesson 1 – meeting Helena

One more walk through Odessa, and in the afternoon a lecture by the Mennonite ship historian titled *Power and Glory*. It was about the glorious Mennonite past: the paintings of Henry Pauls, the city of Ekaterinaslav, dignitaries such as Esau & Janzen & Bergman, the year 1840 when the Mennonites went to the Sea of Asov, the network of Russian bureaucracy, and also about a Mr. Friesen who had established the Alliantie Church in 1905.

The historian went on about the migrations to Poland, that became Prussia, and Catharine II's invitation. Whoever accepted her invitation got land and, tax and conscription exemptions. They were also free to travel, free in their religion, and enjoyed cultural autonomy. Cultural autonomy meant one *Oberschulze* - a colony boss - and a *Schulze* (the village head) for each settlement. In 1789 people went to Chortitza, a previous Cossack settlement, where about 89,000 acres had been made 'available.' In 1804 another 324,000 acres were added to the Molotschna settlement.

However, the historian continued, during Tsar Alexander's reign, around 1804, despite a new Russian territory being established on former Ottoman land, not much land remained. Craftsmen then became the preferred immigrants. While reformations in the Russian government took place, religious and civil schisms arose. The Russian government started to view itself as the government in the New [South] Russia, and wanted to get rid of the local autonomies - such as colony bosses and village heads.

By 1850 half of the Mennonite population was landless, and the landless were not allowed to vote. In 1860 Russia lost one or another war, which resulted in forced - alternative - conscription for the pacifists. After 1870, with the conscription privilege being removed, Mennonites started to vote with their feet: one third immigrated. Among remaining Mennonites splits occurred between the conservatives and progressives; in 1912 there were already nine groups. In 1914 the Mennonites had 300 million acres of land in South Russia, of which one third consisted out of about 500 estates.

The historian described the Mennonite social fabric: people working with silk, bricks, or tiles, in the banks, in social institutes such as schools, old-folks homes, and orphanages. From 1860, Mennonites started to study abroad in Moscow or in Zurich, published the *Odessa Zeiting* and also started to proselytize outside of Russia. In Russia, this was still forbidden.

The historian went on with a stern remark about the Mennonite identity, imitating nobility. He wondered aloud what this said about the simple life Mennonites are supposed to lead?

The lecture ended with one more knotty question: how much would the local [Russian] population have contributed to Mennonite wealth? Any questions?

A dark-haired woman stood up and said that she did not have a question but instead had a remark. She was visibly angry and said that she was not a Mennonite.

'We became serfs, while you, the Mennonites, negotiated with the Russian government. Why don't you call yourself Ukrainian Mennonites? You never lived in Russia.'

An uneasy silence fell over the audience.

The historian finally spoke: 'Back then it was Russia.'

Later Helena, the dark-haired woman, told me that her parents had been ordinary Ukrainians, that they had fled their country after WWII, and that she participated in this cruise because it had looked to her a simple and easy way to see her parents' land of origin. Also, her cousin, married to a Mennonite woman, was also aboard. So, Helena, her cousin, and myself were the only three non-Mennonite passengers.

I mentioned to Helena that when the Mennonites fled the Low Countries, the Spanish/Austrian emperors Charles V and Phillips II had been their rulers.

'Perhaps one can say, that the Russian Mennonites originate from Spain or from Austria?' Helena liked it. The Mennonites I confronted with this new identity option said they had never thought of it this way.

19 September: history lesson 2 and 3

The second lecture was titled *Pathos and Tragedy*. A slide showed the German army in South Russia during WWII. Their arrival in 1914 had been a joyous moment for the Mennonites: the Halbstadters had enthusiastically welcomed them because of their cultural affinity and because they did not like the Bolsheviks. But then Russian nationalism emerged.

The lecture went on, back in time, about the October Revolution of 1917: citizens became targets, politicians showed gangster behaviour, and other global relationships arose. A century of violence was on the rise - what else is new?

The Mennonites established *Selbschutz*-unities to fence off the Red Army, but in 1919 the Germans had to withdraw.

↑ Entrance harbour of Sebastopol, photo Mary E.M.

Self-defence was left to the Mennonite colonies themselves. This did not prevent Nestor Makhno and his band of 15,000 men killing 200 Mennonites in Zagradovka, twenty in Blumenthal, and eighty in Eichenfelt. The historian went on to say that the Mennonites lost about 5000 of their people during the revolution, that 1000 people had suffered from typhus, 100 girls got syphilis, 2000 horses and 1400 cows had 'lost their lives.' Further material damage amounted to 3291000 *rubles*.

Between 1917 and 1921 nine million people had lost their lives. Among these were 10000 Mennonites (about 10% of all Germans in Russia). Initially, they had identified with the Germans, and later associated with the White-Russians. The historian cited from Kroeger's *Hard Passage* that in 1919 the *Verband der Bürger Holländischen Herkunft (Union of Citizens of Dutch Origin)* was formed in South Russia; once again people studied the possibilities of migrating to America. Further, the Mennonite Central Committee (MCC), which had been founded in 1920 in the US, had fed about 40,000 Mennonites and other Russian villagers at about 140 field-kitchens and churches during 1922-1923.

The historian continued about the years 1922 to 1928. A limited ownership had been allowed in Soviet Russia, but was followed in 1928 by collectivization and de-*kulak*-ization: three to five percent of the population was *kulak*, or owner of an estate or a factory. Collectivization entailed that 250,000 collective farms were founded. From 1932 to 1933 between five and ten million people died of famine. Then, in 1941 Germany declared war on Soviet Russia, and the Mennonites enthusiastically welcomed the Wehrmacht. Having arrived at this point in time, the historian let escape a sigh.

In 1943 the Germans were beaten back, and the remaining Mennonites, along with Tatars and Chechnyans, were all treated to a one-way ticket east to Siberia.

That same day, the 19th of September, we were still docked in the harbour of Odessa, and were treated to one more eclectic history class. This time about the Scythians, the Golden Horde of 1453, Russians being kicked out of the Ukraine in 1991, Tatars returning to the Crimea, and Mennonite settlements on the Crimea.

↑ Interior of Tatar palace, photo Mary E.M.

'If these places had memories, they would remember us, and would welcome us,' the historian said wistfully.

Afterwards one of my fellow travellers said that the Mennonites should buy the Crimea and 'we should all go back there, establish a Mennonite state.' I asked him whether he thought that the Mennonites would then be necessitated to establish an army, as soil- and oil-rich countries are prone to predators. It had not crossed his mind, he said.

20 September: Sebastopol and Yalta

After dinner on the 19th, our riverboat left Odessa for Sebastopol across the Black Sea. Moaning and groaning, the ship cleft the wuthering waves through a severe storm. Jellyfish must have been floating to and fro on the black waves-swept decks. A sleepless night passed.

The next morning brought beautiful weather, a flat sea, and Sebastopol's harbour in sight. Only by passing a fort, with numerous protruding canons inviting one to return as soon as possible, this harbour can be entered.

Our ship manoeuvred into this small, natural harbour; its quay lined with pretty restaurants, and a welcoming brass band playing. Immediately after breakfast we boarded a bus. During the most beautiful tour of my life, I could hardly keep my eyes open because of the previous night. Along the way we stopped in Alupta at Count Woronsky's castle and the *dacha* of former president Gorbachov was pointed out. According to the local bus guide, Gorbachov could have chosen to be happy with the *dacha* in Yalta, but, no, he wanted a *dacha* in a secluded area - and now he is no longer president. Something like *good for him* resounded in the guide's voice.

Once in Yalta, we enjoyed an elaborate lunch, peppered with table conversation about kidney dialysis, aunts, and other sores. Hannah and I left early, and strolled for an hour along the boulevard where pathways were being hit by waves. Children warmed their backs on the asphalt while enjoying the spray. On the way back to Sebastopol, we visited the palace of Tsar Nicolas II used by Stalin, Roosevelt and Churchill to sign the 1945 Peace Treaty. One room showed a large photograph of a servant preparing Churchill's bed. Along the road many people were selling ridiculously cheap and extremely good grapes.

After dinner we went to a performance of Russian sailors stationed in a neighbouring little harbour. They were humorous, energetic, athletic, strong voiced, and had impressive calves.

Afterwards, in a pub I had a chat with the dark-haired Helena about nationality and identity. Later a few of the Mennonites joined us. Helena and I continued our discussion:

'Welcoming the invading Germans as friends! How strange is it that you people were deported all the way to Siberia?' I ventured.

'We look after our own interests first. That is our faith. We are sinners.'

21 September: Balaclava

The next day, during the bus tour to Balaclava, location of the infamous 1853-1856 Crimean battles, the local guide talked about the Lenin statue and the Lenin Street we passed. According to the guide, the statue had not been, and would not be, destroyed since it was too expensive to melt all the iron and people still liked Lenin.

In Balaclava we were presented with a beautiful plain full of vine-yards surrounded by higher plateaus. Our guide told us that in 1853 Balaclava was crowded with French, English, Turks, and Sardinians fighting the Russians because the English did not want the Russians to export their grain through the Bosporus (their only seaway).*

Across from the small Balaclava harbour, towered a mountainous wall. The guide whispered that this mountain contained seven more Russian submarines and said in a louder voice that the convent where Florence Nightingale once resided was located behind that mountain side.

Back aboard for lunch, my tablemates asked why I was on this trip. I told them how I had become interested in Mennonite, Hutterite, and Doukhobor history; particularly in the 19th century when the three groups had simultaneously shared a sojourn in south Russia. My explanation did not go over well. They shouted that 'the Doukhobors are such a

* This war inspired Tolstoy to write *The Cossacks*.

small group and look how they behaved in Canada. Arson! Nudity!'

I pointed out that their own Cornies had had an interest, and written about them as well. But this only added to the unease at the table, and evoked more snorting. I was left with the impression that I had been dining with a few moose heads.

22 September: Tatar palace and Kersonesus

In the morning we took off on a bus tour to a Tatar palace housing splendid art, tasteful interior decoration, carpets, carved woodwork & marble, and no shortage of fountains. This palace had been spared while most or all (?) others were destroyed to make room for 'civilization.' In front of the palace the locals conducted a thriving business: postcards, Turkish clothes, bracelets, wooden combs, and embroidered table linens..

We went on to Kersonesus, a Greek settlement dating from 400-500 BC, located right on a splendidly coloured sea, a short distance from Sebastopol. Around the year 1300 the Greeks had been driven away by the Golden Horde, who in turn were driven away by Catharine II. The former settlement is now surrounded by a monastery and a church, features of later civili-, rather 'religizations'

That night we left Sebastopol to set sail for the Dnieper River. Instead of evening prayers people sang hymns again. The conductor told us that on the 24th of September, when the Mennonite centre in Halbstadt was going to be opened, we were supposed to walk, singing loudly, in a procession through the village. During supper I wondered aloud whether 'we, eh, the Mennonites, would not come across as Irish Orangemen.' My table companions looked at me, bewildered. An older table companion urgently asked the waitress whether any more white bread was left and addressed his wife: 'Oh dear, can you believe it. The white is gone first again.'

23 September: sailing the Dnieper and history lesson 4

During breakfast, the Mennonite Brotherhood of Twelve in Vancouver was discussed at our table. At 10:00 a.m. we were treated to another history lecture. Upon entering the crowded

↑ Ruins of a Greek settlement, photo Mary E.M.

room on the fourth floor, Helena and I saw that the choir, which had been practicing for the upcoming Halbstadt event, was still busy singing and stamping their left and right feet. We and the few people that entered with us were invited to participate in the stamping and singing and so we ended up parading on the spot, singing *We are Marching to Zion*.

The lecture was on the interpretation of the difference between the glory and the descent as explained in lectures one and two. According to the historian, 'irony is the prism that looks at the evolution of a society by measuring the plans of the people and the consequences it has or had.' I looked around me to check whether the audience agreed; but most of them were nodding, perhaps tired by marching on the spot to *Zion*.

The irony of going to Russia in the 1870's was that the Mennonites wanted to settle there permanently, but in the end were forced to migrate again. An earlier irony occurred in Germany, where the Mennonites at first kept to their Dutchness, while in 1772 the Poland born Mennonites chose to identify with the Germans. The fact that they had been holding on to German identity later caused their disappearance from Russian soil.

In 1911 about six percent of the 'German' population in Russia, Lutherans and Catholics included, was in possession of twenty percent of the land. No wonder, the historian added, that after the revolution the Russian population perceived these Germans as enemies, despising them for being both religious and German. The historian omitted to add that the 'Germans' did not want to speak Russian, did not intermarry with the Russians, and only saw them as cheap labour - had he added this, no one would have noticed since his audience was still nodding.

He now continued about the population in South Russia: during the 16th century the Slavs had developed a kind of Ukrainian national conscience. In 1649 an independent Tatar state was established in the area, and from 1764 it was part of the Russian empire. The Ukrainians were referred to as Little Russians. On Mennonite immigration he noted that about 18,000 Mennonites had left Russia around 1870, about 20,000 in 1920, about 12,000 in 1943, and some 105,000 in 1972.

↑ Children's' choir, photo Mary E.M.

Subsequently he dealt with the possible return of the Mennonites to Ukraine. Since 1994 there had been a Mennonite Church in Zaprozhye* and in 1998 something was established in Peterhagen. Now, in 2001, we would participate in the opening of a Mennonite centre in Halbstadt. The need for a centre was justified by, 'a need for a new moral and civic order.' The historian said to have learned about this need for 'a new order' from discussions with his fellow Evangelists.

* Whose pastor put his daughter's clothes in my suitcase.

'Why don't you come back?' they had asked him. 'Because of the history you have occasions and obligations.'[51]

The historian subsequently confronted his audience with questions such as: What is a Mennonite? Does it have to do with religion or is it a cultural thing? Does it consist out of values or out of habits? He compared these options with questions about Jewish identity: there are religious Jews and cultural Jews.

The long lecture invited not only for heavy nodding, but also to glance once in a while outside. I saw that we had arrived at the delta of the Dnieper, a very broad river lined or laced by golden beaches with in the flow itself numerous islands. In the end Walter cut the historian's lecture short

---

51 Later, on August 3, 2006, the website of the Government of Canada issued an article: 'ALERT: Mennonite Land Restitution Plan in Ukraine. The Department of Foreign Affairs has been informed of a land restitution and development plan in Ukraine, to which Ukrainian Canadians are being asked to contribute money. The plan involves lobbying the Ukrainian Parliament to consider a "restitution" bill for the return of land confiscated from Mennonites under the former Soviet regime. The company initiating the plan proposes to act as "corporate owner/steward" of these lands, rather than seeking their full restitution to the previous owners or their successors.'

The company has provided the names of three Ukrainian officials to validate its activities in Ukraine, inquiries with these individuals by the Canadian Embassy in Kyiv have found general support for the company's objective of becoming an active investor in Ukraine's economic development, but no support for a restitution bill.

The right of land ownership is a divisive issue in Ukraine. Ukraine's Land Code strictly prohibits foreign citizens, legal entitles, and governments from acquiring agro-industrial lands. The issue of restitution of property confiscated by the Soviet regime is also a sensitive issue. It would appear that only recognized religious organizations have been successful with claims, primarily in the recovery of places of worship.

The Government of Canada strongly advises that those interested in ventures to initiate land restitution in Ukraine to proceed with extreme caution.

↑ Getting entrance? photo Mary E.M.

by barking: 'Mennonites are cosmopolitans; they are partly religious, mostly cultural! Questions?'

Someone asked: 'But when we evangelize, do we have to do it with religious or with cultural Mennonites?'*

Later on the day we boarded a much smaller ship, and sailed along smaller and smaller branches of the Dnieper. The tour ended in a visit to a small fishing community where we enjoyed a marvellous meal spread out over several backyards. We were encouraged by the locals to drink as much vodka as we could. I don't remember returning to the ship, but must have made it somehow.

24 September: gala in Halbstadt

When we woke up, we were docked in Zaparohozhy, literally translated as *Behind the Channels*. With four buses we went across a bridge to the town of Rosenthal on the island of Chortitza. There we were shown an empty school where the first Mennonite Church had been built, and moved on to a former Mennonite school where we were supposed to leave our crayons.

We were received by dancing people, presumably teachers and parents, and a performing children's choir. Standing in a half circle, we watched the children sing *I like to ride my Bike, Old Macdonald has a Farm*, and so on. Behind me our organizers discussed how to get into the school to meet its headmaster. The goal of meeting with him was perhaps to make sure that the next generation of Ukrainian children would sing *I Like Jesus* and *Old MacJoseph has a Son*. The headmaster did not show up. He had it known that our gifts could be left at the doorstep. One young teacher busied himself carrying the crayons inside.

After the dances and the songs, we were invited to stroll along the stalls where the school children handed out apples, pears, and tomatoes. A little boy handed me a hand carved, wooden eagle. A girl held out a loaf of bread sprinkled with salt from which we could take a piece, a hospitality gesture that reminded of the table with salt, bread and water in the Doukhobor centre in Grand Forks.

On we went, now to Schönwies, a village founded between 1793 and 1796 by Frisians from Prussia. On the way we passed

---

* Imagination got a hold of me, forgetting to scribble down the answer, I pictured converted Africans eating borscht and wondered which indigenous spirituality they would have had to trade in for that recipe.

↑ Stalls at the school, photo Mary E.M.

a former Mennonite church, recently renovated and used again as a Mennonite church. Our local guide commented: 'The orthodox priest complained that they took away his people.'

We went on to Halbstadt. The road was intermittently lined with small houses with fenced front yards. Between the road and the yards were large strips of grass with flapping poultry, little goats running in circles around the poles they were tied to. Small cows chewed undisturbed by the dust and blasts of air our busses threw up.

We de-boarded at a little square in front of the Halbstadt town hall in the midst of a crowd of at least one thousand people. The entire village and its surroundings had gotten the day off. Everyone wore the badge of the future Mennonite Centre; children held on to stringed balloons featuring the same light-blue Mennonite Centre logo.

Fortunately, the crowd was too dense for our group to de-board from the four busses, line up, march in close rows, while singing loudly, to the centre. In stead, after some confusion everyone walked to the Mennonite Centre that would be opened that afternoon. Again I felt that togetherness - walking in a crowd, no idea where we going: just trust the throng! On this occasion the throng was headed by mounted Cossacks, militant looking guys, dressed in wide, billowing silk pants and shirts. After a few hundred meters we arrived at our destination.

It was a small building, a former school, with a newly-built deck crowded with dignitaries: among them the ambassadors of Canada and Ukraine (which I recognized from our previous meeting in my Calgary basement), the pastor who had put his daughter's clothes in my suitcase, Walter, and the Mennonite ship scholars such as the historian, the conductor, and the architect. Furthermore an Orthodox priest, the mayor of Halbstadt, members of MCC, and many more. The villagers and the bus people were ushered to the sand-strewn front yard at the front of the building.

The entire program, consisting of twenty-four parts, was executed in English and in Ukrainian, so actually we had to stand on our two legs for 48 parts, which took three hours.

'We are back,' Walter hollered at the crowd. 'We are not here to give you another belief, we are here to strengthen your belief.'

The crowd looked up to the dignitaries. Wondering why he thought that their belief needed enforcement? The dignitaries on the deck, which was one foot higher than the people standing in the sand, praised each other sky-high. Down below there were no chairs, nothing to drink, and no washrooms except for (as I later heard) an extremely filthy outhouse: Gala in Halbstadt!

After the dignitaries thought they had praised one another sufficiently, they graciously descended and lead the crowd down the street. We passed an enormous, neglected mansion with an addition so big, that it made the mansion look small. It had been serving as a ballroom.

'It used to belong to the Wilms family,' someone remarked. 'But then it was well-maintained.'

We ended up at a large field where the crowd formed a circle with one opening. Mounted Cossacks drove into and out of the circle: they stood on their horses, they stood on each other on the horses, and they hung like saddlebags upside down from the sides of the snorting, galloping animals. Very impressive!

Back in the bus a lively discussion arose about the gala event. A soft-spoken seventy-nine year old retired nurse told me about her parents that had owned an estate in Ukraine. They had married in 1922 and arrived in Canada in 1929. Her maternal grandparents had not come along; they had waited until their sons were back from forestry service. When they had finally returned, it had been too late for them to immigrate. After having been imprisoned they were exiled to Kazakhstan.

That night during dinner at the ship our table companions said that they were missionaries. We ate in silence.

25 September: schools, churchyards, and freedom cellars

At breakfast Walter offered apologies. The program had run on because everything had to be bi-lingual. They must only have found that out on the spot. I asked whether there was any more brown bread left, and then we boarded the bus for a rough ride. The local guide told us that in 1789 twelve families had gone to Chortitza, and that in 1916 all churches were confiscated. Driving along the Dnieper through Nieder-Chortitza to Krohnstahl, we learned about the problems of long ago: too many people had arrived, there was not enough land, and the members of the Flemish church, mainly weavers, had kept to their own.

En route we stopped to see a churchyard with the corrugated head stone of some Mr. Rempel. Everywhere sand paths and rectangular houses with the short sides facing the street. And everywhere fruit trees in the front yards. Once upon a (Mennonite, I guess) time, planting fruit trees was required by law. There were also vineyards and watermelons. Geese, chickens and goats roamed everywhere, and once in a while we passed small family autos brim-full of white bags of potatoes (or something). According to the guide, the average income was $50 per month, meat cost $6 per kilogram and one kilogram of bread one *grievna* - equivalent to 20 cents.

Later, in the village of Schönberg, people took pictures of their ancestors' houses. At a crossing, a whole family was seated in front of a barn-like building. Upon seeing us, they waved and ran towards us, said that they were Chechnyan refugees. Never have I seen such poverty-stricken, poor looking, and worn-out people. We all searched our purses, bags, and pockets and gave them whatever we could find: crayons, pencils, notebooks, money, baseball caps, travel wipes, and so on.

In the next village, Krohnstahl, we saw the Rempel factory. In Oisterwijk we were shown the *Zentral Schule*, long ago a school for Mennonite children only. The Ukrainian headmaster, with friendly eyes behind thick glasses, allowed us inside and showed us around. It was a poor looking school, but with children looking very well taken care of. Behind me someone wondered out loud 'How Would We Do If The Stock Market Were To Collapse?'*

We went on, this time to a former Mennonite school in Schönhorst now serving as a community hall. Along the road were trees, their branches heavy with elderberries and plums. After driving on for quite a while through no one's land, we

* Good question! In 2009, the stock market has collapsed.

↑ School children, photo Mary E.M.

ended up at a big factory next to a big house, which was next to an even larger house.

'That was my grandfather's house,' said someone.

We walked around the factory. At the back we met a woman who gave us permission to look inside. She switched on a light in the space now used as storage for tractor parts.

'First my grandparents built this [smaller] house, and then that house,' our travel companion explained.

Upon entering a room, once the living room, we met with four unkempt men and one woman who were wolfing down big, steaming bowls of borscht. Still to go were bowls of steaming hot porridge. We went upstairs, to the former bedrooms, still used as bedrooms: rusty bedsteads covered with rags and the workers' belongings dangling from big nails driven into the walls.

'A real labourers' paradise,' someone remarked.*

We went on to Neuendorp. From the schoolyard there we had a splendid view over a very wide valley. The parents of one of the members of our group had left this village in 1943. When the Germans got there in 1941, they had not bothered these parents, but when the Russians returned in '43, they were bothered. Only much later, only after our visit to Kiev I started to understand the reasons.

Back on the busses. Through the intercom it was suggested that we should not finish our entire lunch box, but instead hand out everything we did not eat to the locals. This suggestion inspired someone to tell a joke:

> Once a Ukrainian had an accident and needed blood. His neighbour, a Mennonite, donated blood. Out of gratitude the Ukrainian gave him a truck. He then had another accident. His neighbour donated blood again and now the Ukrainian gave him a grass mower. He then had a third accident and the Mennonite donated blood again. The Ukrainian gave him a six-pack of Coca Cola. The Mennonite asked him why he now only got such a small present. 'I have gotten too much of your blood,' said the Ukrainian.

We arrived in Franzfeld. The Mennonite church and the school were still around. Inside a woman was mopping up the

---

* Sandra Birdsell describes in *The Russlander* how, after the picking season, the estate owners closed the doors of the labourers' sleeping quarters and people had to sleep in the ditches along the road. Perhaps, in hindsight, we did see a labourers' paradise.

↑ Grandfather's house, photo Mary E.M.

floor, she told us that the school had 119 children. On we went, this time to a mass grave in Eichenfeld. A bit further down the road we saw a statue of Jacob Dijck: a tent preacher who was hacked to pieces by the Nazi's for reasons unknown.

The next village, Kronsweide, no longer had any Mennohouses. Driving back to the ship, we drove past Einlage where the road was lined with big buildings resembling holiday colonies.

'Pioneers camps,' the local guide said. 'During the Soviet period, youngsters between ten and sixteen spent their holidays here, from June until the end of August.'

We saw small children playing in front of a few buildings.

'It is now a boarding school for sick children,' he added.

Lots of new houses had been started along the road, but as far as we could see the construction had stopped a while ago - so lots of half-built houses.

'Such projects are abandoned, because there is not enough money,' the guide duly explained. This explanation was met in the bus with some howls. 'Not to have money to finish a job' would not happen to the howlers.

At the end of the trip we came past a valley full of *dacha's,* very small weekend houses with little gardens. The local plan is that all these *dacha's* will make room for high-rise apartment buildings. The guide explained that eastern European planners find ten-storey apartments, close to industrial areas, ideal housing. It saves time, fuel, and money and it only requires a bicycle to get to work. She went on to say that the government wanted more apartments, but that the population was not growing. 'More people die than are born and then there is immigration. You can buy an apartment for $5000 but then you still have to pay rent, and after you die, you can leave it to your heirs.'

In the meantime, we had seen very many ten-storey apartments. Outside, in the surrounding grass fields along the roads were half-open wooden lids everywhere, covering underground cellars. The guide told us that these outside cellars 'were now allowed. We are now free. The communists did not allow it.'

These cellars function as storage for the fruit and vegetables people grow at their *dacha's*. Inside the apartments there is either no room, or it is too hot, or people do not have refrigerators.

26 September: a gala outhouse

We toured the newer, or later colonies, Gruenfeld and Steinfeld, which villages were established as late as 1874. Along the road were groups of five white buildings close to one another: the remainders of *kolkhozes,* collective farms. Currently the land is leased to anyone. As I understood from the local guide, people are now paid with a part of the harvest (which explained the many people trying to sell fruits and vegetables along the roads). My impression was that this economy lacked somebody such as Cornies: somebody who would buy the produce to sell it in the city.

Neu-Chortitza no longer has a church, just one house dating from 1911. Gnadenthal had one school on the shore of a big, new lake, which, according to one of the travellers was not around in 1940. An old man came out of that one school. He told us that he had been wandering around during the war and had found this building vacant. He had moved in and still occupied it.

In Gruenfeld stood an old Orthodox church, renovated with Mennonite money. An elderly woman let us into the church and said, matter of fact, that the previous priest was still in prison. Inside the text of a memorial sign read that against the outer wall of this church seventeen soldiers were buried. It was signed with a Mennonite name, which irritated one of the Mennonite dignitaries in the bus. He announced, through the intercom: 'That sign is hung there by somebody with a Mennonite name. His name is on that sign, but MCC does not know about this. I will do something about it.'

The next stop was in Deviadoso. We strolled a while along the railway tracks until we, fortunately, saw a green outhouse. The lack of a door, toilet paper, or a latch no longer bothered us; at least it was quite a clean outhouse, almost a gala outhouse.

In 1943, the remaining Mennonites were deported from this station to Siberia. Around me people were telling stories that en route to Siberia the trains sometimes had stopped, a sliding door was opened, and a whole wagon load of

Mennonites had been left free to go, often never to be heard from again. Frozen by King Winter and/or eaten by King Wolf?

27 September: sight-seeing and preaching to a pastor

Breakfast was not very busy. Most passengers were already *en route* to the big estates – among these the former Cornies estates. Someone remarked that the previous day it had crossed his mind that 'the war had been a good thing because otherwise we would still be living in these villages.'

With a few passengers we strolled around in Zaporozhye, an industrial city with beautiful beaches at the banks of the Dnieper. The former Cossack island, Chortitza, was nearby in the middle of the river. In the streets every few meters a woman was seated on a small stool in front of a little chest with a bowl of peanuts or a few melons for sale. At around 4 p.m. we arrived at an open-air market. The vendors were busy packing everything at the end of the day: stockings, shoes, cleaning liquids, vegetables, fruits, shoe polish, flour, cookies, socks, scarves, and etcetera. How much time, energy, gas, and money is wasted daily because the stalls lacked doors and roofs.

That evening we went with about twenty to a ceremony at the University of Zaporzhye where grants were handed out to students who had focused on Mennonite studies.

'From 1991 on it is possible to explore the past,' one of our ship scholars said, 'History includes all the people, also the Mennonites.'

The Ukrainian speakers, the con-rector and a history professor of the Zaparorzhye University spoke briefly. That changed when our historian took the mike. He began, 'We are here as guests, but not as strangers.' A long while later he said that 'Mennonite history is very well documented,' going on saying that 'young students are promising, but can't fulfil their promise because of a slow economy.' Finally, we listened to an overview how the Mennonite grants are spent: archives, publications, and study grants.

After the historian, a Mennonite Central Committee (MCC) representative took the floor and talked just as long as he had on the deck in Halbstadt, again not really saying anything.

↑ Outhouse at Deviadoso, photo Mary E.M.

The students then thanked the MCC for their support, expressed their hope that the MCC would continue its support, and stressed that it was important for Ukrainian students to study the history of groups and minorities. Subsequently the mike went back to our historian, who appeared to be a member of the MCC board and the grant selection committee as well. He said that the studies, for which the students had received grants, had to do with Mennonite industrialization and its influences, Evangelical developments in Russia, the Mennonite population between 1850 and 1917, the social-political life of the Germans and the Mennonites in south Ukraine, and also with library studies. Thereafter, the students were given the opportunity to give thanks again and pose for the camera while signing documents.

There had been no occasion for us, admiring audience, to ask any questions. On the way back to the ship a fellow-passenger and I wondered how many people had applied for a grant and on what criteria the selections had been based. Somehow there never seemed to be an opportunity to speak to one of the ship-scholars.

Back at the ship, the local Mennonite pastor (who had put his daughter's clothes in my suitcase back in Calgary), sitting on a couch near the third floor dining room, stood up and asked me how I was doing.

'Fine,' I said hurriedly. The twenty people and I were heading for a very late dinner. The pastor looked hurt. I repeated 'Fine, and how are you? And thanks for asking,' and walked on.

'I want to talk with you,' he said after me. 'Please sit down.'

I let go of the idea of dinner, and sat down.

'What do you think?' he asked.

'Good weather, nice beaches, excellent food, interesting trips.'

'What do you really think,' he pressured.

'Top-down-organization. The passengers have their own looking-for-their-roots agenda, but the travel organizers' is a different one. They are very busy evangelizing through the presence of the passengers. The travel organizers talked about a new civil and moral order for three hours in . . . eh . . . Halbstadt to a number of dignitaries on a deck while the crowd stood there staring up at them. What is new and civil

↑ Baba statue, photo Mary E.M.

about such order? Anyway, it is good that nothing was served there, because what I heard about that out-house would have troubled me very much to go there. My new order would start with. . . ' and so I went on, realizing that I had become an evangelist.

I went on though. 'Evangelization? The Ukrainians have currently been independent for ten years: why estrange sons and daughters from their parents, and wives from their husbands, and husbands from their wives? Why is it necessary to convince them that children should not be baptized and that they should consider Jesus as their Saviour? Do Ukrainians really need domestic upheavals?'[52]

Strangely enough the pastor agreed with me. Or at least, he nodded and asked me why I did not talk to the travel dignitaries.

'I am here to look and to listen, not to talk.' I preached.

The pastor still urged me to talk to the travel organizers, but I did not. Even if I had wanted to, there would not have been a suitable occasion: most of the time the travel organizers and ship scholars socialized among themselves. The one time I did approach Walter with a question, he had said that 'that day he already answered three questions.'

Dinner was served for me even later (excellent service on that ship!), and again was very good.

28 September: the room in the museum.

After breakfast, we went to Dnieperpetrov, previously called Jekaterinaslav. This town was more of a city, and more prosperous, than Zaporozhy: no more melon- or peanut-selling women were to be seen. We saw the Astoria hotel, Machno's 1919 headquarters. We saw a former KGB building.

---

52 Later, back home I got an e-mail: 'Have a look at: www.mennonitecentre.com "We will do the tea and light food Tuesdays and Fridays but plan by next week to use the space for a drop-in, warm up and reading room on the other days 11-2. On Sat. Dec. 1 we will start an English club (teens-10 and 11 course level) and perhaps also a German club, helped by Marina, a local German teacher. Andrei Utkin, our youth worker, has been showing a video on drug abuse awareness at the high school level and will lead a young people's recreation and religious discussion group starting within two weeks. We are all pretty high right now." Warmest regards.' (Note: In January 2010 this website was no longer functional.)

Stories swirled in the bus about aunts and uncles who had disappeared in that building never to appear again. One traveller ventured out of the bus to photograph the building. Uniformed guards looked on. Times have changed!

Next was a visit to the Historical Museum. Outside were many statues with heads on long torsos with stylized arms holding bowls of milk in front of their bellies. These are the Baba statues of the Polovski, a group that lived in this area between 1000-1300.[53]

We only visited one room. In its' centre was a huge pyramid of 15×15×15 cm blocks. The visible sides of the blocks were covered with photographs of the men that had perished between 1930-1945. In front of each photograph a candle was burning. A number of sides were still unused. Also, the walls, floor, and ceiling of the room were black and also covered with collages of photographs of people being murdered. The murderers were partly covered by a big, white strip of material emblazoned with the number 20,000,000 - the number of people that died between 1930 and 1945 in Soviet Russia.*

In one photograph Nestor Machno stood between two officers; he hardly reached their shoulders. He was a small guy, just like Napoleon or Hitler. Someone laid a few wild flowers in front of a photograph of a Mennonite. By the time we left, the guard had already thrown them out

That evening we enjoyed a share-and-tell evening. A few people had been asked in advance to share their cruise experiences so far. 'Roots stories' ensued about found homes & the feelings when these were found, the poverty experienced before coming to Canada & know-how regarding tomatoes and potatoes.

* I was quite confident that current and future world leaders would know their way with these unused sides: between 2001 and 12 December 2010, 7010 soldiers have officially died in Iraq and Afghanistan, not to mention the hundred of thousands civilians.

After this, I also realized why the 2750 dead on 9/11 failed to make much impact on the Ukrainian front pages.

---

53 It reminded me of Von Haxthausen's account in of these statues *The Russian Empire II*, which had different forms and shapes, but had the same origin. When he visited the Governor in Ekaterinoslaf he inquired about these statues and '[the governor] told me that his predecessor had brought two of them from Kurgans in the neighbourhood of his garden where they lay. . … They are cut out of sandstone [and] the limbs … [rest] upon a sort of pedestal. [The] naked [bodies have a] female character, [either with] no breasts or pendant breasts . … . The first writer hitherto known to mention them is Ammianus Marcellinus, who in his description of the Huns says, "they have singular forms, and might be mistaken for beasts walking upon two legs, or for those roughly hewn columns in human form, which are seen on the shores of the Pontus Euxinus."'

Galyna, one of the Ukrainian travel guides, talked about what it was like to live in the current Ukraine. She had come along on the trips to the rural areas and was 'shocked to see how Ukrainians in rural areas still live. Old people get eighty *grievna's* per month, and one *grievna* equals twenty cents on the dollar.'

Walter later expressed concern about her story. He worried about how it would have come across to the cruisers. Indeed a good question, how did Galyna's story come across? I heard at least a few say again that they were thankful for WWII because it had lead to them not living there any more.

Where the Mennonites once had thrived, the native population was, and is now poor. For these rural people, their life earnings will not match the money we each spent on our trip.

29 September: we're all family now

We enjoyed a lecture by the ship genealogist about genealogy software. Amazing what mankind is capable of! As amazing to see how much some people cling to their roots. The genealogist spoke about 'our grandparents who came from Holland and Germany,' and showed a few examples. Among them was Cornies who had been married to Aganetha Klassen. How can you find out whether you are related to Aganetha Klassen? Some magic with the computer caused several passengers to jump up - they were related, five times removed, from this Aganetha!

30 September: Kiev at last

An efficient system of rotating restaurant groups ensured new table-companions each day. During breakfast a table companion told us about his cousin who had recently emigrated from Siberia to Germany.

'I invited him to come down to Canada and visit. When we sat down for dinner, he insisted that we pray standing up. I told him: "When I stay at your place, I will pray standing up. In my house you can pray standing up, but I pray while being seated."'

That evening slides were shown about another 'roots journey,' this one a bus tour from the Netherlands to Poland. The University of Amsterdam has many Mennonite documents.

A Mennonite *(Singel)* Church was established in Amsterdam in 1639, one in Westzaan in 1647, and one in Edam in 1702. The church of Witmarsum, where Menno Simons originated, was first a catholic church. In Leeuwarden one can find the headstone of some Cornelia Martens. The remainder of the slides showed remnants of Menno Simon buildings in Gdansk, Montau, Christenfelt, and Orlov - all currently in Poland or in Prussia.

Walter took the mike and announced that the new centre in Halbstadt would not carry a fixed ideology. He went on about a 1999 memorial ceremony held in Nieder-Chortitza, and about some monument that will be unveiled in 2001. Walter wondered aloud whether Mennonites could make a difference. The historian added something about needy Russian archives, having to be fair, and having to work for another kind of society because 'our past gives us this opportunity.'

Next was the Mennonite architect who I had already met in the bar while he was organizing his slides. One of them showed a caption saying that 'we finalyze [sic]' this or that. I pointed out that 'finalyze' should be written with an *i* instead of with a *y*. 'I always write it with an *y*,' he said. *

The architect's slides showed an apartment building, a nursing home, a Mennonite church, a thrift shop, and a day-care, all under construction. Our charity underwear, he noted, was going to be sold (so, not given away!) in the second-hand shop, and the profits would go to building the church.[54] During this lecture we were sailing upstream to Kiev. Again the gorgeous beaches lining or lacing the Dnieper could be seen sliding by.

That evening my table companion happened to be the Mennonite choir conductor. I inquired about his singing and

* Somewhere I read that Quakers have never succeeded in converting a Mennonite.

---

54 The whole event made me think of a few lines in the *History of the Hutterites* (a textbook for young Hutterites). Every chapter in this book ends with a section, *Difficult Words*. Page 49 deals with *Indulgences*. The meaning was supplied as 'people paid money to the Church for a slip of paper. The Church claimed that the payment of this money would excuse the purchaser from punishment for his sins. This practice of the Church was known as the selling of indulgences. The money was used to build costly cathedrals.' In this day and age it seems that churches are to be built with the help of my (and my friends') underwear.

marching practices aboard, and commented about us not having been able to march and to sing at the Halbstadt gala event.

'It is too bad; these Mennonites could have set a Orange precedent.' He looked at me and I explained how his activities reminded me of Ireland's singing and marching Orangemen. No, such association had never crossed his mind.

After arriving in Kiev, we visited some enormous onion-dome cathedrals, its entrances surrounded by beggars. A number of these churches had been rebuilt in the last ten years, as the Soviets had blown them up in the 1930's. According to our guide, the World Bank had provided the money for rebuilding. For some reason the World Bank had failed to fork out money for decent housing as well.

After having dealt with the beggars surrounding the entrance, I finally sat on a chair tucked away in a corner in some church, which looked more like a cathedral. For the occasion I was wearing a skirt, but, stupidly, I again sat cross-legged. An old lady approached me and scolded me for it. It made me feel at home; it was like being back in Calgary.

One more visit was to a very large complex of churches, convents, and underground tunnels in a mountainside.* We could only visit these tunnels with our (ladies') heads covered. Be-scarved as if visiting the Pope, we bought an admission ticket and had to buy a candle. We learned that long ago the Soviets had installed electric light in these tunnels, but the Ukrainians had removed it.

Along the tunnels were numerous shoulder-high niches containing coffins. The weather was quite chilly that day, and the many visitors, all carried burning candles, thronged through the tunnels, wore very bulky jackets and scarves. To top off this incendiary situation, we were occasionally rudely pushed aside by exalted Ukrainians throwing themselves against coffins to passionately kiss them.

Having survived this ordeal, back outside street cleaners near the surrounding monasteries were carefully sweeping up every leaf that had fallen from the trees. Two little girls with sores in their faces approached us, holding out their hands. Helena and I watched them as they walked away with a few of our dollars. Around the corner we saw two women check the hands of the girls and take the money. It reminded me of

---

* Sofia Tolstoy also visited these caves. In *My Life* she writes that she walked right behind a guide, an elderly monk. Everyone carried a lit wax candle. After a while she felt like suffocating. In the walls she saw openings where saints voluntarily had walled in themselves: "In these chambers they lived and died, and received food and water through these little openings."

what happened a few days ago, in Zaparovhye, when we gave some money to begging boys. An adult man had reproached us, 'Look what you are doing. You make beggars out of our children.' Damned if you do, damned if you don't.

Our next destination in Kiev was a park with a big war monument. Behind it was a small pathway along a ravine called Babi Yar. A guide told us that on 29 September 1941 the Jews of Kiev had been summoned to gather at this park. Upon arrival they were lined up in rows of five and had a bullet shot through their heads. According to the guide, one bullet can pierce five skulls. After that they were thrown in the ravine. This was how the Nazi's killed 77800 Jews and some Gypsies in just a few days.

Back home

Later back home in Calgary, I watched the video I had bought at the ship from the Ukrainian cameraman who had accompanied us. I enjoyed the splendid images of magnificent Ukraine and was moved by images of the passengers visiting, filming, and photographing the sites of their ancestors.

At the end of the film the screen turned black. Then suddenly, orange flames lit up the foreground. In the background people were moving about on a hillside. A closer look showed that they were throwing lifeless bodies down a very steep hillside. The bodies were trailed by something like burning logs rolling down to. Were these scenes from hell or from Babi Yar in September 1941?

Somehow questions kept popping up.

Conclusion
Answer 3

Pierre,   Calgary 2013

It's me again. I must say, despite me being against proselytizing, I enjoyed the trip. Ukraine is such a beautiful country and has so many troves of cultural treasures. Please find here my overall impression of how the Mennonites are doing, which I hope also answers your question about them.

> The Mennonites still exist and thrive. The Flemish-Frisian schism has become a historical footnote. New splits still occur as currently people just establish a church of their own, vote with their feet, and are no longer being slaughtered as in the good-old-days. The twelve largest Mennonite groups are:[55]

- Mennonite Brethren (300,000 members on 6 continents worldwide)
- Meserete Kristos Church in Ethiopia (120,600 members; 126,000 more followers attending alike churches)
- Mennonite Church USA with 114,000 members in the United States
- Brethren in Christ with 100,000 US and worldwide members
- Communauté Mennonite au Congo (87,000)
- Kanisa La Mennonite Tanzania with 50,000 members in 240 congregations
- Deutsche Mennonitengemeinden with 40,000 members in Germany
- Mennonite Church Canada with 35,000 members in Canada

---

55   See: en.wikipedia.org/wiki/Mennonitism#Schisms (Last accessed April 2013.)

- Conservative Mennonites with 30,000 members in over 500 US churches (2008 CLP church directory)
- Church of God in Christ, Mennonite with 21,765 members in about 19,000 in the US and Canada, with the remaining in members in 32 other countries (2008 data)
- Conservative Mennonite Conference, 11,557 members in North America, plus 33,336 affiliate members in 7 countries worldwide
- Beachy Amish Mennonite, including related Amish Mennonite subgroups, with 10,895 members (190 congregations) in 10 different countries.

As for the Mennonites in general, they help out at whatever humanitarian disaster occurs, by handing out 'Christian Food' and 'Christian Blankets.' At the same time they are not shy to proselytize in any other way, where and when possible, and they are still pacifists. Paradoxically, in many parts of the world proselytizing is a prelude to war, to persecution and killing.

In *40 Days and 40 Nights: Darwin, Intelligent Design, God, Oxy Contin, and Other Oddities on Trial in Pennsylvania*, Chapman phrases his thoughts about proselytizing: 'Even if Christian Evangelicals in America rarely commit violence, their arrogant faith and missionary zeal certainly provoke it.'

Well, that is harsh, but the introduction of another faith often happens to provoke wars.

Of course, proselytizing can be justified, and be seen as part of a grand scheme. One could argue, had there never been a religious war, the world would be overcrowded. In that case many more people would likely have died due lack of food or water, or because of fighting for these necessities. It is regrettable that the most vulnerable are lest capable to access the goods Mother Earth has to offer, and therefore the most open to conversion. They are often in the situation of having to accept food and blankets, free cookies and free lessons, and subsequently suffer most from the resulting struggle for life or religious upheavals. So far Pierre,

Signing off again, Mary. May 2013.

PS. One more thing before you or I die: being converted, evangelized, proselytized or orthodox caused the Hutterites, Mennonites and Doukhobors to flee Europe. Those now in the business of proselytizing, 'sharing the good news,' online evangelizing for God or Allah, will cause others to flee, convert, divide, move, quarrel or radicalize – that is how the world moves on, in circles. In April 2013 we saw in Boston how online evangelizing led to self-radicalization, to loss of life and many maimed limbs.

Bibliography

Aimard, Gustave. 1873. *Les Aventures de Michel Hartmann / Les Marquards.* Paris: E. Dentu.

Bakhuizen van den Brink, Jan Nicholas. 1960-62. *Documenta reformatoria: teksten uit de geschiedenis van kerk en theologie in de Nederlanden sedert de Hervorming.* Publisher s.n.

Bartel, Siegfried. 1994. *Living with Conviction: German Army Captain Turns to Cultivating Peace.* Winnipeg: CMBC Publications.

Bartsch, F. 1993. *Our Trek to Central Asia.* Transl. Elizabeth Peters and Gerhard Ens. Echo Historical Series / MCMBC Publications Manitoba Mennonite Historical Society.

Bieglschmid, U.J.F. 1947. *Das Klein-Geschichtsbuch der Hutterischen Brüder.* Philadephia: The Carl Schurz Memorial Foundation, Inc.,

Berleant-Schiller, Riva. 1999. 'Mahican-Moravian Mission Towns in Eighteenth-Century New York, Connecticut and Pennsylvania, 1740-1772.' In: *Yumtzilob* 11: 2, 145-60.

Chapman, M. 2007. *40 Days and 40 Nights: Darwin, Intelligent Design, God, Oxycontin and other Oddities on Trial in Pennsylavia.* New York: Collins.

Chernenkoff, Mike. (n.d.) 'The Very Truth surfacing.' In: *Assimilating the Doukhobors. Bonner's Method.* P. 7-8. Krestova. B. C.: Comp. Mike Chernenkoff.

——. 1999. 20 October. Letter to Mary E. M.

——. 1999. 8 November. To Mary E. M.

——. 2000. August. 'Premeditated Conspiracy over The Sons of Freedom.' In: *Istina* (17-20).

——. 2000. 15 August. To Mary E. M.

——. 2000. 10 September. To Mary E. M.

——. 2001. 16 January. To Mary E. M.

Chernoff, Michael M. 1982. Excerpt from *Russian Encyclopedia - 'Bolshaya Rooskaya Encyclopedia.'* In: *Symposium Meetings 1974-1982.* Comp. and transl. Eli A. Popoff. Castegar: The Centre for Russian and North American Studies and the President's Office, Selkirk College.

Decavele, Johan. 1975. *De Dageraad van de Reformatie in Vlaanderen (1520-1565) (The Dawn of the Reformation in Flanders [1520-1565]).* Brussel: Paleis der Academiën.

Dijck, J. 1967. Ed. *An Introduction to Mennonite History.* Pennsylvania: Herald Press.

Donskov, Andrew. 1998. *Sergey Tolstoy and the Doukhobors: a journey to Canada.* Com. Tat'jana Nikiforova. Trans. John Woodsworth. Ottawa. Slavic Research Group at the University of Ottawa & Moscow: State L.N. Tolstoy Museum.

Epp, F.H. 1974. *Mennonites in Canada: The History of a Separate People.* Toronto: Macmillan.

Epp, Jacob D.A. 1991. *A Mennonite in Russia: The diaries of Jacob D. Epp. 1851-1880.* Transl. and ed. Harvey L. Dyck. Toronto: University of Toronto Press.

Fretz, Joseph Winfield. 1962. *Immigrant Group Settlements in Paraguay.* Kansas: Bethel College North Newton.

Gemeente-archief Gorcum: Re: Pierre van Paassen. Letter of November 24, 2000.

Goldberg, B.Z. 1958 [1930] *The Sacred Fire: The Story of Sex in Religion.* New York: University Books.

Hawkes, John. 1924. *The Story of Saskatchewan and its People.* Volume II. Chicago-Regina: The S.J. Clarke Publishing Company.

Haxthausen-Abbenburg, August Franz Ludwig Maria, freiherr von. 1968. *The Russian Empire. Its people, institutions, and resources.* Vol. I and II. Transl. Robert Faire. Germany: Frank Cass & Co. Ltd. First published in 1847 as, *Studien über die innern Zustände, das Volksleben; und insbesondere die ländlichen Einrichtungen Russlands.*

Hofer, D. 1982 [1917]. *The Hutterian Brothers in the Military Prison on the Island of Alcatraz in the Bay of San Francisco (1917).* Transl. from Low German Karl and Franziska Peter, Vancouver. Cranford: Lakeside Hutterite Colony.

Hofer, S. 1991. *Born Hutterite.* Sioux Falls: Ex Machine Pub. Co.

Holt, Simma. 1963. 'SVOBODNIKI - Information from Simma HOLT.' www.canadianmysteries.ca/sites/verigin/suspects/peterverigin/1333en.html. Accessed July 2012.

———. 1964. *Terror in the Name of God: the Story of the Sons of Freedom Doukhobors.* McClelland and Stewart Limited, Toronto & Montreal.

Holzach, Michael. 1982. *Des Vergessene Volk: Ein Jahr bei den Deutschen Huttern in Kanada.* Hamburg: Deutscher Tachenbuch Verlag.

Homan, G.D. 1981/1982. 'Pierre van Paassen's Canadian Interlude.' In: *Canadian Journal of Netherlandic Studies.* Fall/Autumn, 1981.

Hoover, Peter. *The Secret of Strength: What Would the Anabaptists Tell This Generation?* Online: www.allgodsword.com/Sos

Inikova, A. Svetlana. 2000. 'Spiritual Origins and the Beginnings of Doukhobor History. In: *The Doukhobor Centenary in Canada.* Ed. Andrew Donskow, John Woodsworth and Chand Gaffield. Ottawa: Slavic Research Group / Institute of Canadian Studies at the University of Ottawa. (pp 1-21).

Jaenen, Cornelius. 1977. 'Missionary Approaches to Native Peoples.' In: *Approaches to Native History,* Ed. D.A. Muise. Ottawa: National Museums of Man, Mercury Series, History Division Paper No. 25, 5-15.

——. 2000. "Others' view the Doukhobors in Canada.' In *The Doukhobor Centenary in Canada.* Ed. Andrew Donskov, John Woodsworth and Chad Gaffield. Ottawa: Slavic Research Group, Institute of Canadian Studies: University of Ottawa. P. 103-13.

Janzen, R. & Stanton, M. 2010. *The Hutterites in North America.* Baltimore: The John Hopkins University Press.

Kirk, H.D. 1997. 'Hitler's Children and Ours: Two Tragic Footnotes to the Politics of Adoption.' Beverly Tansey Memorial Lecture. Lecture Congregation Emanu-El Synagogue, Victoria, B.C.

——. 2002. Ed. and E. Ephgrave *Israel: Democracy's Neglected Ally: 1943 to the Present.* Preface Shnuel Katz. Reprint of *The Forgotten Alley,* chapter 4.

Kirkby, Mary Ann. 2007. *I Am A Hutterite.* Polka Dot Press.

Kolesnikoff, James. 2000. 'Understanding Violent Behaviour: the 'Sons of Freedom.'' In: *The Doukhobor Centenary in Canada: A multi-disciplinary perspective on their unity and diversity.* P. 114-28. Ottawa: Slavic Research Group / Institute of Canadian Studies at the University of Ottawa

Konkin, Fenya. 1997. 'Oral presentation.' In: *Symposium Meetings, 1974-1982.* Comp. and transl. Eli A. Popoff. Castegar: The Centre for Russian and North American Studies and the President's Office, Selkirk College.

Kühler, W.J. 1961. *Geschiedenis der Nederlandsche Doopsgezinden in de Zestiende Eeuw (History of the Dutch Baptists in the Sixteenth Century).* 2nd ed. Haarlem: H.D. Tjeenk Willink & Zoon N.V.

Lavigne, Yves. 1987. *Hell's Angels: Taking Care of Business.* Toronto: Ballantyne Books.

Lee, Jason K. 'The Theology of John Smyth: Puritan, Separatist, Baptist, Anabaptist, Baptist, Mennonite.' In: *The Journal of Baptist Studies* 1.

Legebokoff, Peter Petrovitch. 1997. *Symposium Meetings 1974-1982.* Comp. and transl. Eli A. Popoff. Castegar: The Centre for Russian and North American Studies and the President's Office, Selkirk College.

Liepman, Heinz. 1959. *Rasputin and the Fall of Imperial Russia.* New York: Rolton House Inc..

Livanow, Fydor V. 1869. *Ostrozhniki I Rasskolniki (The Exiled and the Dissenters).* St. Petersburg: s.n.

Maude, Aylmer. 1904. *A Peculiar People: The Doukhobórs.* London: Grant Richards.

——. 1908. *The Life of Tolstoy: First Fifty Years.* Archibald Constable and Co., Ltd.

——. 1910. *The Life of Tolstoy: Later Years.* Constable and Company Ltd.

Mealing, M. 1982. 'Introduction.' In: *To America with the Doukhobors.* Sulerzhitsky, L.A.

Members of the Christian Community and Brotherhood of the Reformed Doukhobors in British Columbia, Canada. 1954. *An Open Letter-Appeal to the Society of Friends (Quakers).*

Murphy, P. Ed. 1996. *Hutterite CO's in World War One: Stories, Diary's and other accounts from the United States Military Camps.* USA: Spring Prairie Printing.

Olson, Nina. 2000. ''No foe, no show'; multiculturalism, the gentle assimilator.' In: *The Doukhobor Centenary in Canada.* Ed. Andrew Donskow, John Woodswort and Chad Gaffield. Ottawa: Slavic Research Group / Institute of Canadian Studies at the University of Ottawa.

Ortt, Felix. 1898. *Christelijk Anarchisme.* Haarlem: Drukkerij Vrede.

Payne Hackett, Alice and James Henry Burke. 1977. *80 Years of Best Sellers.* New York: R.R. Bowker Company.

Peacock, Kenneth. (Coll. and edited) 1970. *Songs of the Doukhobors*. Ottawa: National Museums of Canada. Bulletin No. 231. Folklore Series No. 7.

Penner, G. 1975. *Mennoniten dienen in der Roten Armee*. Steinbach: Carillon Press.

Perepelkin, J.J. and the Fraternal Council of the Union of Christian Communities and Brotherhood of Reformed Doukhobors (Canada). 1959. *Doukhobor problem in Canda: a prototype copy of the Hebrew people in Egypt*. Tr. and ed. by J.E. Podovinikov.

———. 1953 (26/3). 'Doukhobor Problem in Canada: A Prototype Copy of the Hebrew People in Egypt.' Sequel to 'Religious History of the Hebrews: Prototype for the Doukhobors' (Part I) by S.S. Sorokin. 26/3/53. Transl. and ed. J.E. Podovinikov. In: *Assimilating the Doukhobors: Bonner's Method*. Comp. Mike E. Chernenkoff. Crescent Valley. P. 51-87.

Popoff, Eli A. Comp. and transl. n.d. *Symposium Meetings 1974-1982: Report of the United Doukhobor Research Committee in the matter of the Clarification of the Motivating Life-Concepts and the History of the Doukhobors in Canada. A brief summary of the 68 Public Sessions held from 1974 until 1982 in the Kootenay and Grand Forks Areas*. Castlegar: The Centre for Russian and North American Studies and the President's Office, Selkirk College.

———. 2000. 'The Doukhobors: the Enigma' and the Reality.' In: *The Doukhobor Centenary in Canada: A multi-disciplinary Perspective on their Unity and Diversity. Proceedings of a conference held at the University of Ottawa, 22-24 October 1999*. Ed. by Andrew Donskow, John Woodsworth and Chad Gaffield. Ottawa: Slavic Research Group / Institute of Canadian Studies, University of Ottawa.

Rasputin, Maria and Patte Barham. 1977. *Rasputin: The Man Behind the Myth*. New Jersey: Prentice-Hall, Inc..

Reid, Anna. 1997. *Borderland: A Journey Through the History of Ukraine*. Colorado: Westview Press.

Reimer, A. 1985. *My Harp is Turned to Mourning.* Winnipeg: Hyperion Press Limited.

Riazantseva, Tatiana, Ph.D. 'Proselytizing in Ukraine: Positive or Negative?' Kiev: T. Shevchenko Institute of Literature, National Academy of Sciences of Ukraine.

Rimland, Ingrid. 1988. Demon Doctor. Stocton CA: Crystal Books.

Rodzianko, M.V. 1973. *The Reign of Rasputin: an Empire's Collapse.* Florida: Academic International Press. Re impression of the London edition of 1927 with a new introduction by David R. Jones.

Sanborn, Joshua. 2000. A. 'Non-violent protest and the Russian State.' In: *The Doukhobor Centenary in Canada: a multi-disciplinary perspective on their unity and diversity. The Proceedings of an international conference held at the University of Ottawa 22-24 October 1999.* Edited by A. Donskov, J. Woodsworth, and C. Gaffield. Ottawa: Slavic Research Group & Institute of Canadian Studies at the University of Ottawa. P. 83-103.

Shimazaki, Hiroshi Tanaka. 'The Emergence of Japanese Hutterites.' In: *Japan Review*, 2000, 12: 145-164.

Smith, C.H. 1981 [1941]. *Smith's Story of the Mennonites.* Newton/Kansas: Faith and Life Press.

Snyder, C. Arnold. 1997. *Anabaptist History and Theology: Revised Student Edition.* Kitchener: Pandora Press.

Sorokin, S.S. 1956. 'The Epistle of S.S. Sorokin-Yastrebow to the Doukhobors.' Transl. and released by the Fraternal Council Christian Community and Brotherhood of Reformed Doukhobors (19 pages).

Soukoreff, William A. 1982. 'The Doukhobor Movement Before their Settlement in the Milky Water of Tavria Province.' In: *Symposium Meetings 1974-1982.* Comp. and transl. Eli A. Popoff. Castlegar: The Centre for Russian and North American Studies and the President's Office, Selkirk College.

Stahl, Michael A. and Johannas Entz. 1982. Transl. & ed. from Low German to English by Karl en Franziska Peter. *Hutterite Conscientious Objectors and their Treatment in the US Army during World War I*. Vancouver.

Sulerhitsky, L.A. 1982. *To America with the Doukhobors*. Transl. from Russian Michael Kalmakoff. Introd. Mark Mealing. Canadian Plains Studies #12. Gen. Ed. John Archer. Regina: University of Regina. Canadian Plains Research Center.

Tolstoy, Count Lyof N. 1852. *Childhood, Boyhood, Youth*. Transl. by Isabel F. Hapgood. London: Walter Scott, 24 Warwick Lane. Contemporary (Sovremennik).

———. N. d.. *War and Peace*. n.d. Transl. from Russian Constance Garnett. New York: The Modern Library.

———. 1966. *Resurrection*. Transl. Rosemary Edmonds. London: Penquin Books.

———. 1978. *Tolstoy's Letters*. London: Athlone.

Tolstoy, Alexandra. 1933. *The Tragedy of Tolstoy*. London: George Allen & Unwin Ltd.

———. 1936. *The Final Struggle: Being Countess Tolstoy's Diary for 1910*. Preface by S.L. Tolstoy. Transl. with an Introduction by Aylmer Maude. New York: Oxford University Press.

———. 2010. *My Life*. Transl. from the Russian by John Woodsworth & Arkade Klioutchaski. Ed. and introd. by Andrew Donskov. Ottawa: University of Ottawa Press.

Towell, Larry. 2000. *The Mennonites: A Biographical Sketch*. London: Phaidon Press Ltd.

Van Braght, Thieleman J. 1950 [1837]. *The Bloody Theater or Martyrs Mirror of the Defenseless Christians who Baptized Only Upon confession of Faith, and Who Suffered and Died for the Testimony of Jesus, their Saviour, From the Time of Christ to the Year A.D. 1660*. Transl. from the original Dutch of Holland language from the Edition of 1660 by Joseph F. Sohm. Scottdale, Pennsylvania: Herald Press.

Van der Zijpp, N. 1952. *Geschiedenis der Doopsgezinden in Nederland.* Arnhem: Van Loghum Slaterus.

Van Paassen, Pierre. 1939. *Days of our Years.* New York: Hillman-Curl.

——. 1941/1942. *That Day Alone.* New York: Garden City Publishing Co.

——. 1943. *The Forgotten Ally.* New York: The Dial Pres.

——. 1946. *Earth Could Be Fair: A Chronicle.* New York: The Dial Press.

Vicariat de Saint-Boniface. 1902. Transl. from French to English by Mary Eggermont-Molenaar. 'Les écoles galiciennes.' In: *Missions de la congregation des Missionanaires Oblats de Marie Immaculée.* Paris: Typographie A. Hennuyer. P. 20-29.

Voykin, Nathalie. 1998. Comp. and ed. Koozma J. Tarasoff. 'Grandmother Berikoff: a special gift.' In: *Spirit-Wrestlers' Voices: Honouring Doukhobors on the Centenary of their Migration to Canada in 1899.*

Wiebe, Peter. 1977. 'Learning was Hard.' In: *Mennonite Memories: Settling in Western Canada.* Ed. Laurence Klippenstein and Julius G. Toews. Winnipeg: Centennial Publications. (pp. 128-50)

Wiebe, D. 1977. Advisors: John S. Hofer, James Valley Colony. Elias Kleinsasser, Crystal Springs Colony. *The History of the Hutterites.* Manitoba: S.T.E.P. Project. Co-ordinated by Program Development and Support Services, Department of Education.

Wilson, C. 1964. *Rasputin and the Fall of the Romanovs.* New York: Farrar, Straus and Company.

 **Mary Eggermont-Molenaar** was born in the Netherlands in 1945. She received a BA in social work and an MA in law and taught health law. She immigrated to Canada in 1986 and currently works as a freelance writer, editor and translator.